W9-CBA-845

GENDER ISSUES AND CONSUMER BEHAVIOR

To my son, Jason,
whose gendered behavior is often surprising,
generally amusing, and always educational

GENDER ISSUES AND CONSUMER BEHAVIOR

JANEEN ARNOLD COSTA
EDITOR

SAGE Publications
International Educational and Professional Publisher
Thousand Oaks   London   New Delhi

For information address:

 SAGE Publications, Inc.
2455 Teller Road
Thousand Oaks, California 91320

SAGE Publications Ltd.
6 Bonhill Street
London EC2A 4PU
United Kingdom

SAGE Publications India Pvt. Ltd.
M-32 Market
Greater Kailash I
New Delhi 110 048 India

Printed in the United States of America

Library of Congress Cataloging-in-Publication Data

Main entry under title:

Gender issues and consumer behavior / edited by Janeen Arnold Costa.
    p.   cm.
  Includes bibliographical references.
  ISBN 0-8039-5323-2.—ISBN 0-8039-5324-0 (pb)
  1. Consumer behavior. 2. Sex differences. I. Costa, Janeen Arnold.
  HF5415.32.G46 1994
  658.8'348—dc20   94-11313

94 95 96 97 98 10 9 8 7 6 5 4 3 2 1

Sage Production Editor: Yvonne Könneker

Contents

Preface

A S a social dimension affecting consumer behavior, gender has been, for the most part, understudied and misunderstood. Two conferences on gender and consumer behavior held in Salt Lake City, Utah, in June 1991 and June 1993, were moves in the direction of correcting these deficits. This book represents another decisive rectifying step. Primarily drawing on the best papers from the two conferences, as determined by blind review at the time of submission, the chapters in this volume cover some of the most interesting issues in the field of gender and consumer behavior.

We know that men and women behave differently, and consumption is a context in which these differences are often apparent. The contributors to this volume explore why, how, and to what extent these differences are manifest in varying situations and circumstances, addressing issues of biology, psychology, society, and culture as they affect gender constructs and gendered consumer behavior. The chapters presented here are representative of the current breadth and sophistication of gender and consumer behavior studies.

Length limitations prevent the inclusion of even more contributions by researchers who have conducted excellent studies and research projects in this field. Some studies, particularly those presented at the first conference, have been superseded by the authors' own publications in other places; readers who are interested in exploring gender and consumer behavior further are referred to the works cited by the authors in this volume, as well as to the published proceedings of the two conferences from which these chapters are drawn.

It is becoming increasingly common to see special sessions or competitive papers devoted to the issue of gender in consumer behavior at marketing and consumer research conferences, and the *Journal of Consumer Research* devoted part of its March 1993 issue to the subject; nevertheless, the field of gender and consumer behavior remains underexplored. Despite the high quality of the contributions contained herein, it is clear that much remains to be done. Because gender is pervasive, intricate, and interwoven with virtually all aspects of human behavior, further study is necessary if we are to understand more fully this important dimension of society and individual behavior. This book helps to move exploration of these issues forward.

Acknowledgments

I would like to thank all those who participated in the gender and consumer behavior conferences, thereby bringing this book to fruition. Thanks are owed in particular to the many scholars who traveled from abroad to attend the conferences, and whose chapters included in this volume contribute international perspectives and enhance our understanding of cultural variations in gender constructs. The Association for Consumer Research and the Department of Marketing at the David Eccles School of Business, University of Utah, were cosponsors of the conferences. In addition, Eileen Fischer, Barbara Stern, Elizabeth Hirschman, Gary Bamossy, and Russell Belk, as well as Craig Costa, have all been staunch supporters of my efforts and have provided steady encouragement. Finally, I wish to thank Teresa Pavia for her friendship, hard work, scholarly endeavors, and collegial support.

Janeen Arnold Costa

1

Introduction

JANEEN ARNOLD COSTA

Gender and Culture

Gender is a social construct, a dichotomy, that exists in all societies (and has, apparently, for all of human history). Yet, although all societies, all cultures, make social and symbolic distinctions between men and women, the specifics of those distinctions and expected gender-based behaviors vary from one society to the next. A similar marked variation exists in the range of gender differences, that is, in the length of the continuum between "ideal" male and female behaviors. Some societies, for example, are highly dichotomized, with little tolerance for deviation from gender norms. In other societies this is not the case, and greater latitude in behavior, including behavior stemming from sexual orientation, is allowed. In certain societies, lip service is paid to gender equality, but inequalities seethe beneath the surface; in others, there is greater sharing of power, of resources, of decision making (Friedl, 1978).

The observable variations among cultures in this respect point to the malleability of gender constructs and to the cultural rather than biological basis of gender dichotomies everywhere. Although the dichotomy

1

is clearly and obviously based on morphological differences between men and women, cultural gender constructs do not stop there. Moving beyond sex to gender, cultural elaborations of virtually all aspects of behavior are found (Brettell & Sargent, 1993; Rosaldo & Lamphere, 1974). Men are *supposed* to act differently from women, and vice versa—and this is the case throughout all time, in every space, in all groups of people of whom we are aware. In some societies, men are stoic; in others, men are emotional. Some cultural constructs categorize women as generally weak; others place women above men in certain kinds of strength. Other psychological and/or psychobehavioral distinctions abound. In American societies, women are primarily responsible for shopping activities; the opposite is the case in the Mediterranean. Although it has been generally true that women bear and raise the children, this too is changing, at least with respect to raising the children, as responsibilities are shared with or turned over to men in some instances.

Still, despite variation from one society to the next, and individual departures from societal norms, some generalizations about human gender dichotomization are possible. In all societies, there is gender differentiation, and inequality is almost always inherent in the distinction. What is more, the men are superordinate and the women are subordinate within the unequal social order. Despite myths of "Amazonian" matriarchies, there is no indication that such societies, where women dominate in the ways in which we traditionally associate men with domination, have ever existed. Part of this is a Western perspective; that is, Western patriarchal power is nowhere manifest in a female-centered form. Yet there are societies in which women exert and exercise power in specific, often important, circumstances (e.g., Buckley, 1993; Prior, 1993). Among the Hopi, a matrilineal society in which property is inherited and lineage is traced through women, for example, "matriarchs" are responsible for much of the important decision making in a ritual context. Still, in the societies with which we are largely concerned here, the inequality and the differences are marked (see Sanday, 1981, for an interesting discussion of the issues of power and hierarchy).

Consumer Behavior

Consumer behavior is one area in which the differences in behavior between men and women, and often the hierarchical implications of those differences, are evident. Many items or products are associated with one or the other gender. In parts of Greece, virtually all items of the household are associated with women, and tools for working outside the home are associated with men (Costa, 1989). This basic European gender association of objects is manifest in Euro-America as well. Anthropologists have documented numerous instances of ritual objects that are associated only with men or with women, and cannot be used or even touched or seen by members of the opposite sex (e.g., Herdt, 1981; Kendall, 1993).

In addition to gendered objects, behaviors associated with consumption can be gendered as well. In the United States, women are often responsible for consumption activities—shopping, preparing items for consumption, gift buying and gift giving, disposal of used items. Although American men are generally thought to be responsible for production rather than consumption, this axiom does not always hold true. In some cases, American men choose gifts, and they are typically more responsible for the purchase and use of certain types of goods than are women (Belk & Coon, 1993; Fischer & Gainer, 1991; Lavin, 1991; Milner, Fodness, & Morrison, 1991; Rudell, 1991, 1993). Of course, some of this gender dichotomization is currently breaking down, but much of it remains surprisingly resilient to change.

Finally, marketers perform their activities differently when their targets are male than they do when the targets are female, and customers' responses often differ on the basis of gender. Sales personnel learn that alternative methods may be required when a potential customer is male rather than female, for example. The use of color in promotion, advertising, and packaging sends gendered messages, perhaps the most obvious of which is the association of bright, bold colors with toys for boys and pastels and purple with toys for girls in the United States (Pennell, 1994). Given that men and women hold culture-based, dissimilar conceptualizations of reality, disparate worldviews, an assumption of differences rather than similarities in reaction to marketing activities should be expected by marketers.

Nature of Culture; Nature and Culture

Many marketers and academics who study marketing seem unaware of the complexity and pervasiveness of culture in its impact on the behavior of consumers. It has been common in consumer research to focus on individual psychological response to marketing activities, typically emphasizing the processing of information. Beyond efforts to show that findings are generalizable to a larger population, little effort has been made to understand group dynamics of behavior (Costa, 1993). To alleviate the lack of understanding concerning culture and society, a brief description and a discussion of these concepts are necessary at this point.

It must be remembered that humans are, above all, social and cultural animals. That is, humans cannot survive from infancy without contact with other humans. In the rare case in which this human interaction does not occur, where a child is isolated from human contact during the formative years, the child does not develop in a "normal" way, in a way we would recognize as "human." Such a child cannot walk or talk, indeed, cannot control its bowels. The cognitive skills of such a child are extremely limited; the brain does not develop in a normal fashion (Barrett, 1984). Thus it seems that behavior and development that we would categorize as human require interaction with other humans.

In addition, culture is a social phenomenon, requiring the existence of a group. Symbols, constructs, and systems are shared by members of a given society. Culture does not exist in the mind of a given single human; it is learned through contact with others, and it develops and changes in that same context. Humans in a group, a society, or a subgroup of that society share the same culture. Members of this group have markedly similar understandings of reality and respond to actions and events in similar ways. An individual learns culture through contact with other members of the same society, and culture can be said to exist as a manifestation of the group sharing of ideas and beliefs.

A simple definition of culture is that it is everything that is learned. This simple definition has elaborate implications, however. The tabula rasa that is the human mind at birth is ready to be filled with learned information. Some scholars resort to laundry lists to describe everything to which this may refer: Learned behavior includes customs, traditions, behaviors, rituals, morals, values, and so on. Others focus more on the systems of learning, the process of socialization whereby individuals learn societally expected modes and standards of behavior. Still others are concerned with the symbolic systems themselves, characterized as a screen through which members of a society view the world. These systems of arbitrary symbolic associations hold meaning for individuals in a society, providing a means of interpreting all that occurs around them, yielding a guide for behavior, supporting a framework for understanding and action (see Kroeber & Kluckhohn, 1952, for a detailed analysis of concepts of culture to that point in time; see also Costa, 1993).

If culture is everything that is learned, then virtually all aspects of the consumption process must be affected by culture. What we learn we would like to buy, the ads and other promotions to which we respond, the signals sent by various aspects of packaging and presentation of the product, the way we use the product, what we believe the use of the product does for us or says about us—all of this, and more, is affected by culture.

What's in a Role?

Sociologists and anthropologists often analyze social and cultural systems in terms of social roles and statuses (Linton, 1936; Nadel, 1957). A *status* is a social position, and individuals hold numerous statuses at any given moment. Thus I am a woman, a scholar, a mother, a sister, an aunt, a colleague, and a friend all at the same time. Each status carries with it expected behaviors referred to as the *role* of that status. As a scholar, I am expected to conduct research; to read the work of others; to review and comment on that work in certain circumstances; to formulate ideas, hypotheses, and perhaps theories about the behavior I study; to publish my own work; and so on. This is the *role* of a scholar. Each status sustains a similarly elaborate code and system of desired or socially required behaviors.

Of the roles associated with statuses, gender roles are among the most intricate and interesting. Schlegel (1990) describes gender as "the way members of the two sexes are perceived, evaluated, and expected to behave" (p. 23). The definition of gender, it would seem, encompasses a great deal. Temperament, abilities and skills, activities and behaviors, ideal types and accepted and unacceptable deviations from the ideal, sexuality and sensuality, the culture-based essence of what it means to be male or female—all are part of the gender constructs of a given society. The content of the gender role varies from one society to the next; it is composed of culturally differentiated elements. Of course, individual variation exists within societies as well. Still, we may talk about the dimensions of gender roles of a particular society in a general way, discussing the expected parameters of behavior.

Given that cultural assumptions about what it means to be masculine and feminine exist in all societies as elaborate and pervasive belief systems, and given that consumption is also a universal human activity, one that is necessary to survive but that goes beyond survival as an activity in the vast majority of societies, it is not surprising that the two systems of meaning and behavior often overlap. To be specific, consumption is often gendered.

The Ideology of Gender

Ideology refers to a culturally organized system of ideas and beliefs. Obviously, gender falls into this category as an ideological system. However, from a certain perspective, ideology is often analyzed not just as ideas and beliefs, but as a system that serves to maintain the status quo. The issues of power and order then become relevant. When gender involves inequality, as it most often does (despite some counterexamples), gender ideologies are seen to reinforce power structures (e.g., de Beauvoir, 1952; Miller, 1993). From this perspective, ideas and beliefs about males and females are structured such that males continue in a superordinate position and females are consistently subordinated.

Consumer behavior is one area in which this inequality is often manifest. If in many societies men are responsible primarily for production outside the home (at least traditionally), and if production of income is more valued than consumption, then women are believed to be engaging in less-valued activities than are men. The hierarchy is evident. In these societies, when women work outside the home they are expected to conform to male ideals of behavior, dressing in suits rather than loose clothing, acting in authoritative rather than relational ways, and so on. Efforts to show the value of feminine attributes in the workplace often serve only to reinforce the male ways of doing things. The consumption domain of the home, typically (although not always) associated with women, is less valued vis-à-vis the public domain in the ideology of gender (see, e.g., Lamphere, 1993).

Studies in This Volume

The studies reported by the contributors to this book provide consistent support for the contention that gender dichotomizations are elaborately and irrefutably cultural, formulated through learning rather than as functions of universal and inherent sexual, biological differences. The authors draw upon numerous disciplines in providing the backgrounds to their studies, a strategy stemming from the relative lack of gender-focused studies in marketing and consumer behavior. The contributors, then, explore the rich treatment of gender in psychology, sociology, history, anthropology, and other disciplines, thereby pushing back the frontiers of knowledge within our own discipline.

Throughout this volume, it is clear that gender is a pervasive aspect of culture, penetrating deeply and spreading broadly throughout the fabric of society. In Chapter 2, Stern and Holbrook provide an excellent background and general introduction to gender and consumer behavior. Of particular interest in their chapter is the clear manifestation of gendered perspectives—the authors show how gender affects their interpretations of advertising. The conclusion is obvious: Research, approach, and worldview can vary considerably on the basis of gender.

Because gender is a cultural construct, cross-cultural variation is expected. In Chapter 3, Venkatesh provides a detailed and insightful look at gender and consumption in India, with the added dimension of cultural change associated with contact with Western societies. A crucial point in Venkatesh's essay is that, although gender differentiation may exist in all societies, this does not necessarily translate into gender antagonism. In India, gender differentiation seems to be more or less accepted; the political agenda of gender similarity so prevalent in the United States apparently is not sought so fervently in India.

In many societies, women stereotypically are more concerned with their body images and forms than are men. Although her research shows that eating in general is a compensatory activity, Grunert, in Chapter 4, reports that women have a particular relationship to food and eating in the societies she studied. Martin and Kennedy's research in advertising, discussed in Chapter 6, indicates greater emphasis on comparison of self to advertising models in American female subjects than in their male counterparts. Martin and Kennedy also note that the tendency to compare in this particular fashion plays a greater role in self-esteem for women than it does for men.

Gender associations can be linked to objects, activities, even letters of the alphabet used in brand names. Pavia and Costa, for example, report in Chapter 10 that in the United States, females are associated with the attributes of simple, basic, and easy to understand, both through the letters used in names of products and, by extension, in the products themselves. Bamossy and Jansen discuss similar implications in Chapter 8. These researchers found evidence that Dutch male boys are more confident with and less fearful about high-tech products, such as computers, than are girls.

Gender socialization is strong and enduring. Children are socialized into gender roles early in life, as Bamossy and Jansen suggest. The enduring aspect of gender is reflected in Bobinski and Assar's research, reported in Chapter 7, which indicates that, despite some cultural changes in American society in the direction of greater sharing of tasks, men continue to be more involved than women in investment decisions, and women maintain responsibility for routine financial tasks. The research conducted by Fischer and Gainer also points to the maintenance of traditional gender domination in certain domains, in this case, in sports activities. As these authors note in Chapter 5, when women enter this consumption domain, both men and women feel compelled to alter their behavior to adapt to changes and challenges to male control, even ownership, of that province. In Chapter 9, Lowrey and Otnes provide data that indicate consumption in a ritual context can be highly gendered, and their findings support the American social tradition of women as responsible for activities and objects consumed during rites of passage. Gender differentiation and hierarchy are maintained, perhaps even furthered, in these consumption and marketing activities.

In the final essay in this book, Fırat addresses the issues of changing gender roles. He suggests that postmodern society is moving in the direction of less division, less dichotomization, less antagonism. From Fırat's perspective, the gender differentiation characteristic of the recent modern period is breaking down. His discussion moves us beyond the past into the present and future of gender roles.

The contributions to this volume illustrate the diversity and complexity of gender and consumer behavior. It is imperative that scholars and practitioners move beyond the mere statement that gender differences exist and begin to pursue a greater, deeper understanding of gender in this context. Those who are currently engaged in studying gendered consumer behavior are producing works of great sophistication and rigor, but the number of those pursuing this research is still quite small. The publication of this book indicates that a fruitful and important foundation for this field has been laid by the scholars whose work is presented here and by others in the field. The research area of gender and consumer behavior is promising and ripe for further development.

References

Barrett, R. A. (1984). *Culture and conduct*. Belmont, CA: Wadsworth.

Belk, R. W., & Coon, G. S. (1993). Gift giving as agapic love: An alternative to the exchange paradigm based on dating experiences. *Journal of Consumer Research, 20*, 393-417.

Brettell, C. B., & Sargent, C. F. (Eds.). (1993). *Gender in cross-cultural perspective*. Englewood Cliffs, NJ: Prentice Hall.

Buckley, T. (1993). Menstruation and the power of Yurok women. In C. B. Brettell & C. F. Sargent (Eds.), *Gender in cross-cultural perspective* (pp. 133-148). Englewood Cliffs, NJ: Prentice Hall.

Costa, J. A. (1989). On display: Social and cultural dimensions of consumer behavior in the Greek saloni. In T. K. Srull (Ed.), *Advances in consumer research* (Vol. 16, pp. 562-566). Provo, UT: Association for Consumer Research.

Costa, J. A. (1993). *Using the culture concept: A comparison of marketing and anthropology.* Paper presented at the Eighteenth Macromarketing Conference, Kingston, RI.

de Beauvoir, S. (1952). *The second sex*. New York: Vintage.

Fischer, E., & Gainer, B. (1991). I shop therefore I am: The role of shopping in the social construction of women's identities. In J. A. Costa (Ed.), *Gender and consumer behavior* (pp. 350-357). Salt Lake City: University of Utah Printing Service.

Friedl, E. (1978). Society and sex roles. *Human Nature, 1*, 68-75.

Herdt, G. H. (1981). *Guardians of the flutes: Idioms of masculinity*. New York: McGraw-Hill.

Kendall, L. (1993). Divine connections: The *mansin* and her clients. In C. B. Brettell & C. F. Sargent (Eds.), *Gender in cross-cultural perspective* (pp. 353-363). Englewood Cliffs, NJ: Prentice Hall.

Kroeber, A., & Kluckhohn, C. (1952). *Culture: A critical review of concepts and definitions*. Cambridge, MA: The Museum.

Lamphere, L. (1993). The domestic sphere of women and the public world of men: The strengths and limitations of an anthropological dichotomy. In C. B. Brettell & C. F. Sargent (Eds.), *Gender in cross-cultural perspective* (pp. 67-76). Englewood Cliffs, NJ: Prentice Hall.

Lavin, M. (1991). Husband dominant, wife dominant, joint: A shopping typology for the 1990s? In J. A. Costa (Ed.), *Gender and consumer behavior* (pp. 358-366). Salt Lake City: University of Utah Printing Service.

Linton, R. (1936). *The study of man*. New York: Appleton Century.

Miller, B. D. (1993). *Sex and gender hierarchies*. Cambridge: Cambridge University Press.

Milner, L., Fodness, D., & Morrison, J. (1991). Women's images of guns: An exploratory study. In J. A. Costa (Ed.), *Gender and consumer behavior* (pp. 199-208). Salt Lake City: University of Utah Printing Service.

Nadel, S. F. (1957). *The theory of social structure*. New York: Free Press.

Pennell, G. E. (1994). Babes in Toyland: Learning an ideology of gender. In *Advances in consumer research* (Vol. 21, pp. 359-364). Provo, UT: Association for Consumer Research.

Prior, M. (1993). Matrifocality, power, and gender relations in Jamaica. In C. B. Brettell & C. F. Sargent (Eds.), *Gender in cross-cultural perspective* (pp. 310-317). Englewood Cliffs, NJ: Prentice Hall.

Rosaldo, M. Z., & Lamphere, L. (Eds.). (1974). *Woman, culture, and society*. Stanford, CA: Stanford University Press.

Rudell, F. (1991). Boys' toys and girls' tools? An exploration of gender differences in consumer decision-making for high tech products. In J. A. Costa (Ed.), *Gender and consumer behavior* (pp. 187-198). Salt Lake City: University of Utah Printing Service.

Rudell, F. (1993). Gender differences in consumer decision making for personal comput-
    ers: A test of hypotheses. In J. A. Costa (Ed.), *Gender and consumer behavior* (pp. 1-16).
    Salt Lake City: University of Utah Printing Service.
Sanday, P. (1981). *Female power and male dominance: On the origins of sexual inequality.*
    Cambridge: Cambridge University Press.
Schlegel, A. (1990). Gender meanings: General and specific. In P. R. Sanday & R. G.
    Goodenough (Eds.), *Beyond the second sex: New directions in the anthropology of gender*
    (pp. 23-41). Philadelphia: University of Pennsylvania Press.

2

Gender and Genre in the Interpretation of Advertising Text

BARBARA B. STERN

MORRIS B. HOLBROOK

Each person's reading is different, yet there is enough recurrence among readings to make us think some lawfulness is at work. What, then, is the relation between the singularity and the regularity of literary response?

Holland & Sherman, 1988, p. 215

CONVENTIONAL advertising research conducted from the viewpoint of information-processing and decision-oriented choice models presumes that consumers read advertisements in similar ways. These models rest on the assumption that when consumers read an advertisement, they pass through successive response stages to arrive at a "correct" meaning ("Brand X is good"). This meaning, in turn, enables

AUTHORS' NOTE: Barbara Stern would like to thank the Graduate School Newark for the 1993-1994 Research Award that partially funded the study reported in this chapter. Morris Holbrook gratefully acknowledges the support of the Columbia Business School's Faculty Research Fund.

them to perceive the sponsor's intended implications for action ("Buy Brand X") (Lavidge & Steiner, 1961). The processing assumptions underlie those of much post-Aristotelian literary theory by taking as axiomatic a stable and autonomous text, a single meaning, and a correct response on the part of a collective audience of readers.

Our purposes in this chapter are to challenge the traditional assumption of correct consumer responses to a stable advertising text and to propose in its place a postmodern response model (see Stern, 1993) that incorporates the dichotomy of gender as an influence on interpretation. We interpolate gender into the communication triad—source, message, and receiver—to bridge the gap between the source's intention in devising the message, the form and content of the message, and the receiver's response to it. In order to achieve the goal of demonstrating the relationship between analysis of the textual stimulus (the advertisement) and gender-based responses, we draw from several schools of literary theory (Stern, 1989): the new hermeneutics, genre criticism, feminist criticism, and reader-response theory.

We begin by briefly summarizing concepts from the above-mentioned modern and postmodern schools of criticism necessary to understand gender influences on the proposed communication model (Figures 2.1 and 2.2) and to analyze the advertising exemplar. This background material includes a discussion of feminist theory and the romance genre as the theoretical grounding for the exploratory study of male/female readings. Next, we present our exploratory "reader's reading" study, one that uses a male and a female reader of an advertising exemplar as well as material derived from authorial informants. This chapter thus extends previous research on advertising interpretations (McCracken, 1989; Scott, 1990; Stern, 1989) by venturing beyond single-sex readings, by incorporating the author's point of view, and by linking dual-gender responses to textual analysis.

Modern and Postmodern Critical Theory:
Authors, Texts, and Readers

AUTHORIAL INTENTION AND READER RESPONSE

We may represent communication in general, and literary communication in particular, according to the schema shown in Figure 2.1

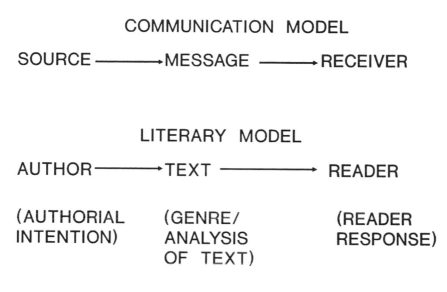

Figure 2.1. The Communication Process

(Holbrook & Zirlin, 1985). Within this general representation, the text, rather than the author or reader, was the object of supreme interest in modern post-World War II critical theory—notably that of the "New Critics" (Berman, 1988). In analyzing a printed text (words-on-a-page), these critics implicitly assumed a passively receptive reader and a disembodied author (Scholes & Kellogg, 1968). This critical perspective is now considered "modern" in contrast to later "postmodern" theory, and the modernist approach provides the fundamental assumptions— often implicit—on which information-processing research on the reading of advertising is based. Processing research assumes a uniform response on the part of readers expected to experience a fixed response to the details of a text.

Notwithstanding the apparent hegemony of this perspective, by the end of the 1960s, the presumption of a static communication process and a stable text was being challenged by several groups of critics, notably those advocating a new hermeneutics, reader-response theory, and deconstruction. The new hermeneuticists were especially interested in reexamining the role of the author—who, following Joyce (1916/1957), was conceived of as "refined out of existence" in the text (p. 215). The new hermeneuticists' aim was to reconsider older ideas about authorial intentionality, for critics such as Hirsch (1967, 1976) turned to nineteenth-century scholarship, reviving and reworking it to suit the texts generated in the twentieth century. This scholarship proceeded on Dilthey's (1972) assumption that readers can be expected to arrive at the meaning that the author intended in his or her expressed words, and that the reader's determination can be accepted as an objective interpretation of meaning. In accordance with the new hermeneutics, the objective interpretation of meaning has three aspects: First, the text means what its author intended the verbal meaning to be; second, the verbal meaning is knowable even when ambiguous; and third, it is comprehensible by the typical competent reader (see Ricoeur, 1974; Todorov, 1968/1981). However, sociologists of literature (Griswold, 1993) are less confident of objective interpretations of meaning, for the "production of culture" approach acknowledges that although authors may try to control the reader's understanding of a text, they do not necessarily succeed.

The assumption of authorial control came into question when the role of the reader was reconceptualized. Whereas formerly readers were considered passive recipients of the author's words, postmodern criticism repositioned them as creative agents actively engaged in making meaning. "Reader-response" criticism arose in the 1960s (see Mailloux, 1982; Suleiman, 1980; Tompkins, 1980), and in the succeeding generation achieved the goal of emphasizing the role of the reader as an active participant in constructing the meaning of a text. Once the communication triad was reweighted to reflect the importance of author and reader as well as that of the text, much postmodern literary criticism (reviewed by Stern, 1989) sought a balanced perspective from which to view the triadic elements as coconstituents of the determination of meaning (Figure 2.1).

THE COMMUNICATION TRIAD REVISITED:
INTRODUCTION OF GENDER

From this postmodern perspective, the communication process expresses a generally accepted sequence of events. However, gender aspects of the triad have been closely scrutinized, especially by feminist critics, and we propose that the model requires revision in order to incorporate these aspects. Feminist studies are responsible for bringing together reader response theory and the sociology of literature (Griswold,

1993), enabling a new perspective from which to view the process of communication. To begin, recall that communication is set in motion by a generative entity—an author—whose intention is expressed in a text. Here, gender issues such as the sex of the author and the sex of potential readers need to be considered. Authorial commentary about gender issues can be found in authorial statements preserved in pre-publication or postpublication material, such as revisions (successive drafts of the work), letters, interviews, and marginalia, all of which contribute to an understanding of what the author intended to do in a text.

These intentions are made manifest in the second triadic entity—a text—a document perceived as an actualized "aesthetic object" that portrays a fictional world as a quasi-reality (see Ingarden, 1931/1973). Perhaps the most salient gender issue in a text is that of genre—the type or species of literature, often called "form" (Abrams, 1988), evidencing features characteristic of one member of the literary family as opposed to others (Fowler, 1982). Textual genre has received renewed attention in recent years in the sociology of literature (Griswold, 1993), where the term "textual classes" (Dubois & Durand, 1989) refers to genres that are classified according to the socially constructed classifications of their different reading publics. Gender is one of the most salient aspects of genre (Stern, 1993), for feminist theory has provided evidence of numerous differences in consumption, appreciation, and interpretation of specific genres by members of one sex or the other (see below). Textual genres have been reexamined as the outcome of formal social structural divisions (Di Maggio, 1987) in that pronounced generic differentiation is considered indicative of a high degree of status diversity and complex role structure in a social system.

The final and crucial member of the triad—now presumed to be central to the interpretation of text—is the reader (Suleiman, 1980). There is no single reader-response theory, but the various groups of critics who focus on the activity of reading emphasize the interpretive role of the reader in making sense out of a text (Staton, 1987; Stern, 1989). These critics define reading as an iterative cycle in which individual differences influence the outcome of the process—the perceived meaning that the reader takes away from the text. These critics believe that the meaning of a text is cocreated by readers, that there is no one indisputably singular and correct meaning, and that perception of the features of the text, such as plot, character, and setting, reflects evolving patterns that continually shift, much like shapes in a kaleidoscope, during the course of the reading experience. Far from being viewed as blank slates, readers are now viewed as *bricoleurs*, making meanings out of the available materials (Griswold, 1993).

Gender is an important facet of the meaning-making process, and most critics nowadays assume that gender influences reader interpretation on many levels. It does so by influencing reader response through interaction among the reader's gender, the textual genre, and the personal/cultural context. In order to discuss the genre-gender relationship as an influence on consumers/readers, we first turn to a pioneering empirical study of contextual influences on reader responses in advertising and consumer research: Mick and Buhl's (1992) meaning-based approach to the interpretation of advertisements.

GENDER AND READING IN ADVERTISING RESEARCH: MICK AND BUHL'S MODEL

In their pathbreaking research, Mick and Buhl (1992) used the reader-response approach to analyze three consumers' responses to five magazine advertisements. Their model advances understanding of consumer responses as an individual phenomenon by drawing on a variety of theories, including those found in Holland's (1975) psychoanalytic reader-response criticism. Their approach rests on the concept of subjective reading (see Bleich, 1978) of advertisements, in that different consumers construct different meanings in response to ostensibly the "same" advertisement, based on their personal histories and their cultural expectations. Ultimately, each consumer actualizes an advertisement's meaning in a personal and idiosyncratic way, based on the individual's personality traits that influence perception and behavior.

However, because the respondents in their meaning-based study were all male, Mick and Buhl's model obviously accounts for response effects only within a single-sex group. With the omission of gender as a response factor, the emphasis falls on idiosyncratic differences among men rather than on communal similarities that might distinguish male readings from female readings. Indeed, Mick and Buhl (1992) acknowledge that their study was limited to single-sex responses and urge evaluation of advertising meanings by consumers of both genders as a "priority for future research" (p. 335). We pursue their suggestion by addressing gender as a component of identity that shapes reader re-

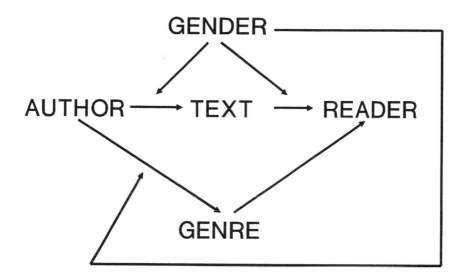

Figure 2.2. Gender and Genre: Revised Communication Model

sponses. In the study presented below, we extend Mick and Buhl's meaning-based approach by adapting their model to include two gender-related dimensions. First, we introduce the aspects of authorial intention and textual genre that relate to gender as a literary framework for analyzing an advertising text. Second, we present the results of our use of a male and a female informant to elicit responses. That is, we revise the communication model (Figure 2.1), adding gender to describe the ways that men and women are inclined to find meaning, as shown in Figure 2.2.

Feminist Theory and the Text-Reader Relationship

GENRE AND TEXTUAL POSSIBILITIES

The addition of gender to the study of the production and reception of text has been the main business of feminist criticism. In the past generation, feminist critics have segmented authors, texts, and readers by gender, engaging in a multilayered quest for literary meaning. Here we note that no matter how diverse critical inquiry may be, the text inevitably plays a central role (although not always an explicitly avowed one) in postmodern literary criticism. No matter what a reader of one or the other gender re-creates as his or her response to a text, most feminist and other critics expect that response to dovetail with the possibilities that a given text offers. That is, the response possibilities are inevitably circumscribed by the text's *genre*—the form and content that permit classification as one or another literary species. Genre classifications identify the textual regularities that govern reading of various forms of literature (poetry as opposed to prose, for example), for reading is not a rule-less activity. As Holland (1975) points out, using the word *matrix* where we would use *genre*:

> The reader is surely responding to *something*. The literary text may be only so many marks on a page—at most a matrix of psychological possibilities for its readers. Nevertheless only some possibilities, we would say, truly fit the matrix. One would not say, for example, that a reader of . . . "A Rose for Emily" who thought [it] described an Eskimo was really responding to the story at all—only pursuing some mysterious inner exploration. (p. 12)

Insofar as genres and subgenres constitute the classification system for literature, much as genus and species do for biology, most critics conceive of genre as a set of conventions that defines an implicit contract between author and reader. The conventions enable the writing of a particular work of literature (even when the writer writes against the prevailing norms) and shape the expectations of the reader (even when these expectations are thwarted). In this way, genre permits readers to derive meaning from a text by relating it to the kinds of texts with which they are familiar as a result of a shared cultural context (Fowler, 1982). When readers experience a text by re-creating it in their own minds, they are presumed to respond to textual details grounded in the genre-governed possibilities that the literary form offers.

FEMINIST PEDAGOGY: GENDER AND READING

Most feminist criticism since the 1970s (Schweickart & Flynn, 1988) has accepted the influence of genre and gender on reading. The prevailing tenets are drawn from reader-response theory, positing readers as central to the interpretation of text (Suleiman, 1980), and from genre theory, positing genre as a determinant of meaning. What feminist scholarship brings to the party is an emphasis on the importance of gender as an influence on the reader's construction of meaning. This emphasis formed the thrust of feminist criticism from the outset, for when feminists began to investigate prior nonfeminist reader-response critical writings, they challenged the unquestioned assumption of a single and uniform correct reading response by readers of both sexes. Here, let us recall that until a generation ago, the search for a "right reading" was premised on a singular male-defined "rightness," with gender unrecognized as a factor that implies multiple possible interactions between reader and text.

Because the early feminist critics considered gender a major reason for differences in reader responses (Schweickart & Flynn, 1988), they insisted on the need to reanalyze "both the text the artist creates and the text of what the audience says" (Holland, 1975, p. 7). At first, feminists engaged in pedagogical research on the reading process challenged the notion of a single right response to text. Much of this pedagogical research was conducted in the elementary school setting, for grade school educators bear the prime responsibility for teaching students how to read (Bleich, 1978). Findings show that from the earliest stages of learning how to read, marked differences in ability, comprehension, and enjoyment of textual types appear to differentiate boys and girls. Once inquiry into gender became a routine part of pedagogical studies, research results most often indicated that girls learn to read more easily and with greater enjoyment than boys (Segel, 1988). Further, boys and girls choose to read different types of texts, with gender exerting an important influence not only on the number and type of texts selected, but also on interpretations of the material at hand.

When feminist literary critics first turned to research on the psychology of reading (Downing & Leong, 1982), their initial goal was to catalog gender-related childhood differences in reading achievement, enjoyment, and cultural valuation as an appropriate sex-role activity (Maccoby & Jacklin, 1974). This body of pedagogical research became the foundation for subsequent feminist study of differences between adult male and female readers of literary texts. One consistent finding has been that childhood differences among North American men and women persist into adulthood in the form of different strategies of reading adopted by male and female readers (Crawford & Chaffin, 1988). The cognitive, emotional, and/or physical reasons for male/female differences in reading are still under investigation (Downing &

Leong, 1982; Philips, 1989), but it is fair to say that gender differences emerge early in life, persist into adulthood, and influence what we read, how we read, and whether or not we enjoy it.

FEMINIST LITERARY CRITICISM:
MALE AND FEMALE READING STYLES

Rosenblatt (1938/1983, 1964) was one of the first feminist critics to study gender-based strategies of reading in the context of literary rather than pedagogical research (Stern, 1993). She formulated a dichotomous schema of male/female differences in reading styles later corroborated in the social sciences, where subcultural masculine/feminine value differences have been found in psychology, sociology, and communication (Chodorow, 1978; Coates, 1988; Kramerae, 1981). Rosenblatt's schema proposes different male and female approaches to interpretation as a consequence of different reading goals. She describes the male style as *cognitive* (directed toward an informational goal) and the female style as *affective* (directed toward an experiential goal). The dichotomy accords with sociolinguistic research on male and female communicative competence reflecting socialized differences in men's and women's conversational aims (Coates, 1988).

Rosenblatt's theory of different reading styles was tested by Bleich (1988) and Flynn (1988), both of whom introduced an empirical orientation into feminist literary criticism by designing studies of student responses to literary stimuli (Stern, 1993). Bleich (1975, 1978, 1988) is perhaps the most notable disciple of Holland (1975), a major figure in psychoanalytic reader-response criticism and the most important source of Mick and Buhl's (1992) meaning-based approach to advertising. Holland (1975) reversed the traditional procedure of analyzing textual content to understand reader responses by arguing that one ought to begin by analyzing reader responses to understand text. When Bleich and Flynn operationalized Holland's ideas in studies of male and female reader responses, they found that differences in student gender influenced the reading styles adopted to make meaning out of novels such as Emily Brontë's *Wuthering Heights* and short stories such as James Joyce's "Araby." In a variant of this approach, Holland and Sherman (1988) fused the interest in reader response, gender, and genre by engaging in a dialogue about the gothic romance genre and using themselves as respondents to analyze male and female reader responses.

We have adapted Holland and Sherman's method for our present purposes and now turn to our interpretation of an advertising exemplar, first analyzing the text and then presenting the male and female readings.

Reader-Response Criticism: An Advertising Exemplar

The exemplar is an advertisement from the 1980s for Paco Rabanne Pour Homme cologne—a fragrance for men introduced in 1973 (see Figure 2.3). The advertisement is titled "Man on a Boat" and is one of six developed in a decade-long campaign featuring men engaged in telephone dialogues. The others are set in an artist's studio, at a beach house, in a Paris apartment, in a photographer's studio, and in a New York apartment. To unify the campaign, each ad followed the same print format (picture and copy the same size, same type style, same colors) and emphasized the same slogan: "What is remembered is up to you."

AUTHORIAL INTENTION: "A ROMANTIC FANTASY"

To analyze the intertwined influence of gender and genre, it is first necessary to demonstrate that the exemplar conforms to genre conventions. To this end, statements of authorial intention are useful adjuncts to within-text elements, for they serve as corroborative evidence of genre. That is, the advertising author's statements about what a text was intended to be lend validity to the internal evidence provided by the text. We determined authorial intention by conducting interviews with the ad's art director, by reading statements found in the fragrance company's public relations releases, and by examining sales-orientation material in corporate training manuals.

To begin, interviews with Alan Sprules, the art director for the ad campaign and a current senior vice president and marketing director at Ogilvy & Mather, elicited his categorization of the advertisement as a member of the romance genre. He called it a "romantic fantasy" (personal communication, December 1992), noting that the picture and copy portray male aspirations by using a fantasized setting and dialogue that features romanticism rather than overt sexual discussion. Company advertorials substantiate the romanticized depictions, for the advertising

Hello?

How would you like to come and make a dishonest woman of me?

Where are you?

If you look out the window...

Porthole.

...porthole, you'll see a pink stucco hotel overlooking the bay. My plane just got in. I'm in Room 16. First bed on the right.

You told me you hated flying.

I didn't know I'd miss you this much.

I never thought I'd hear you say that.

I said to myself, "What am I doing up here while he's down there in the islands? He's probably wearing that Paco Rabanne cologne of his—and damned little else—and flashing that smile at all those able-bodied and weak-minded women he's meeting"

Listen, you've caught me at a bad time. I've got a cabin full of dusky women in skimpy sarongs flying me with papaya and passion fruit. They've been teaching me the secret island ways of love, as handed down from generation to generation. Only four more lessons and I...

Oh, shut up! Room 16. And step on it, sailor!

Paco Rabanne
For men
What is remembered is up to you

Figure 2.3. Paco Rabanne—"Man on a Boat" (used with permission of COMPAR)

treatments accord with the philosophy of Dr. Fernando Aleu, president of COMPAR. He describes fragrance as a "self-gift" rather than as a problem-solving product, and identifies the feeling that the advertisement is supposed to convey: "Fragrances make you feel pleasant, sexy, and identifiable; they promote a feeling of well-being that is actually similar to a mild euphoria and just plain comfort" (quoted in Marshall, 1983). COMPAR's 1991 training manual mingles objective terminology describing the ingredients with emotion-based claims about the fragrance's capacity to stimulate consumer effects: "The unique PACO scent is a clean, dry blend of aromatics with crisp tones of wild herbs and spicy notes . . . light, yet lusty with an intriguing sexy zing [and an] aromatic fern fragrance" (p. 13).

"Light yet lusty" aptly describes the romantic fantasy crucial to the marketing strategy, for it was devised to be as unique as the scent insofar as it targeted both males and females. According to Sprules, this was the first time that a fragrance company had set out to design an appeal targeted to women who buy cologne for men as well as to men who purchase it for themselves or as gifts. Sprules was quite explicit in his statement of a dual-sex strategy, noting that he created a romance— for our purposes, a clear genre identification—to appeal to female buyers. He commented that "romance appeals to women more than does sex" and directed attention to the "idea of relationships" as a strong factor in the ads. He also stated that each advertisement involved humor and mild teasing between the two characters. Sprules gave as a reason for each ad's featuring a sole figure speaking on a telephone the idea that this portrayal would be successful "because of our urges to listen in on other people's conversations."

Although the sole figures shown in the ads were always male, different models were used. Sprules revealed that this, too, was deliberate, saying he wanted to appeal to male buyers by using different models for the campaign. He avoided creating a single identifiable "Paco Man" for two reasons: first, to encourage many different types of males to relate to the ads, and second, to avoid one recognizable spokesman who might have "been a turnoff if the viewer did not generally like the looks of the man." To this end, he positioned the male figure such that he would take up only a small portion of the picture and located him off-center. Thus the authorial decision dictating the pictorial depiction of the model and the companion verbal copy proclaims the intent to create a text designed to appeal to both sexes by guiding male and female readers to construct a romantic fantasy.

WOMEN'S FICTION: ROMANCE FEATURES AND THE EXEMPLAR

Literary history tells us that males and females are unlikely to construct the same romantic fantasies—there is no single "right" reading, but, instead, gendered attitudes toward the genre known as "romance" literature. The reasons are contained in the synonym for this form of text: It is also called "women's fiction." Historically, the romance genre is one that appeals primarily to women (Radway, 1985). Romances (for example, those in the Harlequin paperbacks or those written by Barbara Cartland) have traditionally been written by, for, and about women; additionally, they are purchased almost exclusively by women; and finally, they are nearly always evaluated as a type of fiction that men especially dislike (Holland & Sherman, 1988). The romance conventions (see below) appeal to women on the simplest level by featuring female protagonists. Here, romances run counter to a general tendency of literature to overrepresent male characters and underrepresent female ones—for example, in children's books throughout the twentieth century, the ratio of male to female central characters has been 3:1 (Griswold, 1993). In addition to focusing on a female character, women's romances express themes salient to women, such as the importance of monogamy and marriage as determinants of happiness, the key role that consumption plays in women's lives, and the possibility of "living happily ever after" as a woman's destiny (Radway, 1985).

Not surprisingly, a separate but parallel category of literature called "men's fiction" (see Cawelti, 1976) has been identified, one that embodies a counter set of romantic fantasies designed to appeal to men. Gender preferences extend beyond the romance category to television programs and films as well: Women respond more positively to soap operas and musicals, whereas men respond more positively to football games and war stories (Holbrook, 1993). In order to explain these differences more fully, let us summarize the conventions of the generic romance and then work out their deployment in men's versus women's fiction (Coles & Shamp, 1984; Stern, 1991):

- focus on heroine as main character
- glorification of courtship and premarital love

- idealization of limited sexual activity
- centrality of a love relationship
- importance of consumption (purchases, products, uses)
- presence of fantasy or supernatural elements
- monogamous outcome: success is "living happily ever after"
- reader identification with heroine

On the surface, the Paco Rabanne advertisement appears to incorporate some of these genre conventions, just as the statement of authorial intent indicates. Briefly, it depicts a two-person telephone conversation between a male character, whom we refer to as the "hero" (visible, with his part of the dialogue not italicized), and a female character, whom we refer to as the "heroine" (not visible, with her part of the dialogue italicized). They are involved in a courtship, a romantic relationship that is made manifest by means of sexual innuendo—the sexual activity is allusive rather than explicit. The pictorial displays a compendium of consumer goods defining the good life (a boat, books, chess set, plants, fine fabrics, and nautical accessories), and the dialogue is replete with consumption references (luxury travel, elegant accommodations). Both characters express fantasies about relationships, and the conversation deals with their personal relationship.

ONE ROMANCE FANTASY OR TWO?

It is immediately evident, however, that the most salient characteristic of a romance—focus on the heroine as the main character—is absent. The heroine is invisible. Further, monogamy is relevant to but one of the participants, and the unseen one at that. Whereas the heroine's fantasy involves a single sexual partner, the hero's fantasy involves several. This raises the question of potential contrasts between men's and women's romances, suggesting that what men and women define as "romance fantasy" is likely to differ. Literary history supports this contention, for in narratives from earliest times to the present day, "differences in the norms of courtship behavior specific to each sex" (Pfister, 1991, p. 166) have been found. These differences are so pervasive and replicative that gender (along with age, race, and social class) is considered a universally relevant differentiating feature characteristic of all known literature (Pfister, 1991) and language (Lakoff, 1975). Insofar as each person's language is grounded in a series of culturally determined

TABLE 2.1 Men's and Women's Romance Fantasies

Women's Fantasies	Men's Fantasies
Focus on heroine	Focus on hero

Chaste heroine
    limited sex
    above the waist
    erotic descriptions
	Sexually active heroine
	    abundant and varied sex
	    anything goes
	    pornographic descriptions

Centrality of love theme	Centrality of conquest theme
Passionate consumption	Utilitarian consumption
Fantasy limited to love	Fantasy wide-ranging, sexual
Success is marriage, living "happily ever after"	Success is conquest, finding the grail

Reader identifies with heroine,
    objectifies hero
	Reader identifies with hero, objectifies
	    heroine

and shared beliefs, socialized differences in the belief structures associated with different sex roles for men and women are actualized by different experiences of a text.

In consequence, as shown in Table 2.1, the generic features of romantic fantasies are worked out differently in those designated as "women's fiction" and those designated comparably as "men's fiction," a category including sports stories, westerns, and techno-thrillers (Cawelti, 1976).

In sum, whereas we accept Sprules's genre assignation of "romance fantasy" on the basis of authorial pronouncement and of internal textual evidence (the main features are present), we hypothesize that male and female interpretations and evaluations of the ad's nature and meaning will differ. We now turn to a study conducted to test this assumption by adapting Holland and Sherman's (1988) method to identify differences in male and female readings of "Man on a Boat."

The Study: Method

Holland and Sherman's method of eliciting gender-based readings was to use *themselves* as "readers reading"—that is, they conducted a dialogue with each other to produce male and female interpretations of gothic novels. This method requires some discussion, for it may be unfamiliar outside of literary criticism. In that discipline, this method is an introspective and iterative way of generating a "subjective reading" (Bleich, 1975, 1978) by engaging in a discussion about a text aimed at evoking its rich associations. The respondents illustrate the process of cocreating meaning by discussing the encoded genre elements of a text and by articulating what each one finds in it (Bleich, 1988). The process is often tape-recorded and transcribed/edited at a later date.

Our study departs somewhat from Holland and Sherman's procedure by using written interpretive protocols rather than spoken dialogue. In so doing, it also departs from Mick and Buhl's (1992) method, for they too conducted oral interviews that were tape-recorded and then transcribed. We chose instead to generate written protocols, agreeing in advance that each would write his or her commentary independently and then exchange it by mail with the other in successive rounds of interaction. Our rationale was that independently written protocols would permit each voice to emerge clearly. However, this departure is not especially radical; the method of writing individual response statements has a long history in subjective literary criticism, having been used since I. A. Richards (1929) first studied student responses to poetry.

In acknowledgment of the limitations in our study, we point out, as do Holland and Sherman (1988), that we may not be generally representative of all male and all female readers. Despite this limitation, we echo their affirmation that even if their responses are atypical, "we will never know by simply assuming" so (p. 232). They continue: "One cannot learn about actual responses except by studying actual responses" (p. 232). In this spirit, we present the study as an exploratory effort to elicit male and female reader responses to an advertisement targeted to both sexes. In presenting our responses (labeled W for the woman respondent and M for the man respondent), we claim only to actualize the "potential space" between a sample advertising text and two opposite-sex readers (Holland & Sherman, 1988, p. 225). We thus present the authentic experiences of two real people as a way to begin the exploration of the influence of gender on the interpretation of advertising.

The procedure for eliciting gender differences was to conduct three iterative readings by W and M (Rounds 1, 2, and 3) as follows:

Round 1: W and M each provided an independent reading of the text (typed onto diskettes and cross-mailed in such a way that neither saw the other's interpretation before completing his or her own).

Round 2: W read M's Round 1 interpretation and M read W's Round 1 interpretation; each reacted through a second reading.

Round 3: W read M's Round 2 interpretation and M read W's Round 2 interpretation; again, each reacted through a third reading.

On completion of the rounds, both M and W undertook an interpretive analysis of all the readings. The framework was a set of binary oppositions developed out of the genre conventions applicable to men's and women's fiction (see Table 2.1). These oppositions are organized into an abbreviated schematic presentation of contrasts in Table 2.2, a summary of M's and W's close readings. Note that the terms *hero* and *heroine* are used merely to facilitate clear discussion, and not to imply evaluations of the characters' statures. We now turn to M's and W's interpretations, using categories listed in Table 2.2 to discuss the heroine, the hero, and their relationship.

Interpretations

THE HEROINE

Socioeconomic status. M and W construct very different pictures of the socioeconomic status of the woman. W sees her as a well-heeled businessperson with important obligations:

> What she asks herself is why she is "up here" (civilization, a city, work?) while he is in the islands. . . . We can surmise that she has obligations requiring her to be somewhere other than a tropical island. . . . She has a job perhaps (or a husband and family). . . . I read her as either a wealthy wife who could cat around because her husband was off making money or a businesswoman/professional. . . . She for sure has money. . . . She has money from some source that enables her to travel.

M disagrees, and sees the heroine, whom he calls "Paco Gal," as "unemployed (since she apparently has no reason not to leave town on a moment's whim)" or at least "unoccupied . . . meaning that, to me, Gal seems to have few professional responsibilities that would prevent her leaving town at a moment's notice on . . . a weekday." M elsewhere spells out his assumption that it is a weekday because, if it were the weekend, the real owners of the boat would be on board and the hero,

TABLE 2.2 Gendered Interpretations: Binary Oppositions in Men's and Women's
Readings

Feminine Reading	Masculine Reading
Heroine	
Traits	
ambiguously dishonest	bimbo
unrepressed, not whorelike	a little shady
sophisticated, organized	provincial, bad taste
Social standing	
has obligations	unemployed
wealthy	unencumbered
professional	unoccupied
Sexual identity	
dominant aggressor	aggressive, assertive
overtly sexual	horny
not a feminist	liberated
Overall appraisal	
kind of admire (empathy)	sort of like (scrutiny)
Hero	
Traits	
stickler for accuracy	gigolo
neat	slovenly
sadistic and off-putting	sadistic and off-putting
Social standing	
owns boat	cabin boy
Sexual identity	
ambiguous/role reversal	androgynous/impotent
male chauvinist pig	insecure sexually
Overall appraisal	
don't like	strongly dislike
Attitude toward relationship	
Hero	
won't budge	cruel indifference
couldn't care less	callous disinterest
Heroine	
sexually available	oversexed

whom he calls "Paco Guy," would not be standing around in his
swimming trunks drinking coffee at 11 o'clock in the morning. Insofar
as W is herself an employed professional woman (a college professor),
she identifies with the heroine, characterizing her as a woman of some
status and resources. M, on the other hand, also a college professor,
characterizes the heroine as someone quite unlike himself—a person
who is unemployed or idle.

Personality traits. The divergence in M's and W's attributions of socio-economic status (the externals of life) also pervades their assessments of the heroine's personality and character (internal characteristics). Here, they begin by appearing to agree: Both M and W comment on the heroine's somewhat ambiguously "dishonest" nature, her unrepressed tendencies, and her easy availability as a sexual partner. However, although they converge in agreeing that she is morally ambiguous and sexually expressive, they diverge in their interpretations of what these traits signify. W regards the heroine as rather sophisticated and well organized: "She has sufficient sophistication and organizational skills to orchestrate the trip on a moment's notice. This strikes me as pretty clever and the act of an experienced woman." In contrast, M finds her "provincial or at least not too well traveled (because she hates flying and doesn't know the difference between a window and a porthole)" and accuses her of having bad taste: "Anybody who will travel thousands of miles . . . to pursue an overpowering whiff of a sickeningly sweet men's cologne just does not, in my humble opinion, possess a really refined experiential palate or a carefully calibrated set of values." These divergences support the tendency of W to identify with the heroine by attributing to her traits that are both desirable and self-relevant (sophistication, cleverness, organizational skill) and of M to distance himself from a heroine whose traits are antithetical to those he admires—narrow provincialism, bad taste, and questionable values.

Sexual identity. Perhaps the area where W and M seem most in agreement is in their evaluation of the heroine as far from the chaste maiden of standard women's fiction. Both point out that she articulates the sexual aggressiveness much more typical of heroines in male romantic fantasies. As W points out, "This [sexual aggressiveness] is hinted at in the first six words she says: How would you like to come . . . ?" M goes even further in finding her assertiveness graphically expressed by means of the copy typography: "The italicization of her speeches gives them an added emphasis that his more pallid typeface seems to lack." M defines her as "horny as hell," but also appreciates her "endearing emotional openness" and views her as "an aggressive but basically desirable and overtly available paramour." To this, W adds—somewhat paradoxically—the comment that "her labeling of other women as sound of body/weak of mind suggests that while unrepressed, she is no feminist."

This last comment indicates the divergence simmering underneath M's and W's apparent agreement: W sounds a disparaging note by pointing out that the heroine is not a feminist—from W's perspective (herself an outspoken feminist) and that of most feminist critics, this is not a positive endorsement. The heroine's derogation of other women as sex objects elicits W's disapproval, an interesting contrast to M's lack of attention to the heroine's attitude toward women in general. Even while criticizing what he regards as her bad taste in both men and fragrances, M takes a more approving view of her sexual and emotional accessibility, whereas W faults her not for sexual frankness but for putting down other women who share the same trait. This is, in effect, a variant of "queen bee syndrome," in which a woman sets out to elevate herself as a woman while at the same time derogating other women.

THE HERO

Socioeconomic status. M's and W's differences in reading the heroine are echoed by comparable differences in their readings of the hero. In terms of the hero's socioeconomic status, W tended to take the pictorial representation fairly literally as a view of a wealthy boat owner at play on his vessel:

> Maybe this is a sailboat, which could explain the small living quarters. . . . *sailor* would refer to the person who owns and operates a sailboat. . . . Further, she [the heroine] may not have come straight to the boat for a good reason. . . . There may be only the one narrow bunk on the boat—you [M] assume that it is a large yacht, but what if it is a small (compact) but luxurious sailboat? . . . I see him as the owner of the boat.

In contrast to this flattering view of the hero, M is confident in his beliefs that the boat is a large yacht (because half of it is in front of the mast, and, therefore, behind the photographer), that the hero does not use the main sleeping area, and that he is probably just a cabin boy. M says: "We soon realize that this fellow is actually the cabin boy. . . . A boat this size would have a forward cabin with a big double bed. Obviously, he doesn't sleep there. Equally obviously, somebody else— namely, the boat's owners—does or do sleep there." The vehemence of M's aversive response to the hero can be construed as an instance of anti-identification. It differs both in degree and substance from W's more casual and disinterested assumption about boat ownership. M's overt anti-identification takes the form of denigrating the hero (see below), whereas W's disinterest in tearing him down indicates that identification with him is a nonissue.

Personality traits. Continuing the divergence, W and M disagree as to the personality traits and moral character of the hero. W regards him as a "stickler for accuracy" because he interrupts the heroine ("window") to make a correction ("porthole") in her nautical terminology. W also regards the hero as personally neat, for she views the boat's cabin as tidy: "books neatly arranged on a shelf . . . galley gadgets harmoniously placed." M takes a quite different view, labeling the hero as a gigolo who is also a bit on the slovenly side: "Our hero appears to be just arising for the day. He has not yet had time to drink much of his morning coffee, which is still full nearly to the rim. But the sun has already risen to about the eleven o'clock position. . . . He is too lazy to make his bed . . . and too casual to bother putting on anything more than swimming trunks."

Notwithstanding M's and W's disagreement about sloppiness versus tidiness, both agree emphatically that the hero is "sadistic" and fundamentally "off-putting." W personalizes her disapproving comments about his "sadistic sense of humor": "She flew a long distance and is waiting in bed for him, and he tells her that she's caught him at a bad time. I don't like him at all." M expresses essentially the same reaction to the hero's "sadistic . . . fantasy": "Here Bimbo Gal has followed this creep to God-knows-where, and all he can think of to do is make a bunch of off-putting remarks. How insensitive can you get?" However, M does not directly express a personal opinion about the hero, instead expressing antipathy by calling the hero a "creep."

Thus, whereas the content of M's and W's responses is not dissimilar, their modes of expression corroborate male/female differences found in earlier research (see Stern, 1993). In Bleich's (1988) and Flynn's (1988) studies, female readers were found more likely to interpolate themselves into a story, and male readers were found to express their distaste for a plot or character in stronger judgmental terms. Note here that M's and W's surface agreement is deceptive and must be closely examined for differences in language form (syntax, diction) to make hidden differences visible by exposing the *how* of saying that underlies what is being said.

Sexual identity. Surface similarities masking latent differences also characterize M's and W's interpretations of the hero's sexual identity. Both M and W agree that he is sexually ambiguous or androgynous and that gender role reversal is evident in his actions (he is passive and waits/ she is active and travels to him). W points out that ambiguity is present from the first word in the copy: "The opening greeting . . . hello? . . . is punctuated with a question mark . . . more characteristic of women's language than of men's." W infers that "some gender bending will occur" and moves toward a characterization of the hero as homosexual or bisexual: "There are a lot of things about this guy that are indicative of gayness to me—the cabin decor, his male-modelish body, longish hair, macrame doodad hanging from the lantern. He just isn't all-man to me."

M concurs with W's attribution of androgyny and provides two somewhat subtle pieces of pictorial evidence that W failed to notice: First, on the chessboard, "the king is out of place," and second,

> the phallic symbol . . . at the bottom of the right-hand column . . . is a telescope (penis analogue) in the collapsed (flaccid) and horizontal (impotent) rather than the extended (erect) position. But notice also what a tiny telescope it is. This spyglass—this obvious symbol of our hero's male organ—is literally dwarfed in size by the bottle of eau de toilette next to which it . . . lies.

M's explanation is that the hero verges on impotence, an assessment that does not so much label the hero's sexual identity as deny that he has any.

But whereas M emphasizes the hero's insecure or damaged sexuality, W is less interested in this than in considering the hero's treatment of women. W notes that the hero is a bit of a male chauvinist pig: "His view of women is rather unenlightened—betrays MCP ideology. . . . The women are plying him with fruit . . . and have 'been teaching me the secret island ways of love'—[which] delineates women's place in his mind; they provide food and sex." In sum, M and W interpret the social, personal, and sexual characteristics of the hero and heroine in terms of gender issues specific to their own sexes. W identifies with the heroine, seeing her as a woman like herself, whereas M objectifies the heroine, viewing her from the outside. M interprets the heroine in reference to men in general, not in personal terms. In their interpretations of the hero, M expresses hostile anti-identification, whereas W objectifies the hero by viewing him in terms of his relation to women.

Notwithstanding general agreement about the hero's flaws, the tone of the readings shows a fundamental gender-based difference. That is, W's reading states personal dislike, interpreting the hero as someone who might do her harm in a relationship, whereas M expresses dislike by interpreting the hero as someone whose relational behavior is dishonest.

EVALUATION OF THE HERO/HEROINE AND THE RELATIONSHIP

Before turning to the relationship in the advertisement, let us recall that the central relationship in a woman's romantic fantasy is love (winning a commitment), whereas that in a man's romantic fantasy (Cawelti, 1976) is conquest (winning a sexual adventure). M's and W's interpretations shed light on differences in male and female responses to what is shown and said about the relationship. W remains relatively silent on the hero's attitude toward the romantic relationship, commenting only that he "won't budge" from his boat (the heroine goes to see him) and that he "couldn't care less" (whether the heroine is or is not there). M's response is more aversive: He characterizes the hero as showing "cruel indifference" and "callous disinterest." M says:

> [The hero] begins by correcting [the heroine's] use of the English language, making her feel ignorant and poorly schooled in the Ways of the World. Then he compounds the offense by saying that he never thought he would hear her say something nice. Then, clearly on a sadistic roll and unable to stop himself, he glides into a little self-indulgent fantasy about the kind of females with whom he would ostensibly like to be spending his time (a cabin full of doe-eyed women in skimpy sarongs . . .).

Although M and W agree that the relationship is sexual rather than loving, they do not agree on whether or not it is one of conquest or on who is the conquered/conquering party. M flatly states that the heroine "is still horny *despite* the scary plane ride—in other words, oversexed." W is more ameliorative, saying that "the relationship is from the outset defined by sex (rather than, let us say, love)." W looks for a motivation more complex than sexual hunger for the heroine's behavior: "Perhaps a show of horniness is the only way she can appeal to Guy [the hero]. Maybe she is in love with him, but recognizes that at best his interest in her is sexual. . . . She may be faking sexual desire to cover over her need to see him under any circumstances." These responses suggest that W interprets the heroine's behavior as strategically related to that of heroines in women's fiction, whose success is defined in terms of achieving a marital (or at least a committed) relationship. M, on the other hand, interprets the relationship as one more typical of men's fiction—adventurous sex with no ties, least of all a tie that binds forever after.

To sum up, M's and W's overall assessments of the hero and heroine show latent divergence under surface convergence. They both strongly dislike the man, and W "kind of admires" the woman, whereas M finds her "endearing." However, the important differences occur under the surface, for M tends to distance himself from the hero and heroine (both of whom, the former especially, he finds less than compellingly attractive), whereas W identifies with the heroine empathically. The issue of divergence/convergence is addressed directly in M's and W's dialogue, for W says, "We do agree in liking her, but you see her from the outside (sexy and desirable and available), while I am trying to see her from the inside (hopelessly in love, obsessing, tortured by a louse). Your reading seems more evaluative while mine is more empathetic." Thus the judgmental/empathic dimension that has been found to discriminate between male and female readers of literature (Bleich, 1988; Flynn, 1988) appears to function similarly when an advertisement is the stimulus text.

OVERALL EVALUATION OF THE ADVERTISEMENT

Both readers are marketing professors and approach the advertisement as a persuasive document designed to stimulate a consumption outcome. However, there is a major difference in M's and W's speculations about the strategic rationale behind the marketing campaign. W confines her comments to what has been learned about the target segment(s) from the advertisement's sponsor and author, using this information as evidence of a segmenting strategy based on gender. She refers to the male and female segments that the author identifies as targets ("a two-sex strategy . . . aimed at men and . . . women for their own use"). She goes beyond authorial commentary to add additional gender-oriented material when she points out that bisexuals and gays are also probable targets of an advertisement "aimed at a consumer whose sexuality is ambivalent . . . and . . . designed to inspire empathy with those of indeterminate sexuality." In the absence of authorial identification of a gay target market, W references a retail environment to support her contention: "At Bloomingdale's Men's Cologne Bar . . . the product demonstrators were gay, as were most of the customers."

But whereas W's inferences relate to the demographics of the target markets, M's inferences relate to their psychographics—notably, to the sexual confusion of some consumers who might find the advertisement appealing. In so doing, M begins by hypothesizing a discrepancy between the manifest strategic surface content of the message and its latent meaning to consumers. He describes the surface meaning as follows:

> Most readers, I suspect, would glance at the ad, would see a handsome stud on a luxury yacht, would skim the words enough to figure out that the man is attractive to at least one sexy woman, would notice that he uses Paco Rabanne, and would conclude that this particular fragrance serves as an invaluable tool for enhancing a fellow's ability to appeal to members of the opposite sex. . . . In short, Nice Boat plus Sexy Woman indicates Cool Dude implies Get Paco.

M ultimately detects a somewhat contradictory latent meaning buried below the surface, one that emerges in the juxtaposition of the telescope and bottle of Paco Rabanne in the lower right-hand corner:

> So now—at last—we know the secrets of our tormented hero: a slovenly personal existence, the failure to find a decent self-respecting job, a sexually insecure indifference to heterosexual love, and . . . genitalia whose stature pales in comparison to the true object of the woman's attention and the advertiser's gaze—namely, the bottle of Paco Rabanne. In relative terms, the ratio in sizes of this bottle of eau de toilette versus this telescope as compared with that for a normal bottle versus a normal telescope is about 637 to 1. . . . Thus, clearly, it appears that what is remembered about our hero—as emphasized by the last line of the ad—is not the power of his male sexuality. Rather, it is the sweet and slightly effeminate smell of his Paco Rabanne cologne.

Here, M's uncovering of his own responses to meanings latent in the advertising message resembles that of Bleich's (1988) and Flynn's (1988) male readers, in contrast to W's experiential reading, typical of female readers who interject their own experiences to make sense out of text.

Conclusions

This study yields insight into the ways that readers of opposite sexes construct interpretations of an advertising exemplar. The foregoing interpretations reveal the tension between convergence and divergence in terms of agreements and disagreements between the two readers. The following lists provide a summary.

Agreements

- The overall evaluation of the hero is that he is sadistic and off-putting.
- The overall evaluation of the heroine is that she is unrepressed, admirable, endearing.
- The hero is sexually ambiguous or androgynous.
- The hero is cruelly indifferent.
- The heroine is interested primarily in sex.
- The heroine is overtly aggressive or dominant.

Disagreements

- W: The hero is neat and tidy, wealthy, and a bit of a male chauvinist pig.
  M: The hero is sloppy and lazy, menially employed as a cabin boy, and sexually insecure.
- W: The heroine is sophisticated, professional, but no feminist.
  M: The heroine is provincial, an unencumbered free spirit, and liberated.
- W evaluates the ad in terms of target markets of diverse sexual orientations.
  M evaluates the ad as an overt appeal to macho males, but decodes a latent subtext that appears likely to attract those of confused sexual identity.

However, what is perhaps the most striking feature of the dialogue abstracted in the preceding section is the inability of M and W to agree on the issue of whether or not there is divergence or convergence. After Round 1, M proclaimed: "Amazing! . . . I find myself gratifyingly surprised by the extent to which our independent interpretations of the Paco Rabanne ad converged on the very first round." At the same time, W insisted that "her reading is very different" and even suggested that "sometimes I was not sure that we were reading the same ad." As the dialogue proceeded, M devoted more of his attention to efforts to convince W that the two basically agreed, whereas W spent more energy denying apparent convergence in interpretations.

The controversy can be framed as a question: Do M's and W's readings agree or disagree? M feels that the answer lies somewhere in between. On the other hand, W is more insistent on differentiating interpretations based on gender. W states: "It is true that you are more intent on seeing convergence and that I am more interested in seeing divergence, but this could be the glass half empty/glass half full point of view." The convergence argument rests on agreement about details, for when support was found in clear textual evidence, these two close and careful readers reached near unanimity. However, diverging views remained despite a lengthy dialogue that extended to about 50 double-spaced typed pages and that is only hinted at by the summary of key points above.[1]

The final question is whether the differences reflect meaningful contrasts in reading styles flowing from gender differences. Here again the two readers—now wearing their hats as researchers—tend to disagree. W tends to regard her reading as demonstrating the feminine virtue of empathy as opposed to M's more distanced propensity to pass evaluative judgment. M tends to regard his reading as supported by pictorial details concerning the design of the boat, the positions of objects in the cabin, and the juxtaposition of the bottle with a small telescope (below the copy, bottom right) that W failed to notice. In other words, M views his reading as fairly neutral with respect to sexual stereotyping and refrains from labeling W's reading as "typically feminine" in any way, whereas W views M as more typically masculine in his efforts to dominate the text by judging the characters and by distancing himself from them. What W and M agree on is that the truly wonderful thing about interpretive research on advertising is that there is obviously no single correct answer to the questions raised about meaning. Rather, this study can be seen as a fruitful beginning. In Flynn's (1988) words:

> In order to make conclusive assertions about the relationship between gender and reading we need to look at a large number of response statements, at the responses of women and men readers from a variety of backgrounds, and at responses to numerous kinds of texts at various stages in the reading process. (p. 285)

In this spirit, we end by encouraging other readers to engage with advertising texts, to converse about them, to perform their own close readings, and—ultimately—to continue the dialogue about gender and genre in the hopes of advancing our understanding of advertising meanings.

Note

1. Interested readers may obtain a copy of the full written protocols by writing to Barbara Stern at the Faculty of Management, Rutgers, The State University of New Jersey, 180 University Avenue, Newark, NJ 07102; or to Morris Holbrook at the Department of Marketing, Graduate School of Business, Columbia University, 504 Uris Hall, New York, NY 10027.

References

Abrams, M. H. (1988). *A glossary of literary terms* (5th ed.). New York: Holt, Rinehart & Winston.

Berman, A. (1988). *From the New Criticism to deconstruction: The reception of structuralism and poststructuralism*. Urbana: University of Illinois Press.

Bleich, D. (1975). *Readings and feelings: An introduction to subjective criticism*. Urbana, IL: National Council of Teachers of English.

Bleich, D. (1978). *Subjective criticism*. Baltimore: Johns Hopkins University Press.

Bleich, D. (1988). Gender interests in reading and language. In E. A. Flynn & P. P. Schweickart (Eds.), *Gender and reading: Essays on readers, texts, and contexts* (2nd ed., pp. 234-266). Baltimore: Johns Hopkins University Press.

Cawelti, J. G. (1976). *Adventure, mystery, and romance*. Chicago: University of Chicago Press.

Chodorow, N. (1978). *The reproduction of mothering: Psychoanalysis and the sociology of gender*. Berkeley: University of California Press.

Coates, J. (1988). Introduction. In J. Coates & D. Cameron (Eds.), *Women in their speech communities: New perspectives on language and sex* (pp. 63-73). London: Longman.

Coles, C. D., & Shamp, N. J. (1984). Some sexual, personality, and demographic characteristics of women readers of erotic romances. *Archives of Sexual Behavior, 13*, 187-209.

Crawford, M., & Chaffin, R. (1988). The reader's construction of meaning: Cognitive research on gender and comprehension. In E. A. Flynn & P. P. Schweickart (Eds.), *Gender and reading: Essays on readers, texts, and contexts* (2nd ed., pp. 3-30). Baltimore: Johns Hopkins University Press.

Dilthey, W. (1972). The rise of hermeneutics (F. Jameson, Trans.). *New Literary History, 3*, 229-244.

Di Maggio, P. (1987). Classification in art. *American Sociological Review, 52*, 440-455.

Downing, J., & Leong, C. K. (1982). *Psychology of reading*. New York: Macmillan.

Dubois, J., & Durand, P. (1989). Literary field and classes of texts. In P. Desan, P. P. Ferguson, & W. Griswold (Eds.), *Literature and social practice* (pp. 137-153). Chicago: University of Chicago Press.

Flynn, E. A. (1988). Gender and reading. In E. A. Flynn & P. P. Schweickart (Eds.), *Gender and reading: Essays on readers, texts, and contexts* (2nd ed., pp. 267-288). Baltimore: Johns Hopkins University Press.

Fowler, A. (1982). *Kinds of literature: An introduction to the theory of genres and modes*. Cambridge, MA: Harvard University Press.

Griswold, W. (1993). Recent moves in the sociology of literature. *Annual Review of Sociology, 19*, 445-467.

Hirsch, E. D., Jr. (1967). *Validity in interpretation*. New Haven, CT: Yale University Press.

Hirsch, E. D., Jr. (1976). *The aims of interpretation*. Chicago: University of Chicago Press.

Holbrook, M. B. (1993). Nostalgia and consumption preferences: Some emerging patterns of consumer tastes. *Journal of Consumer Research, 20,* 245-256.

Holbrook, M. B., & Zirlin, R. B. (1985). Artistic creation, artworks, and aesthetic appreciation: Some philosophical contributions to nonprofit marketing. In R. W. Belk (Ed.), *Advances in nonprofit marketing* (Vol. 1, pp. 1-54). Greenwich, CT: JAI.

Holland, N. N. (1975). *Five readers reading*. New Haven, CT: Yale University Press.

Holland, N. N., & Sherman, L. F. (1988). Gothic possibilities. In E. A. Flynn & P. P. Schweickart (Eds.), *Gender and reading: Essays on readers, texts, and contexts* (2nd ed., pp. 215-233). Baltimore: Johns Hopkins University Press.

Ingarden, R. (1973). *The literary work of art: An investigation on the borderlines of ontology, logic, and theory of literature* (G. G. Grabowicz, Trans.). Evanston, IL: Northwestern University Press. (Original work published 1931)

Joyce, J. (1957). *A portrait of the artist as a young man*. New York: Viking. (Original work published 1916)

Kramerae, C. (1981). *Women and men speaking*. Rowley, MA: Newbury House.

Lakoff, R. (1975). *Language and woman's place*. New York: Harper & Row.

Lavidge, R., & Steiner, G. A. (1961, October). A model for predictive measurements of advertising effectiveness. *Journal of Marketing, 25,* 59-62.

Maccoby, E. E., & Jacklin, C. (1974). *The psychology of sex differences*. Stanford, CA: Stanford University Press.

Mailloux, S. (1982). *Interpretive conventions*. Ithaca, NY: Cornell University Press.

Marshall, C. (1983, May 16). O&M relate secret of success. *Advertising Age,* p. 37.

McCracken, G. (1989). Who is the celebrity endorser? Cultural foundations of the endorsement process. *Journal of Consumer Research, 16,* 310-321.

Mick, D. G., & Buhl, C. (1992). A meaning-based model of advertising experiences. *Journal of Consumer Research, 19,* 317-338.

Pfister, M. (1991). *The theory and analysis of drama*. New York: Cambridge University Press.

Philips, S. U. (1989). Introduction: The interaction of social and biological processes in women's and men's speech. In S. U. Philips, S. Steele, & C. Tanz (Eds.), *Language, gender, and sex in comparative perspective* (pp. 1-11). Cambridge: Cambridge University Press.

Radway, J. A. (1985). *Reading the romance: Women, patriarchy, and popular literature*. Chapel Hill: University of North Carolina Press.

Richards, I. A. (1929). *Practical criticism: A study of literary judgment*. New York: Harcourt Brace.

Ricoeur, P. (1974). *The conflict of interpretations: Essays in hermeneutics* (D. Ihde, Ed.). Evanston, IL: Northwestern University Press.

Rosenblatt, L. M. (1983). *Literature as exploration* (4th ed.). New York: Modern Language Association of America. (Original work published 1938)

Rosenblatt, L. M. (1964). The poem as event. *College English, 26,* 121-128.

Scholes, R., & Kellogg, R. (1968). *The nature of narrative*. New York: Oxford University Press.

Schweickart, P. P., & Flynn, E. A. (1988). Introduction. In E. A. Flynn & P. P. Schweickart (Eds.), *Gender and reading: Essays on readers, texts, and contexts* (2nd ed., pp. ix-xxx). Baltimore: Johns Hopkins University Press.

Scott, L. M. (1990). Understanding jingles and needledrop: A rhetorical approach to music in advertising. *Journal of Consumer Research, 17,* 223-236.

Segel, E. (1988). As the twig is bent . . . : Gender and childhood reading. In E. A. Flynn & P. P. Schweickart (Eds.), *Gender and reading: Essays on readers, texts, and contexts* (2nd ed., pp. 165-186). Baltimore: Johns Hopkins University Press.

Staton, S. F. (1987). *Literary theories in praxis.* Philadelphia: University of Pennsylvania Press.

Stern, B. B. (1989). Literary criticism and consumer research: Overview and illustrative analysis. *Journal of Consumer Research, 16,* 322-334.

Stern, B. B. (1991). Two pornographies: A feminist view of sex in advertising. In R. H. Holman & M. R. Solomon (Eds.), *Advances in consumer research* (Vol. 18, pp. 384-391). Provo, UT: Association for Consumer Research.

Stern, B. B. (1993). Feminist literary criticism and the deconstruction of advertisements: A postmodern view of advertising and consumer responses. *Journal of Consumer Research, 19,* 556-566.

Suleiman, S. R. (1980). Introduction: Varieties of audience-oriented criticism. In S. R. Suleiman & I. Crosman (Eds.), *The reader in the text: Essays on audience and interpretation* (pp. 3-45). Princeton, NJ: Princeton University Press.

Todorov, T. (1981). *Introduction to poetics* (R. Howard, Trans.). Minneapolis: University of Minnesota Press. (Original work published 1968)

Tompkins, J. P. (1980). *Reader-response criticism: From formalism to post-structuralism.* Baltimore: Johns Hopkins University Press.

3

Gender Identity in the Indian Context: A Sociocultural Construction of the Female Consumer

ALLADI VENKATESH

THIS chapter addresses gender identity issues and rising consumerism in India, and their joint implications for our understanding of the emerging Indian female consumer. In the first part of the chapter, I present a theoretical and conceptual analysis of gender as it pertains to Indian society, using a sociocultural framework of gender theory. Although the term *gender* includes both male and female, my focus in this chapter is on women, because most changes are occurring in regard to their roles and status in the Indian context. In the second part of the chapter, I discuss consumer trends in India and the construction of the identity of the emerging female consumer by the media.

Provision of a comprehensive account of the "condition of women" in India is beyond the scope of this chapter. There is ample literature available in this regard, in terms of both quality and quantity (see

AUTHOR'S NOTE: This research was supported by a Senior Fellowship grant from the American Institute of Indian Studies.

Anant, Rao, & Kapoor, 1986, for a detailed bibliography; for some relevant areas of discussion, I refer to Krishna Raj & Chanana, 1990; Parikh & Garg, 1989; Rose, 1992; Sharma, 1986). Just as the scholarly and critical literature is impressive and growing, so are the number of popular magazines in India (*Femina, Women's Era, Savvy,* and others) that focus on women's issues, from the serious to the glamorous and even to the more sordid.

At the risk of oversimplification, the gender question in India may be encapsulated in two opposing, yet parallel, themes. The first is the significantly emancipatory nature of women's condition in certain urban contexts (especially the urban middle-class group, or career women, or educated/professional segments), where changes are occurring in a dramatic fashion; the second is a corresponding lack of development among women in various other social categories (e.g., urban poor, rural, agrarian workers), primarily because of severe structural, cultural, and economic impediments (Mies, 1986; Wignaraja, 1990). (There are, of course, some intermediary positions within these two extremes.) In this chapter I examine the implications for consumer behavior of the changes taking place among the women in the former group.

The Ethnosociological Context

An important way to analyze the situation of women in India must be broadly framed within its own historical, social, and cultural contexts. I use the term *ethnosociological context* after Marriott (1990), who recently coined the term to provide an intellectual legitimacy to sociological and anthropological research in cross-cultural contexts. Following the serious concern expressed by researchers such as Marcus and Fischer (1986), ethnographic research took an intellectual tailspin in the wake of self-doubt and critical introspection. Although not in direct reference to Marcus and Fischer's work, Marriott (1990) has addressed this issue in an admirable manner, that is, by constructing social knowledge about other cultures on the basis of categories unique to their cultural ethos.

At this point, one is entitled to ask whether Western feminist questions and theoretical paradigms are applicable to the Indian situation— more specifically, are debates in the United States (or the West) relevant to India (or the Third World)? The answer to the question is both yes and no. There are no doubt similarities and differences—the realities are based on respective cultural, social, and historical factors, but at the same time point to certain commonalities in terms of universals such as gender hierarchy, patriarchy, and women's family roles. If similarities exist, they may be at the structural or superstructural level, that is, at the level of broad categories but not specific levels of empiricality. Although one must not attempt to impose Western etic models on Indian situations, one must not neglect to find commonalities within bounds of reason and reasonableness, if this helps us to understand the Indian question. Otherwise, there cannot be a dialogue between cultural discourses.

The Historical Context

Indian scholars and reformers who address the gender issue divide the relevant history of India into three periods: the preindependence period, or the first period (i.e., from the beginning of the mid-1800s to the 1940s—the so-called historical period of modern India), the second period (from 1947, the year India gained freedom from British rule, to 1980), and the third period (from the early 1980s to the present). This division is generally accepted in the consciousness of historical writing on India on various social and political topics.

The first period involved the awakening of the Indian spirit, its articulation, and the unfolding of the fight for freedom from British colonial rule. The gender issue was buried under the overall issue of colonial resistance, without any separate identity of its own. Women were, indeed, invited and encouraged to participate in the freedom struggle at national and local levels, and many upper-caste and educated women did (e.g., Sarojini Naidu, Vijayalakshmi Pandit, Aruna Asaf Ali, and Indira Gandhi).

The postindependence period (after 1947) established constitutional guarantees for all citizens, particularly women and underprivileged castes and classes, with a view to ensuring universal participation in the political process, in education at all levels, and in appointment to the civil service. During this period, the social condition of women improved in urban areas but not in rural areas. Considering that nearly 70% of Indians live in rural areas, the improvements seen in the urban areas could not be generalized. Even in the urban areas, the changes for the better were experienced mostly by upper-caste women, who were better situated historically and socially to take advantage of economic and educational opportunities.

In the third period, which began in the early 1980s, a new feminist consciousness seems to have awakened in India. Educated women from urban areas with strong activist or leftist leanings have begun to get involved in rural and village direct-action reform movements (Bhushan, 1989; Mies, 1986; Rose, 1992). Included in this activist group are women who have been influenced by the rising global feminist consciousness and various theoretical ideas originating in the West. They refuse to see the women's question in India at a benign reformist level; rather, they see it in transhistorical and foundational terms. This macrosystemic perspective is combined with an urge to deconstruct women's positions at an everyday, mundane level.

Theoretical Issues:
Construction of Gender and Identity

My analysis of the theoretical issues is based on some central works on Indian women and my own theorizing based on my ethnographic work (Banerjee, 1991; Bhushan, 1989; Brock-Utne, 1989; Krishna Raj & Chanana, 1990; Liddle & Joshi, 1986; Marriott, 1990; Mies, 1986; Parikh & Garg, 1989; Rose, 1992; Saradamoni, 1992; Sharma, 1986; Wadley, 1977; Wignaraja, 1990). For the Western (especially the U.S.) audience, a clear issue is how the gender question in India is different from (or similar to) that in, say, the United States.

FAMILY, KINSHIP ISSUES

First, the gender question in both India and the United States is based on respective historical, political, cultural, and social-structural conditions. Traditional Indian culture (specifically the dominant Hindu culture) very clearly specifies the role of women in terms of its household structure, kinship relationships, and caste hierarchies (Dumont, 1980). As Lardinois (1992) describes, Hinduism represents a "socially differentiated religious culture based on caste." For example, the most universal model in terms of kinship structure, holding the caste constant, is the tridependent relationship. From birth until marriage, a woman is under the protection of her father; during married life, her husband; and during later years, her son (whether her husband is alive or not). These relationships have made it impossible for a woman to be independent of male omnipresence in theory and practice, or to claim her own social space during her entire life. Her unmarried life is completely spent in preparation for a life after marriage, and in relative seclusion. In this condition, she is differentiated from a male child, because sons do not leave their biological families after marriage and are socialized from early on to be an integral part of their families, whereas women are not. Thus the status of women is marked by a liminality, as the conditions of possibility require women to live on borrowed time and the social space of the other.

In the West, women pretty much choose their own life partners, with relatively little input from their families; if there is any dependency relationship at all, it is played out in ways somewhat different from those found in India. There is no gender-based differential preparatory status for unmarried women in the West, because both men and women leave their families to establish their respective future lives upon reaching adulthood—sometimes even earlier. That is, compared with Indian culture, in the West neither males nor females have more privileged status within their families of origin. Much of Western discourse on gender focuses on the politics of difference, but not so much prior to adulthood (although this certainly exists) as during adult life.

MATRIARCHAL RELIGIOCULTURAL TRADITION

Another major difference between Western and Indian discourse is how the politics of difference are played out. In the West, the politics of difference are the focus of much debate and discussion, whereas in India the focus is more on the discourse of dependence and exploitation. The politics of difference are so obvious in India that they do not generate much energy in discourse. Differences in gender constructions are accepted by both men and women, and to some extent they are welcomed at the theoretical level. Because of this, it is difficult to import the ideas of Derrida, or Kristeva, or Irigary wholesale into the Indian scene, for these ideas are based very much on specific constructions of gendered differences without regard to kinship patterns or the sociocultural realities of Indian family life. For example, in India, there is not much dispute as to how women are written about in literature or religious texts. As evidence of this, the power of matriarchal religious tradition is quite strong in India (Liddle & Joshi, 1986). In contemporary India, female goddesses are worshipped by both men and women with equal fervor. The Hindu pantheon is full of goddesses, and Hindu India is full of temples that are the exclusive preserves of female deities. In many of these temples, female deities are more important and given a higher status than some of their male equivalents. Goddess worship represents a supreme form of ritual act and metaphysical exercise.

THRESHOLD THEORY OF
WOMEN'S POSITION IN INDIAN SOCIETY

In a complicated element of life in India, one also finds a curious phenomenon not found in the United States or the West in general. When women do manage to attain high positions in political and social life, Indians are willing to give them coequal status and the same esteem accorded men in the same positions. I use threshold theory to explain this. Because Indian society is basically hierarchical (Dumont, 1980), Indians give a lot of weight to the position itself. Consequently, any-body who occupies the position is given the same high regard, inde-pendent of that person's individual background. At higher levels, the gender of the occupant is less material. Thus Indians may resist giving a higher position to a woman (or, for that matter, to a man if he is from a lower caste), but once the person attains the position, any resistance melts away. I call this *threshold theory* because there is a threshold that operates between the person and the position. Once the individual crosses the threshold, he or she is no longer the same subordinate individual as before, but a different persona in a new position. This kind of transfiguration from individual to status position seems to be re-sisted in Western egalitarian societies, where women are still deemed as women (and perhaps rightly so, but that's not the issue here) and positional statuses are not given great importance (there may, of course, be some exceptions to this, e.g., in the military). It is the individual as an individual, and his or her characteristics, that is most pertinent in the West. In India, the individual is easily idealized into the position itself. Threshold theory is related to the religiocultural theory mentioned above; both address the issue of the individual's position.

RECENT SIGNIFICANT DEVELOPMENTS

How has all this changed over the past few years? There are two aspects to the recent developments in India, or two extreme profiles, as I mentioned in the beginning of this chapter. One consists of the dramatic developments that are taking place in certain sections of the urban communities, and the other is a relatively slower pace of change, or none at all, among rural women and the urban poor. I shall report primarily on the developments taking place among women in the first segment.

Ethnographic Account of Changing Identity Formation

First, I will present a summary from relevant ethnographic work I conducted in Madras, India, a city of about 5.5 million people. My stay in Madras lasted seven months, from June 1992 to January 1993. Madras is considered more conservative than Bombay and Delhi, although many local informants seemed to agree that the rate of change in the past five to eight years has been nothing short of dramatic. It is hard to believe that, in a country where one talks of social change in terms of decades or centuries, people are using single digits to refer to periods of change. This is the reason contemporary India is so interesting and affords a great opportunity for many social scientists to study the momentous changes that are likely to occur in the next two or three decades.

India is certainly witnessing some significant changes in the economic and social status of women and the nature of household structure in the urban areas. For the first time, we are able to see trends that transcend the caste hierarchy and reflect a more class-based system. This means that caste hierarchy is disappearing among the upper strata of society. This does not, however, mean that caste differences are themselves disappearing. In other words, economic prosperity has touched people belonging to different castes, and educational levels are increasing along similar lines. Many women from different castes attend colleges and universities, and many are gainfully employed. This has given them both economic and social status. Many young women, in contrast to past custom, are choosing their own marriage partners, either directly or through some sort of consensus with their parents. Even though many marriages today are still arranged, men and women exercise equal choice in the decision. Selection of a suitable partner remains a family decision more by consensus than by an imposition from the parents.

The attitudes of women with respect to marriage, career, and economic status, are undergoing so many changes that there seem to be intragenerational differences among women within narrow age categories. That is, there are not merely the differences between parents and daughters that one might expect to find, but differences among groups of younger women whose ages are not very far apart. The views and modes of behavior of a 30-year-old woman in establishing her own identity may be radically different from those of a 25-year-old, and the views of a 25-year-old may be different from those of a 20-year-old, and so on down to even younger age groups. These changes are extremely vibrant and turbulent at the same time. They have important repercussions and perhaps healthy ones in the reconstitution of the Indian family system and the society at large.

A major contributory factor in maintaining both patriarchy and gender hierarchy has been the nature of controls in the household system and the generating and sharing of resources. The joint family system is certainly a major structural arrangement that ensures male domination within the household through traditional gender-based household patterns of behavior. More and more, the joint family system in India is giving way to a nuclear family system. In India, the nuclear family system has both narrow and broad definitions. In the narrow definition, it includes husband, wife, and their unmarried children, or couples in the empty-nest stage. The broader definition includes grandparents also. When we combine this shift to the nuclear family system with the emergence of career roles for women and their ability to generate independent income for the family, there is no question that women's role in household management and decision making is getting stronger. This does not necessarily mean that the nuclear family system can by itself cause these changes, but it is one of the facilitating factors. The other factors are career opportunities for women, women's income-generating power, the presence of the elderly in the household or in close physical proximity, the family's adherence or nonadherence to traditional norms of behavior, and attitudes toward changes that have the potential to alienate the families from traditional patterns causing anxieties in daily lives. Add to these the attitudes of friends and families that are part of the social network. If the attitudes within the social network are progressive (or conservative), the attitudes of the families will also be progressive (or conservative). One cannot, therefore, minimize the social interaction effects in these matters.

I also observed an interesting revival of religious worship and participation among young and old alike. Modernization and changing family structure seem to be accompanied by a search for internal cultural processes as appropriate mechanisms of change. Thus one has to be very careful to describe the progressive tendencies in India in purely secular, or nonreligious, or even Western terms. If anything, women in India derive more power by appealing to the religiocultural aspects of life, for here the freedoms are plentiful. Women are able to separate the religious from purely ritualistic practices, and even in the latter case, many women feel privileged in terms of their ritualistic roles. Religion has suddenly become a refreshing avenue for exploration among the liberated middle class. Today, there is a lot more close reading of Indian epics and mythological stories (e.g., *Ramayana* and *Mahabharata*) and an incredible and almost revolutionary search for cultural icons that give women immense spiritual strength. Such revivalism can be seen in music, art, and other cultural practices, access to which had, in a very interesting way, never been theoretically denied to women, but had not found expression in practice. In other words, women in India are now looking at their religiocultural roots, selectively picking up threads of possible support, exercising their options in areas that have been up for grabs for centuries, untouched by masculine control, and exploring this virgin territory for their own adoption. Such social spaces are denied to women in the Western context, where religion is so organized, so male oriented, that every move on the part of women to capture an inch of religiocultural space meets with strong resistance.

What I have seen among the urban middle-class people is that the oppressive element of Indian family seems to have been taken out, and more healthy elements seem to have been put in its place. The preservation of the family system at any cost seems to be the motivation for these changes. Much of this arises from what Indians have heard about the West (whether true or not)—that families are breaking apart, older parents are being sent away to the purgatory of nursing homes, detached from their families when there is the utmost need for people to be together. As Indians modernize (whatever that term means) or seem to approximate Western-oriented independent behavior, it is important to remind ourselves that the individualist philosophy of the West is not totally embraced by Indians. If I were to describe how the individualist and collectivist principles are being played out in contemporary modern India, I would have to say that collectivism is still the preferred model, with various adjustments to individual desires. This is the cardinal principle of the difference between India and the West, and the indications are that it will remain so even as India is changing. I do not think there is anything in contemporary thought and practice in India to suggest that an individualist framework will be incorporated into the Indian ethos. There is an important message here for Western feminists (particularly Anglo-Americans) that Indian women's questions cannot simply be forced into the Western antagonistic model of male versus female, however tempting this might appear. Gender hierarchy does not mean gender antagonism. I find less hostility in male-female relationships in comparable groups in India than in, say, the United States. No doubt, the situation of many women in India still leaves a lot to be desired, but one cannot assume that this is based on a politics of difference. Systemic changes can be brought about in many ways, and in India it is simply not the politics of difference.

Rising Consumerism in India

INDIA AS A CONSUMER SOCIETY: SOME GENERAL ISSUES

Recent work on consumerism in so-called Third World cultures and in India shows that this is not an epiphenomenon (Belk, 1988; Joy & Dholakia, 1991; Mehta & Belk, 1991). There has also been much publicity in the past two years regarding marketing and consumerist-oriented developments in these societies. However, attaching the label of "consumer society" to India begs some questions. What is a consumer society, and why apply that label now—as if to say there was no consumption in India prior to recent history or that there were no consumers to speak of? I use the term *consumer society* in a contemporary sense, in the way Fox and Lears (1983), McKendrick, Brewer, and Plumb (1982), and Marchand (1985) have used it in their sociohistorical analyses.

As is evident from the available literature, what constitutes a consumer society is difficult to define but perhaps easier to describe. India has been known for centuries for its trade, exotic markets, and bazaars

(Subrahmanyam, 1990). However, until European penetration, the market structure in India showed no evidence of being a "spatially sophisticated economy with production and consumption zones" that characterize modern industrial economies (Subrahmanyam, 1990). In the colonial period, which coincided with the Industrial Revolution, India was basically a primary goods-producing economy, and most consumer outlets were small distribution centers for indigenous products. It was only after independence that India began to develop as a major consumer economy, and only recently have many aspects of consumerism begun to surface with remarkable ease and diffusion.

SPECIFIC FACTORS ACCOUNTING FOR INDIAN CONSUMERISM

Several factors combine in India to create what may be described as an emerging consumer society. Although the following list is not to be considered exhaustive, these factors are representative of the movement of India toward a consumer-oriented society:

- a burgeoning middle class, with changing values and pent-up consumer demand
- changing women's roles, including labor participation, financial independence, and the changing structure of the family
- rising consumer aspirations and expectations across many segments of the population and particularly among women
- increased consumer spending on luxury items, aided by past savings and the introduction of the credit system
- new types of shopping environments and outlets
- media proliferation: satellite and cable TV, and the thriving film industry
- emergence of traveling Indian consumers—immigrants in the United States and England, overseas workers, tourists, business professionals and their exposure to worldwide consumer products
- the resurfacing of hedonistic cultural elements after centuries of dormancy
- the entry of multinational corporations into India

The size and economic strength of the Indian middle class have received much attention recently, both within India and in the foreign press. Estimates place the numbers of people with the ability to afford many standard consumer goods, if not luxury items, anywhere between 200 million and 250 million. An interesting aspect of the Indian middle class is that its median age is lower than that of the middle class in most Western countries, as is the case with many Third World countries, thus suggesting the potential for rapid growth in income generation and wealth accumulation.

Because of a number of economic, cultural, and social/family factors, the savings rate of the middle class has been slightly on the high side. Among the relevant economic factors are various government schemes for savings, the availability of a limited number of brands in consumer markets, and the emphasis on utilitarian goods rather than symbolic goods. Cultural factors affecting the economic strength of the middle class include norms that discourage borrowing and spending within one's means, as well as conservatism in clothing, fashion, and physical appearance, and general discipline of body and mind. Social/family factors include the joint family system, in which resources are pooled and assets are shared to minimize multiple purchases of the same products. Many of these traditional features are now undergoing change. Families are becoming more nucleated, and so-called middle-class cultural norms are undergoing major transformation.

For a number of Indians, participation in a consumer society means becoming more modernized or Westernized in dress, food, and the use of many grooming products and cosmetics. While showing such preferences, Indians are also conscious of Indianizing their experiences, for too much Westernizing means giving up their unique cultural identity. Consequently, we are witnessing an interesting development of what might be called an Indian version of modernization. Western ideas and products are adopted with an Indian twist, as can be seen in many television commercials and print ads.

For residents within India, who may not travel abroad, global consumerism is also rendered possible by the diffusion of satellite and communications technology, which brings with it exposure to international advertising for the latest products on various cable TV channels—CNN, BBC, MTV, and the like. This global participation is further enhanced by familiarity with English, the universal language of late twentieth-century commerce and culture. Not far behind these forces are the proliferation of local media within India and their marketing activism.

THE FEMALE CONSUMER

India is witnessing some significant changes in the economic and social status of women. The attitudes of women with respect to marriage, career, and their roles in the family and society are undergoing radical changes, as several researchers have described (e.g., Liddle & Joshi, 1986; Sharma, 1986; Wadley, 1977). The changing roles of women are accompanied by similar changes in the family structure and household systems (Saradamoni, 1992).

Many women, especially in the urban areas, are becoming educated and are entering professional or career-oriented jobs once reserved for men. There has been a rapid increase of women in the labor force. Women's income has now been recognized as a major factor in the creation of a family's wealth. Women's magazines have multiplied in unbelievable numbers, both in different languages and for different role groups (Figure 3.1 shows the covers of some representative magazines in English, Hindi, Telugu, and Tamil). Women are independent across many dimensions—in transportation, career choice, marriage, and family responsibilities. Recent advertising aimed at women has recognized these changing roles, yet the pull toward maintaining tradition remains quite strong among Indians (see Figure 3.2). This tension between developing a more progressive element and maintaining what is desirable and acceptable in the traditional context is nowhere more evident than in the case of changing women's roles. The clash between traditionalism and modernism, or the blending of the two, is a perennial theme that one discovers in studying India, and is played out in different ways, depending on the social and historical contexts. From an etic point of view, one can find Indian women who are traditional, or modern, or progressive, or even Westernized, or some combination thereof (Chakraborty, 1991). From an emic point of view, similar labels are used by Indian women to describe themselves, although the term *Westernized* seems the least favored (based on personal interviews). Indians use a combination of terms to represent the notion that in some aspects of their lives they are modern, whereas in others they are quite traditional. Among many middle-class women, this ontological tension exists regardless of age, signifying the fear of a possible loss of cultural identity in moving away from imagined notions of Indianness. Figure 3.3 reproduces some print ads showing how consumers are depicted as having a combination of traditional and modern values. Elsewhere, I have discussed in greater detail how the play of gender roles in contemporary India is marked by this tension.

There is demand in India for a number of household appliances. The concept of a *modern* home as both a physical and a symbolic space has

Figure 3.1. Indian Magazines Devoted to Women's Issues in Different Languages (top left, *Women's Era*, English; top right, *Chitralekha*, Hindi; bottom left, *Swati*, Telugu; bottom right, *Mangai*, Tamil)

Figure 3.2. Depiction of Women in Traditional Roles: A Key Aspect of Indian Advertising (in English and Tamil)

Figure 3.3. Examples of Advertising Depicting a Combination of Traditional and Modern Roles for Women (in English and Hindi)

NOTE: The ad on the top right reads, "She's modern. She's traditional. She's you."

not been a generally accepted theme in the Indian cultural context until recently, although traditional physical spaces have always projected very high symbolic meanings of their own. (For some interesting accounts of recent Indian immigrants and their relationships to their homes and household possessions, see Joy & Dholakia, 1991; Mehtha & Belk, 1991.) With families nucleating and women taking on independent or coequal financial responsibilities and making consumption decisions on behalf of their families, women's roles have been dramatically augmented; they are acquiring goods and making purchases for their homes in a manner not seen before. With the rise of the population, the emergence of nuclear families, and the growth in family incomes, more Indian nuclear families are opting for separate, independent households. The problem of urban space is so acute that land developers and architects have had to come up with innovative schemes and new buildings to meet this demand. In a number of urban communities, older homes are being torn down, giving way to multiapartment or high-rise complexes. These apartments are being built by professional architects who have been exposed to many Western ideas about use of space and construction materials. Thus one can see many modern-style apartments with many gadgets and appliances.

Historically, Indian tradition allowed for hedonism in various aspects of life. The Hindu religious texts are full of goddesses and gods whose physical appearance has been a major subject of textual description. In this respect, Indian culture presents a seeming contradiction to the Western eye. First, there is an asceticism in the East that seems to suggest that all material possessions and goods are to be avoided. At the same time, Indian culture is known for its joviality and eroticism. To Westerners, these characteristics seem to stand in opposition to each other, because in the modernist West, the body and mind are separated, the body being considered inferior to the mind. In Indian thought such dualisms exist, but not in any antagonistic way. Contemplation of the human form in Indian culture is as important as contemplation of spiritual forms (see the seventh-century Sanskrit religious work of Sankara, *Soundaryalahari*, or *The Ocean of Beauty*). The exploitation of erotic themes, in both electronic and print media, has a liberatory appeal to Indians that arises out of new sensibilities. For one thing, the younger generation no longer feels compelled to obey traditional authorities on these matters. This is particularly true of women, whose exposure to Western media, combined with their search for Indian cultural norms/

forms of the past, has given them a certain amount of legitimacy and cultural pride in these matters.

Traditional Market Segments

In the past, there have been three traditional target groups in Indian marketing: young adult male earners, young marrieds, and people 45 years of age and older. These classifications were employed from the early 1960s to the mid-1980s, and to some extent they exist even today in some markets.

Young adult male earners. Young adult males were considered important consumers of a number of personal items—clothing, shoes, shaving cream and other personal grooming products, and so on. For anything more expensive, such as bicycles or transistor radios, it was customary for young men to seek the opinions of their fathers. This deference was considered natural and desirable.

Young marrieds. In this category, the wife chose the brands of products used for family consumption—cooking oil, detergent, toothpaste, the family bath soap ("one cake for all"), and so on. If she needed face powder or makeup, she could choose that—but only after her family's purchases were completed and she had money left over. The purchases for "us" came before any purchases for "me." Decisions on high-ticket items such as radios or ceiling fans were deferred to the husband, and the wife accepted this very naturally. In fact, she would have been surprised had her husband asked for her opinion.

People 45+ years old. This group was by and large ignored by marketing people, except as approvers of the purchases of younger adult male earners.

Members of all three of the target groups usually lived under one roof, as a joint family. In sum, the market segments for many products were simple, themes of borrowing and credit were totally absent, and the advertising media were mainly newspapers, magazines, and cinema. Older people were never depicted as having material needs (a cultural value) in the traditional culture. At the most, for the elderly market, one saw occasional ads for savings and retirement plans.

After the Dawn of the Consumer Revolution

As mentioned above, the Indian consumer society has been shaped by a number of forces. As a result, the media have begun to identify some emerging consumer segments, which are described below. It should be noted that some of these roles have always existed in the traditional social organization, but the focus on them as "consumers" is a recent occurrence. Much of this has no doubt been aided by the traditional cinema verité that has inspired television, the new defining medium of Indian consumer culture.

Sociologically "conditioned" female consumers. This category consists of the consumer as a wife, providing emotional support and partnership to her husband; the consumer as a daughter-in-law, preserver/protector of traditional values; and the consumer as a mother, the nurturer.

Newly rich urban Indians. This category includes Indian men or women who have either traveled abroad and returned with new tastes and insights or are homegrown consumers who have acquired new sophistication and tastes. Such a consumer may be characterized as the new thinking man, young adult, single or married, or as the thinking woman, a self-achiever, single or married. In the latter case, the consumer is vocal about what she wants, confident in herself but not a feminist (as the term is popularly understood), yet. She is presented as a role model for upper-middle-class women or for women with aspirations. As an Indian woman, she is no longer unidimensional. She may be a wife, mother, or girlfriend, but she is now conscious of her individual persona. The boom in women's beauty products also shows that she has none of the earlier guilt about spending money on herself.

Conclusions

This chapter represents an attempt to integrate gender construction from a sociocultural perspective and the emergence of the female consumer in India. Women belonging to either traditional upper castes or upper economic strata are forging ahead and heralding changes that are likely to continue into the next century. In the meantime, we are also seeing how consumerism is shaping Indian society in general and, more specifically, females as consumers. Major challenges facing Indian women seem to be how to combine traditionalism with modernism and how to combine the best that is available within the culture with emerging change phenomena.

As I have noted, in the analysis of the condition of women in India, imported feminist theories cannot be applied without due regard for India's particular historical and sociocultural factors. I have discussed how these factors come into play through historical continuities as well as discontinuities. Indian women are of course subject to the politics of patriarchy and gender hierarchy, much as are Western women. In addition to these two factors, Indian women are also subject to caste hierarchy and its own imperatives. Students of gender studies should be careful in understanding these forces, because they do not act in the same way as in some other cultures. Indian women believe that there is a lot to be preserved in the traditional family system and that many Indian cultural values have much to offer. Ignoring these values would be self-defeating; there is always the danger of throwing out the baby with the bathwater.

References

Anant, S., Rao, S. V. R., & Kapoor, K. (1986). *Women at work in India*. New Delhi: Sage.

Danerjee, N. (1991). *Indian women in a changing industrial scenario*. New Delhi. Sage.

Belk, R. W. (1988). Third World consumer culture. In E. Kumcu & A. F. Firat (Eds.), *Marketing and development. Toward broader dimensions* (pp. 109-127). Greenwich, CT. JAI.

Bhushan, M. (1989). Vimochana: Women's struggles, nonviolent militancy and direct action in the Indian context. *Women's Studies International Forum, 12*, 25-33.

Brock-Utne, B. (1989). Women and Third World countries: What do we have in common? *Women's Studies International Forum, 12*, 495-503.

Chakraborty, S. K. (1991). *Management by values: Towards cultural congruence*. New Delhi: Oxford University Press.

Dumont, L. (1980). *Homo hierarchicus: The caste system and its implications*. Chicago: University of Chicago Press.

Fox, R., & Lears, T. J. (Eds.). (1983). *The culture of consumption: Critical essays in American history, 1810-1980*. New York: Pantheon.

Joy, A., & Dholakia, R. R. (1991). Remembrances of things past: The meaning of home and possessions of Indian professionals in Canada. *Journal of Social Behavior and Personality, 6*, 385-402.

Krishna Raj, M., & Chanana, K. (1990). *Gender and the household domain*. New Delhi: Sage.

Lardinois, R. (1992). Family and household as practical groups: Preliminary reflection on the Hindu joint family. In K. Saradamoni (Ed.), *Finding the household: Conceptual and methodological issues*. New Delhi: Sage.

Liddle, J., & Joshi, R. (1986). *Daughters of independence: Gender, caste and class in India.* London: Zed.

Marchand, R. (1985). *Advertising the American dream: Making way for modernity, 1920-40.* Berkeley: University of California Press.

Marcus, G., & Fischer, M. (1986). *Anthropology as cultural critique: An experimental moment in the human sciences.* Chicago: University of Chicago Press.

Marriott, M. (1990). Constructing an Indian ethnosociology. In M. Marriott (Ed.), *India through Hindu categories* (pp. 1-40). New Delhi: Sage.

McKendrick, N., Brewer, J., & Plumb, J. H. (1982). *The birth of a consumer society: The commercialization of eighteenth-century England.* Bloomington: Indiana University Press.

Mehta, R., & Belk, R. W. (1991). Artifacts, identity and transition: Favorite possession of Indians and Indian immigrants to the United States. *Journal of Consumer Research, 17,* 398-411.

Mies, M. (1986). *Indian women in subsistence and agricultural labor.* New Delhi: Sage.

Parikh, I. J., & Garg, P. K. (1989). *Indian women: An inner dialogue.* New Delhi: Sage.

Rose, K. (1992). *Where women are leaders: The SEWA movement.* New Delhi: Sage.

Saradamoni, K. (Ed.). (1992). *Finding the household: Conceptual and methodological issues.* New Delhi: Sage.

Sharma, U. (1986). *Women's work, class, the urban household.* London: Tavistock.

Subrahmanyam, S. (1990). *The political economy of commerce: Southern India, 1500-1650.* Cambridge: Cambridge University Press.

Wadley, S. S. (1977). Women and the Hindu tradition. In D. Jacobson & S. S. Wadley (Eds.), *Women in India: Two perspectives* (pp. 113-140). New Delhi: Manohar.

Wignaraja, P. (1990). *Women, poverty and resources.* New Delhi: Sage.

4

On Gender Differences in Eating Behavior as Compensatory Consumption

SUZANNE C. GRUNERT

MY purpose in this chapter is to discuss "normal" eating behavior (i.e., not deviant aspects, such as anorexia or bulimia) as an important aspect of daily consumer behavior, with the objective of stimulating research in this neglected area. The emphasis here is on eating behavior that has a compensatory function. I pay special attention to gender differences, with a focus on women's particular relationship to food and eating. This focus seems justified for a number of reasons. First, women still have the main responsibility for their families' food supplies and meal preparation, and thus most still have the gatekeeper function (Lewin, 1963) in this area. Second, advertising for food products is very often targeted to women in a way that supports the traditional housewife role. Third, women's magazines publish both recipes and diet plans, thus perpetuating the paradox of the great cook who is at the same time physically attractive, with a slim figure. Fourth, psychological research aimed at eating behavior has concentrated mainly on women, based on the implicit assumption that women are more willing than men to indulge in the compensatory and compulsive sides of eating behavior.

This chapter is divided into three main parts. The first consists of a review of the literature on the connotative meanings of food and a short note on the concepts of purposes, needs, and compensation. I do not explicitly address the gender issue in this part of the chapter, partly because of the general character of the concepts described, and partly because of the lack of specific gender-focused or feminist approaches appearing in the literature. In the second part of the chapter, I explain the concept of compensatory eating behavior and how it has been measured so far. I then present results from several studies conducted in both Germany and Denmark, concentrating on gender differences. The third part of the chapter outlines a research program on gender differences in compensatory eating behavior.

The Connotative Meanings of Food

People seek food, not nutrients. If this statement were false, why would there be so many culturally different ways of preparing the same foodstuffs, so many societal rules and norms about when and how to serve what kinds of meals, so many distinct individual food cravings and food aversions? Hence the eating behavior of an individual, a group, or a culture should be regarded as a phenomenon in which a multitude of physiological, sociocultural, psychological, and economic factors interact, thus transforming the existential need for nutrients into complex food habits and patterns.

Researchers have proposed several classifications of connotations to explain these patterns and to emphasize how different the meanings of food and eating can be. The common beliefs underlying all these classifications are that food has social and psychic meanings, that meals serve as communicative symbolism, and "that eating is an experience that may be invested with many intellectual and emotional values quite apart from metabolic utilization of the food" (Babcock, 1948, p. 390). Often based on anecdotal evidence that stems mostly from psychoanalytic or therapeutic work, these classifications are claimed to denote the *emotional meanings of food*. Use of the term *emotional* implies that the pure physiological need for food—that is, the need for nutrients—is a nonemotional state, whereas the above-mentioned influencing factors refer to emotional states.

Babcock (1948) distinguishes among three main connotative dimensions: food as a reliever of anxiety, food as a (re-)gainer of acceptance and security, and food as a means of influencing others, especially children. Kaufman (1954) characterizes food connotations with the labels "security," "reward," "fetish," "show-off," and "grown-up." Woods (1960) describes prestige, maturity, status, anxiety, hedonic, and functional connotations of foods. Jelliffe (1967) classifies foods as cultural superfoods, prestige foods, body-image foods, sympathetic magic foods, and physiological group foods. McKenzie (1974) distinguishes food connotations on the grounds of social and economic status of consumers, noting that food can be an aid to security, a substitute for maternal creativity, a demonstration of group acceptance, an indication of conformity and prestige, a form of compensation, and a way to show mood and personality.

In an attempt to extract the underlying dimensions of these and other classifications, I have proposed the following four principal categories of connotative meanings: *security*, in which eating serves ego-defensive purposes; *pleasure*, in which food is a means of ego actualization; *prestige*, in which food is used for ego enhancement; and *status*, in which food increases ego-environment integration (Grunert, 1993). Whereas the first two categories refer to the self, the last two relate to a social relationship between the self and its surroundings. Universally applicable connotations of food are thus derived in which the different determinants of eating behavior are intertwined.

PURPOSES, NEEDS, AND COMPENSATION

Individuals associate various emotional meanings with food, emphasize different values in eating, and hold numerous attitudes toward food consumption. In a nutshell: "Food feeds the ego, not merely the body" (Pumpian-Mindlin, 1954, p. 577). However, all this has usually been neglected when it comes to describing or explaining human needs. In need hierarchies and lists of needs, food and eating usually have been assigned only to the category of basic or existence needs, probably because of their necessity for maintaining bodily functions. They are not associated with other need-satisfying qualities by Alderfer (1969), Maslow (1943), or Murray (1938). I am inclined to suspect that these three men were not very much interested in food and eating—and this suspicion seems to hold true at least for Maslow (1981, p. 220), who describes the self-actualizing individual as giving food and eating a low importance in his or her life plan.

Another reason the manifold functions of food and eating behavior have been disregarded in need theory may lie in the difficulty of defining needs. I would like to propose a need concept grounded in living systems theory (Miller, 1978), in which *purpose* is the more fundamental concept, and needs are derived from purposes in a fairly complex way:

> A need of a living system is a lack of a specific resource which is useful for or required by the purposes of that system. A resource may be matter, energy, or information. Purposes are defined by living systems theory as preferred steady state values for various resources. Purposes, and therefore needs, may be innate, or learned, or innate but modified by learning. (Tracy, 1986, p. 212)

The only assumptions made in this definition are that living systems exist and that they are purposeful. There is no necessity to assume that needs always lead to behavior, or that they are ordered in hierarchies, or that they are either true or false.

To analyze eating behavior in the context of living systems theory, it is necessary to focus on the *resources* a living system draws on when pursuing its purposes. Although *need* refers to a lack of a specific resource that would relieve the deficiency if it could be obtained, that particular resource may not be the only one capable of doing so. From this perspective, a need is not deterministic, because a system may choose from various *alternative resources* to relieve a deficit, and because the same resource may be useful for several *different purposes* of the system. This applies especially to eating behavior and food habits.

Compensatory Eating Behavior: The Concept

An individual may feel a deficit or lack of tenderness and affection, associated with feelings of loneliness and boredom. To overcome this lack, he or she could turn to the resource of contacting close friends to arrange a date. Another way to take care of this need may be to go to a movie, perhaps one full of passions and "dangerous liaisons" or one that is humorous and suited for laughing away unpleasant feelings. Yet another resource could be a particular food that may relieve the individual's feelings of loneliness and boredom—be it marinated herring, ice cream and butter fudge, or a T-bone steak. Turning this example around, the second case mentioned above arises; that is, food can serve several different purposes. Food, and therefore eating, can be a resource for specific nutrients influencing mood, a resource for regaining good humor through preparing a delicious meal, or a resource for rewarding oneself for an achievement.

In general terms, the phenomenon is that a lack of x could be cured by a supply of x, but may also be cured by a supply of y. If y is used, this process is called *compensation*. This term is neutral and is not intended to discriminate between so-called true and false, conscious and unconscious, or good and bad purposes, needs, and resources. In the context of the theory of living systems, in which purpose rather than need is the basic concept, it is only important that a system's purposes are met, by whatever resources available. This conceptualization of compensatory behavior is more general than the approach taken by Grønmo (1988), who defines compensation mainly as an attempt to make up for a general lack of (Maslow's needs for) self-esteem and self-actualization. Here it is proposed that virtually every kind of need derived from a lack of resources can be fulfilled by various resources as long as these are useful for or required by a system's purposes.

Compensation is mainly associated with the alleviation of negative emotions, but positive emotions also play an important role in food consumption. Hirschman (1982) has labeled foods the "truly nondurable goods" that provide pleasures that are simple, familiar, yet intense, and indefinitely renewable, because these pleasures are based on the body's recurring physiological need for energy: Foodstuffs disappear precisely when conveying their energy to the organism, and their disappearance is essential to the pleasure felt in the act of consumption. It is this pleasure experience one might seek to maintain or intensify by eating. *Compensation* in this regard would mean that an individual eats to prolong agreeable emotional states such as happiness or joy—or, in terms of the purpose concept, to maintain a preferred steady-state value of resources. This is the case when lovers may feel like having a delicious snack after they have savored sex together (eating and eroticism have been closely connected throughout the centuries and in many different cultures; see Kleinspehn, 1987), when business partners enjoy a gourmet dinner after a successful meeting, or when festive occasions such as birthdays and wedding anniversaries are celebrated with special meals.

Assuming that the resource chosen by a living system—an individual, a consumer—is food, required for the purpose of *regaining or maintaining* a preferred steady state of *mental homeostasis,* what are the reasons for selecting food and not another resource—matter, energy, or information? In attempting to answer this question, it is helpful to recall that an individual's eating behavior is the result of his or her structuring and processing of various external and internal determinants, none of which has an independent and direct influence, but all of which interact at any given time (Diehl, 1980). Examples of external factors are the availability of food, the individual's relationships to family members and other reference persons, influences through media, and times and places of meal intake. Physiological needs, nutritional knowledge, attitudes, self-concept, emotions, and personality traits are internal determinants. Factors that influence behavior both internally and externally include education, culture, religion, and social status.

When eating behavior is mainly determined by physiological factors, it is not compensatory, because in a state where nutrients and energy are lacking, the organism needs this specific resource—food—to survive. Hence we have to look at the (social) psychological factors determining eating behavior in order to explain compensation. The process of compensation can be described in terms of *schema theory* (e.g., Bartlett, 1932; Grunert, 1991a, 1993; Selz, 1913): A person-environment encounter activates an appraisal schema to evaluate the situation. When the situation is appraised as either harmful or beneficial, an emotion schema is activated. Then, a regulation of the emotion is called for. This is achieved through the activation of a regulation schema that consists of guidelines on how to change, maintain, or enhance the emotional state. If emotional feelings lead to the activation of a regulation schema that calls for eating without the organism being physiologically hungry, the ensuing food intake will be the result of *emotionally induced compensatory eating.*

The concept of emotional eating is not new, but it has been discussed exclusively in the context of misbehavior patterns leading to such eating disorders as obesity, bulimia, and anorexia (e.g., Conrad, 1970; Herman & Polivy, 1975; McKenna, 1982). Overeating has been described as a means of sedation, of diminishing anxiety, of counteracting feelings of being unloved, and of competition avoidance (Kaplan & Kaplan, 1957; Menzies, 1970). Moreover, emotional eating has been used as an explanation of why obese people eat more than normal-weight people. But it has never been taken as a phenomenon in its own right.

A concept closely related to emotionally induced eating is that of external eating. This is based on Schachter's (1964) cognitive-physiological theory of emotions, suggesting that the eating behavior of some individuals can be relatively independent of internal body signals of hunger and satiety, and, thus, is largely controlled by external stimuli. Many studies have investigated this phenomenon, with sometimes contradictory results (e.g., Coll, Meyers, & Stunkard, 1979; Goldman, Jaffa, & Schachter, 1968; Nisbett & Kanouse, 1969; Rodin, 1975, 1981). It is related to emotionally induced eating, because states of arousal can considerably enhance the susceptibility to external stimuli (Ganley, 1988). Hence this type of behavior is called *externally stimulated compensatory eating.*

There are two possible explanations for these processes. The first concerns *learning experiences.* Experiments have shown that the food intake of the sane young infant is regulated primarily by internal body stimuli (Davis, 1928, 1939). With increasing age, learning experiences have a growing influence on the perception of hunger, appetite, and satiety feelings. These experiences are linked to certain external stimuli interacting with internalized attitudes, educational effects, and sociocultural norms. When they receive a signal function, the external regulation of food intake can lead to a marked deconditioning of responsiveness to internal states. Emotional experiences accompanying the nutritional interactions between a child and his or her feeder(s) shape behavioral patterns that influence the child's ability to identify hunger as a clear signal not to be confused with other emotional states (Bruch, 1971). This occurs when food gains connotations such as reward or security in the context of stressful experiences. In terms of living systems theory, this is how purposes are learned. The consequence of such learning experiences is the development of schemata linking food intake to emotional states.

The second possible explanation concerns what may be called *affective stability.* Individuals differ in their emotional makeups, that is, in the ways they react to various daily encounters, manage difficult situations, and handle personal relationships. This is usually referred to as temperament (e.g., Derryberry & Rothbart, 1988) or as general arousability, that is, the extent to which an individual is aroused by any increase in the information rate of his or her surroundings (e.g., Mehrabian, 1987). Affective stability is a personality trait associated with genetic predisposition rather than with learned patterns of coping or behavior across a wide range of situations. On the contrary, the feelings responsible for compensatory eating are emotional states of acute, dynamic, and temporary character. Hence the trait is the frame of reference within which feeling states are handled. It is likely that a low degree rather than a high degree of affective stability results more often in compensatory consumption activities.

Compensatory eating behavior should not be regarded as an eating disorder, but as one facet among others in normal food habits. It is a phenomenon we can all observe in ourselves if we pay close attention. Compensatory eating behavior is similar to some of the different aspects of self-gifts described by Mick and DeMoss (1990). It is not necessarily a sign of neurosis or psychosis, as occasional compensatory strategies seem to facilitate individuals' adaptation to environmental conditions. For example, respondents in a nationwide survey in West Germany who described themselves as "very satisfied" with their lives reported more sporadic *compensatory buying* than the less satisfied, whereas those declaring they were "not too happy" more often admitted *compulsive buying* (Scherhorn, Grunert, Kaz, & Raab, 1988). Hence positive judgments of subjective well-being are, to some extent, associated with compensatory consumption behavior, whereas compulsive consumption behavior is related to negative judgments of subjective well-being, indicating the inability of individuals to cope with prevailing circumstances. A continuum is therefore suggested: One end denotes no inclination toward compensatory eating, the middle range contains some emotionally induced/externally stimulated eating behavior from time to time, and the other end describes the addictive extreme in which compensatory strategies are the rule rather than the exception. This extreme can result in compulsive food consumption patterns that imply eating disorders such as obesity and bulimia.

HOW TO MEASURE COMPENSATORY EATING BEHAVIOR

No survey instrument has been developed so far that measures *compensatory eating* as an aspect of normal eating behavior. Most eating behavior questionnaires are concerned with eating disorders (Garner & Garfinkel, 1979; O'Neil et al., 1979; Wollersheim, 1971). A few refer to the concepts of emotional and/or external eating and could be helpful for testing whether the theoretical considerations outlined above find empirical support.

The Dutch Eating Behavior Questionnaire (DEBQ; van Strien, Frijters, Bergers, & Defares, 1986) is an example of an instrument used to measure emotional and external eating. Examples of statements in the DEBQ on emotionally induced compensatory eating include "I have the desire to eat when I am bored or restless," "I wish to eat when I am emotionally upset," and "When I am anxious, worried, or tense, I want to eat." Externally stimulated compensatory eating is measured with statements such as "If food smells and look good, I eat more than usual," "If I see others eating, I have also the desire to eat," and "If I walk past a snack bar or a café, I want to buy something delicious." Respondents rate 20 statements on 5-point scales using the responses *never, seldom, sometimes, often,* and *very often.* The questionnaire is self-administered.

It should be noted that the statements on emotionally induced compensatory eating in the DEBQ cover only more or less unpleasant emotional states; no positive feelings are probed, although these are included in the concept of compensatory eating. The scale on externally stimulated compensatory eating, however, also covers pleasant aspects in mentioning hedonic attributes, such as "delicious" and "good smelling." These limitations of the questionnaire have to be considered in the evaluation of the analytic results. A future task therefore lies in further improving this instrument to ensure that all theoretically relevant aspects of compensatory eating behavior are operationalized.

Factor analysis of the instrument reveals that the items of the emotional eating dimension load on two different factors: Three items measure the tendency to eat because of *diffuse emotions,* whereas the other seven items assess eating intentions caused by *clearly labeled emotions.* The term *diffuse* here refers to moodlike emotional states, such as boredom or loneliness, that are of rather low intensity. *Clearly labeled* means that the actual emotion is so distinct from the preceding emotional state and is felt with such intensity that it can be precisely termed disappointment, irritation, or the like.

GENDER DIFFERENCES IN COMPENSATORY EATING

Table 4.1 presents results from four studies. Samples I, II, and III stem from studies conducted in West Germany in 1987 and 1988; Sample IV is from a study conducted in Denmark in 1990. For these studies, the DEBQ was translated into German and Danish and somewhat modified (Grunert, 1989a). Principal-component analysis reproduced in all samples the

TABLE 4.1 Gender Differences in Self-Reported Compensatory Eating

		Emotionally Induced Eating			Externally Stimulated Eating
	n	Clear	Diffuse	Clear/Diffuse	
Sample I (undergraduates)					
women	132	14.74	—	22.98	—
men	93	11.61	—	19.21	—
Sample II (nationwide representative)					
women	484	.53	.69	1.21	—
men	508	.28	.46	.75	—
Sample III (convenience)					
women	64	13.39	—	23.53	18.37
men	62	10.00	—	19.05	16.58
Sample IV (business school personnel)					
women	21	13.14	6.35	20.33	—
men	45	10.53	4.98	16.76	—

expected loading patterns, with high loadings on the three factors, and Cronbach's alpha was in all cases and for all scales above .92, thus indicating that the operationalization of the concepts was successful and stable over samples, time, and cultures. As can be seen in the table, where only differences of mean values significant at the 5% level (*t* test) are reported, women consistently show a higher degree of emotionally induced eating than men, especially with regard to clearly labeled emotions. Note that the low mean values in Sample II are caused by the use of a shortened version of the two scales.

Gender Differences in Compensatory Eating as Symptoms of Gender Roles: Outlining a Research Program

Relatively few studies have examined gender differences in eating behavior. It is common to focus solely on female subjects when studying eating disorders such as anorexia and bulimia. Moreover, explanations are concentrated on general mechanisms underlying these disorders, but very seldom clarify why women seem to be more affected than men. Aspects of normal eating behavior are even less frequently studied, except perhaps in anthropological investigations (see Grunert, 1989b), and, if studied, gender differences are mentioned only in the context of gender-dependent physiological needs (nutrition physiology), food distribution within the household (food aid policy), use of convenience products (food marketing), and the like. As for the specific question of compensatory eating behavior, this concept has only recently been introduced (Grunert, 1991a, 1991b; Scherhorn et al., 1988). All of this justifies the following suggestions for explaining gender differences in compensatory eating. The central assumption underlying these speculations is that *gender differences in compensatory eating behavior reflect, as well as result from, gender-specific roles that society assigns to women and men.* The focus is on learning experiences and affective stability.

Given the general importance of socialization processes in the development of values, attitudes, beliefs, and behavior patterns, it is plausible that learning experiences account for gender differences in compensatory behavior as well. This refers mainly to sociocultural norms of femininity versus masculinity. Concepts such as values, personality traits, the number of roles an individual considers central to his or her identity, and body image (physical appearance and attractiveness) will be addressed in this context. Concerning affective stability, a more indirect effect is supposed. As a trait, affective stability is, to a large extent, linked to genetic disposition and thus is less susceptible to socialization influences. Learning experiences may, however, influence the way an individual handles her or his temperament. Important concepts here are coping strategies, emotional control, and vulnerability to negative affect. The relationships among these different concepts are summarized in Figure 4.1, in which the first level of concepts refers to learning experiences that are considered as social factors, and the second level relates to affective stability aspects as individual factors.

LEARNING EXPERIENCES: VALUES, PERSONALITY TRAITS, ROLE DIVERSITY, AND BODY IMAGE

With regard to learning experiences, the first concept mentioned is that of values. The value concept attempts to assess those patterns by which individuals orient themselves in and adapt to their environments. Values are both self-centered and social-centered in the sense that they are at the intersection of individual and society. They reflect a culture's orientation standards, where culture can be defined as being expressed in collectively shared cognitive structures that direct behavior mainly through automatic cognitive processes (Grunert, Grunert, &

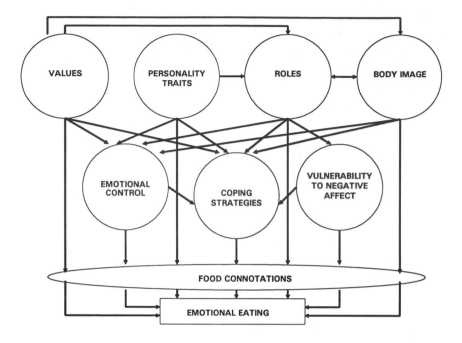

Figure 4.1. Relationships Among Coping Strategies, Emotional Control, and Vulnerability to Negative Affect

Kristensen, 1992). Values can be deficit values, as when an individual accentuates a certain value, such as security or harmony, because he or she does not get enough of it. A number of studies have revealed that values are linked to various aspects of consumer behavior, and it has been shown that they influence compensatory eating as well (Grunert, 1991b). However, no studies have attempted to probe gender-related aspects of values, although results show differences in the importance attached to various values by women and men (e.g., Grunert & Juhl, 1991; Grunert & Wagner, 1989; Scherhorn et al., 1988). Examples include values such as "sense of belonging," "warm relationships with others," "true friendship," and "security."

Assuming (a) that values embrace gender-specific norms acquired during childhood and adolescence under the influence of parents, peers, and popular media; (b) that the function of values is to guide the individual's adaptation to the surrounding conditions; and (c) that the actual situation in modern societies is characterized by dispersing and, particularly for women, often contradictory gender roles, it is probable that the more an individual feels a deficit in certain values or resents the diminishing order of things in general, the more he or she is inclined to compensatory (food) consumption. On the other hand, hedonistic values such as pleasure, fun, and enjoyment become increasingly important. It is therefore also likely that individuals strongly endorsing a hedonistic attitude toward life will use compensatory eating as a resource to prolong pleasurable emotional states.

Another concept that relates to learning experiences is that of personality traits. Like values, personality traits are acquired during childhood and adolescence, although they are to some extent genetically determined. Personality traits can be either self-focused or socially oriented. Research has shown that some traits are more prominent for women than for men and vice versa (Buss & Finn, 1987): Women score higher on traits such as empathy, guilt, fear, and altruism, whereas men score higher on such traits as dominance, aggressiveness, excitement seeking, and anger. With regard to eating behavior, personality traits are conceived as intervening variables in the psychological control of food intake. Squires and Kagan (1986) found that, in contrast to common beliefs, compulsive eating of American men seems to reflect profound psychological disturbances, as it is clearly associated with an addicted profile, whereas women's compulsive eating seems to express a reaction to the stress inherent in a Type A personality. Another study showed that the higher Dutch women scored on a scale of emotional eating, the more they reported feeling anxious, lacking self-esteem, being sentimental, being worried and emotionally unstable, lacking patience, and having a high preference for sweet foods (van Strien, Frijters, Roosen, Knijman-Hijl, & Defares, 1985). Other research has revealed a distinct relationship between emotionally induced and externally stimulated eating and the personality trait of social anxiety, which indicates that individuals marked by a high degree of uncertainty in social situations are more inclined to react to emotional cues and external stimuli (Grunert, 1989b). These examples lead to the following hypothesis: If those personality traits that have been suggested to be related to eating behavior in general can be shown to discriminate between genders, then they will also be linked to compensatory eating behavior in a gender-specific manner.

The number of roles an individual considers central to his or her identity is the third concept suggested to result from gender-specific learning experiences. The potential distress associated with role diversity may lead to compensatory eating behavior. This hypothesis builds mainly on results of an exploratory study on possible relationships between roles and eating behavior (Timko, Striegel-Moore, Silberstein, & Rodin, 1987). Although the multiple-roles literature is usually interested in the ramifications of the three major roles of women—mother, wife, and worker—women may have a large number of other more specific roles. Timko et al. (1987) found that women who felt that many roles were highly relevant to their self-esteem were more likely to place greater importance on their own appearance and reported significantly more symptoms of eating disorders than women who reported only a few roles as central to them. These authors suggest that their results refer to the "superwoman" cliché. Superwomen are expected to encompass traits of both traditional masculine and traditional feminine gender role stereotypes. They do not seem to prioritize their various roles, but rather consider successful performance in all roles to be important for their self-esteem. A situation in which new role expectations emerge while the old ones still remain may therefore call for some compensation through relatively easily achievable pleasures, such as eating—be it to intensify pleasure experiences or to cope with stress or to reward oneself for an achievement.

The final concept in the context of learning experiences is body image, or physical appearance and attractiveness. This is an important constituent of perceived femininity that has strong influence on females' feelings of well-being and satisfaction. As early as 1935, Schilder stressed the significance that social norms have on the formation of an individual's body image. Women seem to be much more preoccupied with their body weight and physical attractiveness than men, and this preoccupation stems presumably from general sociocultural pressures toward slimness as the current beauty ideal (Rodin, Silberstein, & Striegel-Moore, 1985). Male and female judges who ranked photographs of females on an aesthetic basis preferred ectomorphs to esomorphs, who, in turn, were preferred to endomorphs (Stewart, Tutton, & Steele, 1973). Similarly, an archival study revealed that *Playboy* centerfold models have been significantly thinner than the average woman over the past 20 years and have also become progressively thinner during this period (Garner, Garfinkel, Schwartz, & Thompson, 1980). Women's feelings of being fat and dissatisfied with their bodies have been found to be significantly related to striving for perfectionism, engaging in social comparison with other women regarding body weight, and perceiving social pressure toward thinness (Striegel-Moore, McAvay, & Rodin, 1986).

An experiment based on the hypothesis that "eating lightly" is a gender role conforming behavior for women demonstrated indeed that women, but not men, "are what they eat" (Chaiken & Pliner, 1987). Both female and male judges regarded a woman who ate small meals as significantly more feminine and significantly less masculine than a woman who ate large meals. Furthermore, meal size information influenced the judges' tendencies to attribute stereotypically feminine personality traits. Women who ate smaller portions were perceived as considerably more expressive, kind, and understanding of others, as being more concerned about their appearance, and as significantly better looking than the women who ate large meals. In contrast, the amount eaten by men was irrelevant to the male gender role and therefore not used in judging masculinity and femininity in men. This social norm of equating thinness with attractiveness is responsible for misbehavioral eating patterns such as continuously going on and off diets, which can finally lead to disorders like anorexia or bulimia. Polivy and Herman (1987) emphasize this concern, stating that the permanent restriction of food intake has become such a ubiquitous phenomenon that it could be regarded now as "normal" eating deserving therapeutic treatment. Even though beauty ideals have changed throughout the centuries (see Grauer & Schlottke, 1987), it seems plausible that a certain percentage—although not the same segment—of women will always suffer from eating disorders in order to keep pace with socially imposed body norms, whether of Twiggy-like shapes or more Rubenesque proportions. The relationship to compensatory eating is expressed in the hypothesis that the more women tend to accept current beauty ideals, the more they are inclined to engage in frequent diet efforts, and, thus, to compensate for this stressful life with temporary eating binges.

AFFECTIVE STABILITY: COPING STRATEGIES, EMOTIONAL CONTROL, AND VULNERABILITY TO NEGATIVE AFFECT

The second concept that may shed light on gender differences in compensatory eating is that of affective stability, which relates to individual differences in emotional response style and dispositional levels of emotional intensity. There are hints that these individual differences are to some extent gender related, influencing, for example, which *coping strategies* a person chooses when confronted with stressful life events. Psychological research has been interested in the interaction of coping and emotions, concentrating mainly on the ways in which emotions can interfere with cognitive functioning. But, as Folkman and Lazarus (1988) point out, coping can also mediate emotions arising during an encounter and transform the original appraisal and its attendant emotion in several ways. These authors found three types of coping strategies to be strongly associated with changes in emotion: planful problem solving, confrontive coping, and distancing. The first was associated with positive emotions, but the other two contributed to a negative emotional state. Unfortunately, Folkman and Lazarus do not report on gender differences. However, it is very likely that women and men differ according to the coping strategies they adopt and how their choices mediate the emotional outcomes of an encounter. Both strategy and outcome are supposed to influence whether eating will be one of the behaviors used to regulate emotions. This relationship can be explained within the schema theory approach briefly mentioned above (Grunert, 1991a, 1993).

Closely related is the phenomenon of stress and stress-induced eating. Stress results from an imbalance between environmental load and the ability of an individual to cope, leading to heightened physiological arousal that is accompanied by augmented levels of adrenaline. This in turn decreases hunger sensations, and the stressed individual loses his or her normal appetite. However, many individuals respond to arousal with excessive intake of food. If this type of compensatory eating occurs frequently, it may result in weight gain. One Dutch study revealed that the midterm effects of high emotional eating on body mass index (weight/height,^{2} which is a more reliable indicator than body weight) occurred only for men when assessed six months after a negative life event had happened. There was neither a mid- nor long-term interaction found for women, which indicates that there may be several coping strategies operative in a given period of stress. It is also conceivable that there are gender-related differences in the subjective appraisal of undesirable life events such as divorce, accidents, or the death of a close relative or friend.

In addition to possibly different subjective appraisal, concepts such as emotional control (Roger & Nesshoever, 1987) and affect intensity and self-control (Flett, Blankstein, Bator, & Pliner, 1989) may play a role in how an individual handles emotions. *Emotional control* is defined as the tendency to inhibit the expression of emotional responses, which may delay recovery from the arousal associated with emotion, which, in turn, may further the transition from distress to illness. *Affect intensity*, a dimension of temperament, refers to individual differences in the intensity of experiencing emotions. It is significantly positively related to emotional expressivity, emotional sensitivity, and social sensitivity. One striking gender difference is the finding that higher affect intensity has been associated with lower general self-control in males but not in females (Flett et al., 1989); this result, however, rests on a student sample of only 96 respondents, and thus calls for further substantiation. Nevertheless, it is possible, corresponding to prevailing social norms, that men score higher on emotional control than women (e.g., a man is not allowed to weep, at least not in public). To the extent that affect intensity can be linked to differences in cognitive appraisals of emotions (Flett, Boase, McAndrews, Pliner, & Blankstein, 1986), it is possible that this temperament dimension is more prevalent in women than in men. Both hypotheses imply that higher emotional control and higher affect intensity are related to eating as a compensatory strategy.

A final speculation concerns gender-dependent differences in self-focused attention and thus *vulnerability to negative affect*. It has been demonstrated by Ingram, Cruet, Johnson, and Wisnicki (1988) that women show a stronger propensity to self-focus than men in response to stressful events, and that gender role differences may account for this difference: Feminine gender role individuals of both sexes in Ingram et al.'s study were more likely to display negative affect and to self-focus in response to stressful events than were masculine individuals. These results help to explain the findings that women are much more likely to be depressed than are men. With regard to food habits, it seems evident that those individuals who are more prone to self-focus in stimuli response will, to a corresponding extent, be more open to compensatory eating. For the time being, it appears these individuals are most likely to be women. However, there is an intriguing alternative interpretation, that rather than femininity serving as a vulnerability factor per se, masculinity may serve as a buffer for stress (Nezu & Nezu, 1987): Instead of women being more vulnerable to negative events and affects, men may be more invulnerable because they are less willing or able to engage in introspection when situational factors would call for such internal focus. If so, such a behavior should increase the tendency to react to external stimuli in the form of food cues. In other words, invulnerable men are likely to display externally stimulated eating when they tend to direct their attention elsewhere, outside themselves.

Conclusion

The ideas presented here to account for observed gender differences in compensatory eating are speculative, and only some of them are backed up by several empirical findings. I should add that the concepts are of a rather general and fundamental character, which makes operationalization and combination with specific aspects of eating behavior more difficult. This, however, should not impede further research. Additionally, more theoretical work is needed to elucidate the potential influence that gender-related social norms may have on compensatory eating. These limitations notwithstanding, I have attempted to show in this chapter that the topic merits greater attention from gender and consumer behavior researchers. This will not be only an academic exercise, but of practical importance, considering the economic effects of food expenditures and advertising claims as well as the societal costs of curing the consequences of harmful food consumption patterns leading to organic disease that may result from eating as a means of reaching psychological well-being.

References

Alderfer, C. P. (1969). An empirical test of a new theory of human needs. *Organizational Behavior and Human Performance, 4*, 142-175.

Babcock, C. (1948). Food and its emotional significance. *Journal of the American Dietetic Association, 24*, 390-393.

Bartlett, F. (1932). *Remembering*. Cambridge: Cambridge University Press.

Bruch, H. (1971). Family transactions in eating disorders. *Comprehensive Psychiatry, 12*, 238-248.

Buss, M., & Finn, W. (1987). Classification of personality traits. *Journal of Personality and Social Psychology, 52*, 432-444.

Chaiken, S., & Pliner, P. (1987). Women, but not men, are what they eat: The effect of meal size and gender on perceived femininity and masculinity. *Personality and Social Psychology Bulletin, 13*, 166-176.

Coll, M., Meyers, A., & Stunkard, A. J. (1979). Obesity and food choices in public places. *Archives of General Psychiatry, 36*, 795-797.

Conrad, E. H. (1970). Psychogenic obesity: The effects of social rejection upon hunger, food craving, food consumption and the drive-reduction value of eating for obese vs. normal individuals. *Psychosomatic Medicine, 32,* 556.

Davis, C. M. (1928). Self-selection of diet by newly weaned infants. *American Journal of Diseases of Children, 36,* 651-679.

Davis, C. M. (1939). Results of the self-selection of diets by young children. *Canadian Medical Association Journal, 41,* 257-261.

Derryberry, D., & Rothbart, M. K. (1988). Arousal, affect, and attention as components of temperament. *Journal of Personality and Social Psychology, 55,* 958-966.

Diehl, J. M. (1980). *Ernährungspsychologie* (2nd ed.). Frankfurt am Main: Fachbuchhandlung.

Flett, G. L., Boase, P., McAndrews, M. P., Pliner, P., & Blankstein, K. R. (1986). Affect intensity and the appraisal of emotion. *Journal of Research in Personality, 20,* 447-459.

Flett, G. L., Blankstein, K. R., Bator, C., & Pliner, P. (1989). Affect intensity and self-control of emotional behavior. *Personality and Individual Differences, 10,* 1-5.

Folkman, S., & Lazarus, R. S. (1988). Coping as a mediator of emotion. *Journal of Personality and Social Psychology, 54,* 466-475.

Ganley, R. M. (1988). Emotional eating and how it relates to dietary restraint, disinhibition, and perceived hunger. *International Journal of Eating Disorders, 7,* 635-657.

Garner, D. M., & Garfinkel, P. F. (1979). The Eating Attitudes Test: An index of the symptoms of anorexia nervosa. *Psychological Medicine, 9,* 273-279.

Garner, D. M., Garfinkel, P. F., Schwartz, D., & Thompson, M. (1980). Cultural expectations of thinness in women. *Psychological Reports, 47,* 483-491.

Goldman, R., Jaffa, M., & Schachter, S. (1968). Yom Kippur, Air France, dormitory food, and the eating behavior of obese and normal persons. *Journal of Personality and Social Psychology, 10,* 117-123.

Grauer, A., & Schlottke, P. F. (1987). *Mu der Speck weg? Der Kampf ums Idealgewicht im Wandel der Schönheitsideale.* Munich: dtv.

Grønmo, S. (1988). Compensatory consumer behavior: Elements of a critical sociology of consumption. In P. Otnes (Ed.), *The sociology of consumption: An anthology* (pp. 65-85). Oslo: Solum Forlag.

Grunert, S. C. (1989a). Ein Inventar zur Erfassung von Selbstaussagen zum Ernährungsverhalten. *Diagnostica, 35,* 167-179.

Grunert, S. C. (1989b). Personality traits as elements in a model of eating behavior. In K. G. Grunert & F. Ölander (Eds.), *Understanding economic behavior* (pp. 309-332). Dordrecht, Netherlands: Kluwer Academic.

Grunert, S. C. (1991a). The cognitive representation of emotions: How schema theory may explain emotional eating behavior [abstract]. In *Interdisciplinary approaches to the study of economic problems* (IAREP/SASE 1991 Proceedings) (pp. 85-86). Stockholm: Stockholm School of Economics.

Grunert, S. C. (1991b). The influence of values on compensatory eating behavior. *British Food Journal, 93*(9), 4-9.

Grunert, S. C. (1993). *Essen und Emotionen.* Weinheim: Psychologie Verlags Union.

Grunert, S. C., Grunert, K. G., & Kristensen, K. (1992). The cross-cultural validity of the List of Values (LOV): A comparison of nine samples from five countries. In J. J. G. Schmeets, M. E. P. Odekerken, & F. J. R. van de Pol (Eds.), *Developments and applications in structural equation modelling* (pp. 89-99). Amsterdam: Sociometric Research Foundation.

Grunert, S. C., & Juhl, H. J. (1991). *Values, environmental attitudes, and buying of organic foods: Their relationships in a sample of Danish teachers* (Series H, no. 60). Århus, Denmark: Århus School of Business, Department of Information Science.

Grunert, S. C., & Wagner, E. (1989). *Beziehungen zwischen Werthaltungen, Einstellungen, Schenken und Freizeit: Generationen- und Geschlechtsunterschiede im kulturellen Vergleich* (Working paper). Stuttgart: Universität Hohenheim.

Herman, C. P., & Polivy, J. (1975). Anxiety, restraint, and eating behavior. *Journal of Abnormal Psychology, 84*, 666-672.

Hirschman, A. O. (1982). *Shifting involvements: Private interest and public action*. Princeton, NJ: Princeton University Press.

Ingram, R. E., Cruet, D., Johnson, B. R., & Wisnicki, K. S. (1988). Self-focused attention, gender, gender role, and vulnerability to negative affect. *Journal of Personality and Social Psychology, 55*, 967-978.

Jelliffe, D. B. (1967). Parallel food classifications in developing and industrialized countries. *American Journal of Clinical Nutrition, 20*, 279-281.

Kaplan, H. I., & Kaplan, H. S. (1957). The psychosomatic concept of obesity. *Journal of Nervous and Mental Disease, 125*, 181-201.

Kaufman, W. (1954). Some psychosomatic aspects of food allergy. *Psychosomatic Medicine, 16*, 10-40.

Kleinspehn, T. (1987). *Warum sind wir so unersättlich?* Frankfurt am Main: Suhrkamp.

Lewin, K. (1963). *Feldtheorie in den Sozialwissenschaften*. Bern, Switzerland: Huber.

Maslow, A. H. (1943). A theory of human motivation. *Psychological Review, 50*, 370-396.

Maslow, A. H. (1981). *Motivation und Persönlichkeit*. Reinbek: Rowohlt.

McKenna, R. (1982). Some effects of anxiety level and food cues on the eating behavior of obese and normal subjects: A comparison of the Schachterian and psychosomatic conceptions. *Journal of Personality and Social Psychology, 22*, 311-319.

McKenzie, J. (1974). The impact of economic and social status on food choice. *Proceedings of the Nutrition Society, 33*, 67-73.

Mehrabian, A. (1987). *Eating characteristics and temperament: General measures and interrelationships*. New York: Springer.

Menzies, I. P. (1970). Psychosocial aspects of eating. *Journal of Psychosomatic Research, 14*, 223-227.

Mick, D. G., & DeMoss, M. (1990). To me from me: A descriptive phenomenology of self-gifts. In R. Pollay, G. Gorn, & M. Goldberg (Eds.), *Advances in consumer research* (Vol. 17, pp. 677-682). Provo, UT: Association for Consumer Research.

Miller, J. G. (1978). *Living systems*. New York: McGraw-Hill.

Murray, H. A. (1938). *Explorations in personality*. New York: Harper & Row.

Nezu, A. M., & Nezu, C. M. (1987). Psychological distress, problem solving, and coping reactions: Sex role differences. *Sex Roles, 16*, 205-214.

Nisbett, R. E., & Kanouse, D. E. (1969). Obesity, food deprivation and supermarket shopping behavior. *Journal of Personality and Social Psychology, 12*, 289-294.

O'Neil, P. M., Currey, H. S., Hirsch, A. A., Malcolm, R. J., Sexauer, J. D., Riddle, F. E., & Taylor, C. I. (1979). Development and validation of the Eating Behavior Inventory. *Journal of Behavioral Assessment, 1*, 123-132.

Polivy, J., & Herman, C. P. (1987). Diagnosis and treatment of normal eating. *Journal of Consulting and Clinical Psychology, 55*, 635-644.

Pumpian-Mindlin, E. (1954). The meanings of food. *Journal of the American Dietetic Association, 30*, 576-580.

Rodin, J. (1975). Causes and consequences of time perception differences in overweight and normal weight people. *Journal of Personality and Social Psychology, 31*, 898-904.

Rodin, J. (1981). Current status of the internal-external hypothesis for obesity: What went wrong? *American Psychologist, 36*, 361-372.

Rodin, J., Silberstein, L. R., & Striegel-Moore, R. (1985). Women and weight: A normative discontent. In T. B. Sonderegger (Ed.), *Psychology and gender: Nebraska Symposium on Motivation 1984* (pp. 267-308). Lincoln: University of Nebraska Press.

Roger, D., & Nesshoever, W. (1987). The construction and preliminary validation of a scale for measuring emotional control. *Personality and Individual Differences, 8,* 527-534.

Schachter, S. (1964). The interaction of cognitive and physiological determinants of emotional state. In L. Berkowitz (Ed.), *Advances in experimental psychology* (Vol. 1, pp. 49-80). New York: Academic Press.

Scherhorn, G., Grunert, S. C., Kaz, K., & Raab, G. (1988). *Kausalitätsorientierungen und konsumrelevante Einstellungen: Bericht über die erste Phase des Forschungsprojekts Konsumentenverhalten und postmaterielle Wert-haltungen* (Working paper). Stuttgart: Universität Hohenheim.

Schilder, P. (1935). *The image and appearance of the human body.* London: Kegan, Trench, Trubner.

Selz, O. (1913). *Über die Gesetze des geordneten Denkverluufs.* Stuttgart: Spemann.

Squires, R. L., & Kagan, D. M. (1986). Personality correlates of disordered eating. *International Journal of Eating Disorders, 5,* 363-369.

Stewart, R. A., Tutton, S. J., & Steele, R. E. (1973). Stereotyping and personality: Sex differences in perception of female physiques. *Perceptual and Motor Skills, 36,* 811-814.

Striegel-Moore, R., McAvay, G., & Rodin, J. (1986). Psychological and behavioral correlates of feeling fat in women. *International Journal of Eating Disorders, 5,* 935-947.

Timko, C., Striegel-Moore, R., Silberstein, L. R., & Rodin, J. (1987). Femininity/masculinity and disordered eating in women: How are they related? *International Journal of Eating Disorders, 6,* 701-713.

Tracy, L. (1986). Toward an improved need theory: In response to legitimate criticism. *Behavioral Science, 31,* 205-218.

van Strien, T., Frijters, J. E. R., Bergers, G. P. A., & Defares, P. B. (1986). The Dutch Eating Behavior Questionnaire for the assessment of restrained, emotional, and external eating behavior. *International Journal of Eating Disorders, 5,* 295-315.

van Strien, T., Frijters, J. E. R., Roosen, G. F. M., Knijman-Hijl, W. J. H., & Defares, P. B. (1985). Eating behavior, personality traits and body mass in women. *Addictive Behaviors, 10,* 333-343.

Wollersheim, J. P. (1971). Effectiveness of group therapy based upon learning principles in the treatment of overweight women. *Journal of Abnormal Psychology, 76,* 462-474.

Woods, W. E. (1960). Psychological dimensions of consumer decision. *Journal of Marketing, 24,* 15-19.

5

Masculinity and the Consumption of Organized Sports

EILEEN FISCHER

BRENDA GAINER

THE recent spread of feminist ideas and theories has prompted a rapid expansion in research on women. A diversity of both philosophical viewpoints and substantive concerns has surfaced. For instance, liberal feminist thought has prompted investigation of the ways in which women have been disenfranchised; women's voice/experience in feminism has given rise to examination of women's experiences and knowledge that were previously marginalized and denigrated; poststructuralist feminism has led to a consideration of how dominant discourses reinforce the subordination of women and of how those discourses can be challenged in ways that undermine this subordination (Bristor & Fischer, 1993). Most feminist writing and research has one feature in common, however: It centers its attention on women.

AUTHORS' NOTE: Our names are listed here alphabetically; each of us contributed equally to this work.

This tendency to focus primarily or exclusively on women in gender studies following in the wake of feminism is, not surprisingly, evident in the field of consumer research. For instance, studies in this field inspired by liberal feminism have looked at women's (usually wives') work status as a predictor of their consumption behaviors (e.g., Schaninger & Allen, 1981). Studies rooted in social feminism have typically looked at the manner in which consumption sustains and reinforces socialized feminine gender roles (e.g., Fischer & Gainer , 1993). Research infused by poststructuralist feminist thought has looked at how the dominant signification practices in marketing may sustain the devaluation of women and, indeed, of the feminine-gendered role of consumer (e.g., Firat, 1991; Fischer & Bristor, 1993; Stern, 1993).

This new focus on women, both within and beyond the consumer research literature, has been of immense value in adding to our knowledge of women's lives and of the role that institutions (such as consumption) play in shaping and constraining them. However, as a number of scholars have noted, if feminism inspires research exclusively on women, it runs the grave and ironic risk of reinforcing a notion it eschews: that men, and the male experience, are the norm (Messner & Sabo, 1990). If men are conceptualized simply as an abstract category, only women appear to be gendered beings, and the idea of gender as a *relational process* is lost. To conduct a thorough critical examination of the socially structured inequities women face, it is necessary to study both masculinity and femininity as they develop in relation to one another (Gerson, 1986; Kimmel, 1986).

The study we report in this chapter represents one attempt to understand how a form of consumption may shape and reinforce men's socially defined gender roles. We focus on sports, a consumption domain that is widely regarded as the purview of men, just as earlier studies examining the relationship between consumption and women's gender roles focused on consumption domains viewed as the purview of women (e.g., home shopping parties; Gainer & Fischer, 1991). Our goal is to illuminate how the consumption of sports contributes to, and is affected by, the relational process of defining masculinity and femininity.

We begin with a review of the literature on how organized sports is interconnected with the definition and maintenance of the "gender order." Based on insights from this literature, we note a number of themes that we anticipated would arise in the empirical study conducted. We next describe our research and interpret it according to these a priori themes and according to some emergent observations related to these themes. We end with a general discussion of the relationship between consumption and masculinity/femininity in light of what we have gleaned from this study.

Before we review insights from studies on the history and sociology of sports, it bears mentioning that we began by distinguishing analytically among participation in organized sports as one form of consumption, watching organized sports as a second, and following news about organized sports as a third. We believed that these distinctions would help us capture differences among these forms of consumption; however, we also looked for continuities among the three forms. Some might regard participation in organized sports as something other than consumption. We regard the distinction between consumption and production as an arbitrary one and view the two as inseparable (see Featherstone, 1991). However, because much of the literature we reviewed focuses on participation rather than on spectatorship, we will emphasize the latter to some extent.

A second point of clarification concerns our focus on *organized* sports. Most of the literature on sports is centered on sports played by groups and/or organized by community groups, schools, or professional leagues. Although we wished to follow in this tradition to capitalize on the existing literature, we could not and did not attempt to restrict the informants in our study from discussing sports that would not be viewed as organized team sports. Thus we begin with, but do not remain strictly tied to, a discussion of the connection between organized sports and masculinity.

Historical Connections Between
Organized Sports and the Gender Order

Sports historians have documented that organized sports constitute an institution in which colonial, class, and racial power relations are played out (Messner, 1992). Most pervasively, however, organized sports is an institution in which a sharp divide between men and women is defined and reinforced (Lenskyj, 1986; Twin, 1979): Struggles over power and meaning within organized sports have been fought almost exclusively among men since the early forms of modern organized sports emerged in England between 1820 and 1880 and in the

United States between 1840 and 1890. Feminist sports historians argue, in fact, that the rise of sports at this time is connected to the concurrent challenges to the gender order and to the power of privileged white males that was then taken for granted in these countries (Crosset, 1990; Kimmel, 1990).

In the mid-nineteenth century, the urban Industrial Revolution transformed the family unit such that men's and women's social roles both came into flux. For a time, women took on such roles as brewer, merchant, mill worker, and missionary as well as that of homemaker (Ryan, 1975). Although these changes did not lead to a widely shared new ideology about the role of women, many women did experience greater economic independence and political influence during this period. At the same time, rapid industrialization radically altered men's relationships to their work. Self-employment and economic autonomy for men dropped off quickly after the midpoint of the century; control over and ownership of the labor process rapidly diminished as the routinization of paid labor increased.

The changes some women were experiencing helped give rise to a women's political movement that challenged patriarchal institutions and sought for women the right to divorce, to have abortions, and to vote (Smith-Rosenburg, 1985). Middle-class white men, simultaneously, were "jolted by changes in the economic and social order which made them perceive that their superior position in the gender order and their supposedly 'natural' male roles and prerogatives were not somehow rooted in the human condition, that they were instead the result of a complex set of relationships subject to change and decay" (Hartman, 1984, p. 13, quoted in Kimmel, 1990).

These challenges to the gender order, of course, proved to be tempo rary. Many factors helped to displace women from the positions of power they had briefly gained and to mute women's political demands (Lesbock, 1984; Ryan, 1975; Smith-Rosenburg, 1985). Dunning (1986) has proposed that male hegemony is strengthened to the extent that fighting skills and physical strength are honored in a society and that men have their own social institutions, whereas women do not; he argues that organized sports served as one male-only social institution that took on this role in the late nineteenth century and thereby helped reconstitute the subjugation of women.

Quasi-scientific theories (e.g., Darwinism, Freud's psychoanalytic theories) that became popular during this period shaped or reinforced a perception of women as naturally biologically and rationally inferior to men. Dominant thinking also suggested, however, that men might become delicate and effeminate without rigorous, disciplined physical exercise such as sports offered. If the Industrial Revolution had led to the "enervation" of young men, sports could be counted on to help these same youngsters in their struggle for manliness (Crosett, 1990; Kimmel, 1990). Manhood had to be proven, and demonstration of achievement in organized sports could constitute such proof (Adelman, 1986). These notions justified the rise of early modern sports as a male-only purview, and in turn, organized sports socialized its participants to accept the idea of male superiority.

Bryson (1987) has argued that organized sports, particularly in its more violent forms, supported male dominance both through the exclusion or marginalization of women and through the linking of men and manliness with the sanctioned use of aggression. Modern sports naturalized the equation of maleness with power, dominance, and aggression.

Contemporary Connections Between Organized Sportsand the Gender Order

The past 30 years have seen a rise in women's economic and political power more pervasive than that of a century ago. Some would argue that men's roles have, as a result, changed dramatically as well. In the face of this and the statistical increase in women's access to and involvement in organized sports as both players and spectators, we might speculate that some of the associations between masculinity and sports would have eroded. Studies of men's and women's participation in contemporary organized sports, however, suggest otherwise. For many males, sports appears to be a primary socializing experience that shapes and reinforces in them their sense of masculinity.

Studies conducted during the 1970s and 1980s suggest that the initial connection between sports and masculinity is forged simply because many young men are introduced to sports by their fathers, older brothers, or other male role models (see, e.g., Fasteau, 1980; Messner, 1992; Sabo & Panepinto, 1990). Moreover, for a significant portion of boys, sports provides the context for the only close and sustained connections between them and their fathers. Boys thus are likely to form initial views of sports that cast it as primarily or exclusively a male activity. Further, they may feel that participating (successfully) or showing interest in organized sports is one of the few ways they can gain the attention and approval of fathers or other male role models. Further analyzing the importance of this connection, Messner (1992) argues that active participation or interest in sports is one of the ways boys differentiate themselves from female caregivers and thus define themselves as "not feminine."

In a similar vein, research suggests that participation in organized sports is one of the major ways in which boys can form close bonds with other boys and, if they are talented athletes, gain their respect. Particularly because organized sports, as structured by adults, are typically sex segregated, the "bonding" that sports affords is almost exclusively male bonding (Messner, 1992). This encourages boys to think of sports as a male-dominated if not male-only activity. It also encourages them to see interest in sports—or, better, success at playing sports—as one of the few ways in which they may forge connections to other men. Learning the "rules" of sports, and more subtly the values sports enshrines, thus becomes an important way of gaining authenticity as a male.

What are the traits valued by and reinforced through organized sports? As these sports have evolved in our society, they have been found to reward those who demonstrate the greatest levels of need for achievement, respect for authority, dominance among peers, self-control, and low sensitivity to other people (Ogilvie & Tutko, 1971). Other characteristics promoted by sports include the demonstration of physical and psychological aggression toward opponents and high tolerance for physical pain (Sabo & Panepinto, 1990). Not surprisingly, this list conforms virtually completely to the inventory of personality traits Bem (1974) found to be socially stereotyped as masculine in American society, and includes none of those traits she found to be stereotyped as feminine.

It is important to stress that sports encourages more than the mere demonstration of masculine virtues. Sports encourages demonstrating these virtues in order to compete and win. To gain attention and connection with others, boys learn that they must be better than others. And as Messner (1992) puts it, "Given the fact that one's own 'success' is the flip-side of another's 'failure,' organized sports encourages boys to view other boys not as intimates, but as rivals" (p. 34). Thus the form of the social bond that sports facilitates between boys is more hierarchical than equalizing, and more self-distinguishing than commonality reinforcing.

The above-noted findings from the literature lead us to our first two a priori themes:

1. The consumption of sports helps men to develop and reinforce their masculine self-identities.
2. The consumption of sports promotes and reinforces a hierarchical form of social bonding among men.

Other portions of the sports sociology literature suggest that different types of masculine self-identities are forged through the consumption of sports. First, the "pecking order" created by the competition inherent in organized sports leads to very different experiences of sports for those who are "winners" and those who are "losers." Ironically, it appears that the more successful a man is in organized sports, the greater his sense of isolation from or lack of close connection to other people (male and female). This occurs because successful athletes increasingly learn that it is not bonding with other guys, but beating them, that counts. Moreover, the more integrated into the culture of organized sports men become, the greater the pressure on them to refrain from close emotional relationships with women, because such relationships are said to interfere with performance in sports (Connell, 1990; Hoch, 1980; Sabo & Panepinto, 1990). Messner (1992) stresses how differences in race and class figure into the development of differentiated masculinities: Middle-class white men are less likely than lower-class men, particularly lower-class black men, to derive the majority of their self-defined masculinity from sports. Black male athletes in particular have forged through sports a uniquely expressive version of masculinity referred to by sports sociologists as "cool pose" (Majors, 1990). Pronger's (1990) research suggests that homosexual men develop ironic senses of themselves and their masculinity through involvement in sports. Kidd (1990) suggests that even among white, heterosexual, middle-class men, sports may promote versions of masculinity that emphasize different "manly" traits. For instance, preferences expressed for different sports, different positions in sports, and different styles of play are in part statements about whether higher valuation is placed on the traits of discipline and self-control versus the traits of aggression and indifference to pain (one's own and that of others).

At the same time different versions of masculinity emerge through organized sports, however, it is clear that the sporting culture as a whole distinguishes most sharply between the nature of masculinity and femininity. Specifically, sports values the traits associated with masculinity and devalues those associated with femininity, such as empathy, cooperativeness, and nurturance (Kidd, 1990). This disdain for femininity, and more broadly for women, is clearly expressed when coaches, supporters, and commentators in organized sports chastise whole teams or specific individuals for playing like girls, sissies, poofters, or fairies (Bryson, 1987; Sabo & Panepinto, 1990). It is reinforced by the fact that male athletes on professional teams engage together in such practices as "beaver shooting" (attempting to look up women's dresses) and bragging about their exploitative sexual conquests (Hoch, 1980), and by the "cheerleading" role to which women are typically relegated in professional sports.

Bryson (1987) suggests that organized sports promotes an ideology of male dominance and female inferiority in two general ways: by linking masculinity to highly valued and visible skills, and by linking maleness with the positively sanctioned use of aggression and violence. Her research shows that when women do become involved in sports, they are likely to avoid (and to be encouraged to avoid) contact sports or the demonstration of aggressive behavior and physical strength. Women who violate these norms are presumed to be inordinately (and unappealingly) masculine. In many cases they are simply barred from opportunities to display their valued skills or aggressiveness by competing with men in men's leagues (Bryson, 1990). These observations lead to our other two a priori themes:

3. Through their choices or constraints in the consumption of sports, men will display a varied range of masculinities.
4. Women will experience feelings of marginalization in their consumption of organized sports.

Our Study

To explore these themes and others that might emerge, we undertook a series of focus groups. Specifically, we conducted four focus groups with 8 to 12 participants in each: Two of the groups were male only, one was female only, and one was a mixed-sex group. Participants were drawn from an M.B.A.-level marketing elective class. They ranged in age from early 20s to early 40s.

Professional moderators followed a detailed question guide and audiotaped all sessions. Informants were asked about their levels and types of physical participation in sports, their viewing of sports (live and televised) and reading of sports news, their personal motivations for all forms of sports involvement, and the perceived motivations of others. They were asked who they shared their consumption of sports with under different circumstances, and about the relative importance of social aspects of sports. All groups were also asked whether they believed men and women differ with regard to what they derive from the consumption of sports. The audiotapes of all groups' discussions were transcribed.

After the focus groups met, we asked each participant to write a two-page report on what he or she thought the session had been about and whether the moderator had missed anything pertinent to the topic. We then separately analyzed these write-ups and the transcripts of the focus groups, before sharing our independent interpretations and working together to synthesize a joint interpretation.

THEME 1

The first a priori theme was that consumption of organized sports helps men to develop and reinforce their masculine self-identities. Evidence in support of this point comes in the following extended quotation from a male informant who is a rugby player:

> When I was younger, rugby was a very safe atmosphere. I had a lot of cooped-up frustrations as a kid, and that was the biggest relief I had. I played six days a week and I loved it. . . . As the years went on, I lived for rugby. . . . Rugby has always been associated with crazy beer-drinking parties and being really rowdy. Most of it is a purely male-dominated sport, although women are getting much more involved in it. When I first started you just get out with a whole bunch of guys who had no worries about anything, doing the same thing, venting their frustrations and trying to kill each other. And then when you are finished you are the best of friends. . . . The game is, I find it very challenging. It is a very physical game, it is not even just running and hitting, it is full contact. It is a challenge to make it through without getting hurt. So—male ego, big

thing, can I get through 90 minutes of physical activity without hurting myself. In order to do that, you have to hit harder than the guy across from you, run a little faster, be a little smarter. When you play, you play to save your life. You don't want to get hurt. But at the same time you don't have much care for the other person.

This informant clearly links the sport of rugby with masculinity (the male ego) and specifically with dominance, self-control, insensitivity to others, and capacity for physical violence.

We derived a related observation concerning the link between masculinity and organized sports by noting the frequency with which our informants, particularly the women, noted that men denigrate organized sports that are not male dominated. Gymnastics and figure skating were the two sports that a number of men seemed to belittle as "not real sports." A typical example came from a female informant, who reported: "My boyfriend says gymnastics is . . . well, I like to watch gymnastics by myself because I don't want to have to explain why it is a good sport. I just want to enjoy it." It is noteworthy that, like many male-dominated sports, gymnastics is highly competitive and requires considerable physical skill, self-discipline, and respect for authority, all of which are noted above as being stereotypical masculine traits. However, gymnastics does not require dominance, insensitivity, or aggression toward others. It may be, then, that sports that reinforce too small a proportion of masculine stereotypes are considered "lesser"; alternatively, it may simply be that any sports that are not male dominated are undervalued.

We developed two interesting additional insights relevant to this theme from our interpretations of the interviews. The first concerns how sports help women to define themselves as "sufficiently" masculine. The second concerns how sports contribute to a very central aspect of self-definition that is not uniquely masculine.

We developed the first insight from our interpretation of the remarks of a number of female informants who suggested that they consumed sports—both as participants and spectators—in order to gain acceptance as equals in male-dominated settings such as the workplace. Remarks made by informants that are relevant to this point include the following:

Sometimes we come in to the . . . office, and you hear about a guy that got a really good stick to the face and needed 27 stitches and we will talk about a good fight. [I keep track of sports] from listening to what is going on, or watching the news the night before. [I would have such a conversation] mostly with guys, because I hang out with guys. (female)

I know at work, also at school, I used to be in a hockey pool, and then I was right into it. I went haywire. So we would talk about it every day almost, during the playoffs, and it's mostly with men. (female)

Well, I worked at a site with all men, I used to listen to every single game in the car religiously, so I had something to say at coffee break. You know, that I knew which team won, because I had never paid much attention. . . . When some big event occurred then you would have to because then everyone would talk about it at coffee break. So you had to say like, "Oh yeah, isn't it true" or something. It was a social fit-in type of thing. (female)

Our second insight was that many informants, male and female, drew a distinction between exercise (as derived, for instance, from aerobics) and sports (usually defined as organized, competitive team activities such as baseball). Whereas sports was typically associated with developing or demonstrating strongly stereotyped masculine traits, exercise was largely associated with developing or maintaining the "shape" (a term used by many informants) deemed by society as appropriate to one's gender role. Typical was one female informant who said: "I don't really do any competitive sports. More of a recreational thing, aside from the aerobics which I do to stay fit."

The theme that the consumption of exercise (versus sports) helps participants be "in shape" is pervasive. Clearly, this theme relates to the establishment or maintenance of a desired self-image: The "shape" for which people are striving is that defined by society as appropriately lean and muscled. Both male and female informants stressed that they engage in exercise to help achieve their desired physiques; although the body shape and degree of muscularity defined as desirable differ for men and women, the consumption of exercise (versus sports) as a means of achieving attractiveness is at least as important to defining femininity as it is to defining masculinity.

THEME 2

The second a priori theme was that the consumption of sports promotes and reinforces a hierarchical form of social bonding among men. Many men said that sports was an activity they undertook with close male relatives, and one indicated particularly strikingly that it was through sports that he formed a connection with his closest male relatives:

> From my relationships with my father and grandfather, I think the only time I ever had a serious conversation with either of them is when we are playing golf together. Because for them it is something that they really want to do. It is an outlet. And for me it is a chance to get to talk to them and I see a different side of them because they are very relaxed. It is just the three of us . . . and we have really interesting conversations, really get this male bonding. Father, son, grandfather, we play 18 holes. It is a really interesting atmosphere.

A number of the male informants stated that sports is important to them, at this stage in their lives, at least in part because it allows them to maintain contact with male friends with whom they would otherwise find it difficult to interact. One stated:

> The only way I keep in touch with my group from undergrad is our sports. And the people I used to work with, [the way I keep in touch] is through sport. . . . I am going skiing with a friend of mine from high school on Friday. Normally we wouldn't spend 12 hours together. It would drive us both crazy. This is an opportunity to do that, and to have something to do while you are together.

Another said:

> Guys usually don't call up each other and say, "Hey, you want to talk?" you know. But a sporting event is a good outlet to talk. You are talking about sport, but other things come up. . . . So, sporting events, people talk about male bonding, it is true, it does exist. So many areas are being opened now to women, which I am not saying is bad, but it is sort of taking away from men just being with men and being themselves. Because you sort of have to put on an act if women are there, a lot of the time.

This informant's last remark suggests that the social bonding that occurs among men in such settings is *exclusively* "male bonding": The presence of women is problematic because the communities formed by men through sports exclude or at least marginalize women.

Some men gave clear indications that the bonds they formed through the consumption of sports are important and hierarchical. One said: "What keeps me doing it [participating in triathlon] I guess is I have some very close friends, I guess my two best friends, are both involved in the sport, so that is sort of a rivalry between us. That is always good and it keeps it interesting." The rugby player quoted above also emphasized how the social bonds he forged through participation were inextricably linked with attempting to establish dominance over his friends. As he summed it up, "I love going out there and trying to kill somebody and then buying them a beer."

One observation builds on the insight that the male bonding achieved through the consumption of sports is hierarchical and exclusively male: Some men use sports consumption to reinforce the social hierarchy of all men over all women. That is, the worldview shaped by sports categorizes women as "the lowest of the low." This point is reinforced by the following remarks of a male informant:

> I have a lot of female friends who are good in sports and as much as they are my friend or my wife or my sister, if they beat me at a sport I hate it. I despise them at the minute that they beat me. It is an ego thing. It's a male thing to be competitive toward sports. It always takes a chunk out of me. It is like, oh man, so off I go working away on my own so next time I make sure I can beat them.

It seems that to be beaten by male peers would be much less threatening; to be beaten by a woman is incompatible with his image of men's general superiority. Even to have a woman demonstrate comparable knowledge of sports would threaten the male-superior worldview reinforced by organized sports, as one informant suggested when he stated:

> Through high school, you play with all guys. When you are watching sports at a professional level, not even playing—although most men put themselves in the position that they are playing—and so a woman comes in and it is like, "I know this team. I know football. You don't know football."

One male informant made it very clear that establishing masculinity through the consumption of sports involves displaying superiority (of either skill or knowledge) and that if a woman displays knowledge equal to his own, not only his masculinity but the general camaraderie is threatened:

> [Sports] is just a place for men to pretend they are more than they are, and they are more intelligent. In a room full of men talking about sports, the

stories get bigger and better, I mean I love it, every story he tells is better than the next guy's and it is a really good atmosphere, a lot of fun. But then the woman enters, then her stories are probably just as good but it is coming from a woman and . . . she is infringing on your territory. And when a woman comes in and seems to suck it all away, you're just going, "Ah, man, here goes the story." I don't think it is the fact that we don't think they know anything. I think it is the fact that they know just as much as we do and it is embarrassing. . . . I have very great respect for women in sports, I think it is great and I respect their point of view. I just find that when I am with guys it infringes on my territory because they know just as much as I do. It is an ego thing.

This theme is also reinforced by men's answers to questions concerning what they believe men versus women derive from sports:

For men, basically I think [attending sports] is to do with the boys, an outing. For females [it is] a way to get men, see what men want, a way to participate in something males enjoy, a way to understand males better. (male)

For females, [they watch sports] so they can impress men. (male)

The maintenance of both individual masculinity and male bonding through the consumption of sports clearly involves a sort of performance on men's part. A form of one-upmanship appears to be de rigeur when it is exclusively men who are in a joint consumption setting. When women are present, men appear to have to establish (in their own minds and those of their peers) that they are superior to women as a class. The success of this performance is threatened by an awareness that some women may well be as just as knowledgeable and skilled consumers as most men. Maintaining the role of the superior "player," however, appears to be imperative to the presentation (and preservation) of the masculine self (see Goffman, 1959).

THEME 3

This theme suggested that, through their choices or constraints in the consumption of sports, men will display a varied range of masculinities. The range of responses by men to questions about their reasons for and type of involvement in both organized and other sports certainly seems to support this notion. At one extreme was a male informant who engaged in no organized sports but who biked fairly regularly. He said: "Bike riding is just so relaxing. You can go along Lakeshore Road to Oakville and you see a lot about history. It is very peaceful." The pursuit of such tranquillity could be deemed the very opposite of a search for a means to demonstrate one's masculinity. A contrast can be drawn between this attitude and that of the rugby player, who stated, "The biggest reason I play rugby is just a way for me to vent my frustrations." Although both men are saying they find their chosen sports a physical release, the former projects a passive (more stereotypically feminine) image, and the latter an aggressive (stereotypically masculine) one.

One male informant who consumed a wide range of sports clearly drew the line at sports he considered to be expressive of excessive dominance and aggression: "Each sport has a different attitude. Like boxing, that is one sport that I have to admit I would never watch. Because it is a waste of time, watching two people kill themselves, knock each others' brain cells all over the mat." This informant reported that he enjoyed beating his friends in competition (which would serve to reinforce a masculine image of himself as more skilled than his friends), but distanced himself from other masculine traits, such as physical aggressiveness.

An emergent observation that should be noted under this heading is that women, too, display a range of masculinities through their involvement in sports. For instance, one woman said:

> When I was younger, you play and you defeat this person because they score all the goals or they tripped you on purpose or something, so that was carried on after the game. But now that I am getting older and sort of understand how the other person is, you are going into a game and you are playing as hard as you can and when you step off the ice you are fine and you talk to the other person.

This woman's words suggests that she identifies with the "masculine" traits of aggressiveness, self-discipline, and dominance. Several women mentioned that they liked to consume sports because they enjoyed competition—a stereotypically masculine trait. Women expressing this point varied, however, with regard to whether they expressed a preference for competition with others (which is more stereotypically masculine, because it involves "beating" someone else) or competition with themselves (which involves no insensitivity to others' feelings).

THEME 4

Our final a priori theme was that women experience feelings of marginalization in their consumption of organized sports. Some of our female informants did report such feelings. At one extreme were those women who never played organized sports, and who rarely took on the role of spectator. Typical of this group was one woman who said:

> [Sports] is kind of like being in a country where nobody told you what the language was. You can only go on playing the dumb blonde for so long, and you can only sort of go, "What is the name of the puck you use in baseball?" You annoy the people around you when you are saying, "Why do they do this and why do they do that?"

Another said, "A lot of times I feel out of place [at baseball games] because I don't think that anything relates to me."

Others reported that, despite their interest in and knowledge of sports, they were marginalized by men when they played sports or watched sports with men. One stated: "When I go to baseball games with females I can ask questions and I get answers like I am an intelligent human being. If I ask a guy it is like they talk down to you. Women who love sport talk about it in a way that is understandable to everybody."

One accomplished female athlete who had participated extensively in such "masculine" organized sports as soccer and football, having learned them as a young child from her father and brothers, reported that male acquaintances belittled her as a consumer of sports when they watched certain games together:

> I find that during a baseball game, my boyfriend's friends automatically assume, "Oh, she is into baseball because the team is doing really well and they are going to take the series this year." But I have been watching since opening day, like I follow spring training and everything that they do. Yet they think, "Oh my God, she knows what four balls mean." They are really shocked.

Some informants noted that men reinforce their masculinity by establishing (or conveying the impression) that they know more than the females with whom they consume sports:

> There are people that I go [to sporting events] with, let's say they are boyfriend and girlfriend or husband and wife, the wife will be asking

questions and they [men] often like to tell them how it is played because they like to show that they know what is going on. (female)

Even women who were avid consumers of organized sports and who denied being personally marginalized reflected a perception that in the broader society, men and women alike regard women as having less than full status as consumers of sports. For instance, a heated outburst occurred in one focus group when one woman objected after another woman remarked that she disliked watching football because she didn't understand it: "It bothers me to hear women talk like that because there is nothing tricky or challenging about figuring out any of these sports. . . . I think there [are] too many people that think women don't know anything about sports."

It seems fair to interpret our informants' comments as a whole as evidence that if women do wish to be involved in sports, they must "play by men's rules." That is, rather than organized sports changing to be consistent with social stereotypes of femininity (e.g., cooperative, nurturing), women must become or act "masculine" if they wish to gain status as either participants or spectators. They must demonstrate such male-stereotyped traits as displays of superior knowledge if they wish to feel any sense of inclusion in sports and be regarded as authentic consumers.

There was no evidence from our interviews that organized sports were adapted by women to achieve similar ends as are served by female-stereotyped consumption activities. All of the female inform-ants who were asked whether they would socialize with other women at a sporting event suggested that they could not see it as serving the same relationship-reinforcing purposes as, for instance, an evening spent shopping or dining out. As one woman put it, "I wouldn't just sit watching sports with girlfriends." Another said: "The women from my office, when we go out, we mostly go out to try new restaurants or something like that; we went out to a ballet one time, and to a few plays. But I have never been to a sporting event with a group of female friends."

Mixed-sex groups did, in a manner of speaking, socialize through sports, but informants appeared to experience tension in trying to "visit" while attending games or watching them on television. Male informants believed attention should be focused on the sport so long as play was occurring; female informants suggested that they were relegated to the "back of the box" (in stadiums) or to the kitchen if they wished to communicate other than about the game being watched while play was ongoing.

In summary, it seems that at present, the consumption of organized sports continues to be linked with the development or expression of masculinity—and male superiority—and with the devaluation of femininity—and of women.

Implications of the Sports-Masculinity Link for Other Forms of Consumption

The foregoing discussion suggests that the consumption of sports is deeply associated with defining what *is* masculine and, concurrently, what *is not* feminine. It has been noted that participating in and watching sports lead to a range of masculinities, and each of them relies for its definition on being distinct from femininity.

This insight raises the question of how other forms or venues of consumption contribute to, and are affected by, the relational process of defining masculinity versus femininity. As one example, Firat (1991) has suggested that shopping, once stereotyped as a woman's pastime and therefore a feminine activity, remains feminine in its connotations even though men now form a significant portion of shoppers. It seems that in the shopping domain, men are "feminized" by participation, just as in the sporting domain, women are "masculinized" by participation.

A challenge for scholars interested in the connection between gender and consumption will be to consider whether any "gendered" consumption domain or activity can become "gender neutral" if, for example, sufficient numbers of people of both sexes come to participate in the domain or activity. If we find, as we suspect, that most consumption domains and activities are gendered, and not particularly susceptible to revision in this regard, we will begin to have a better appreciation of the ways that consumption practices are shaped by (and support) other mutually reinforcing social practices that contribute to the current gender order. If exceptions to pervasive and persistent gendering of consumption practices are found, they will be worth much scrutiny for the insights they may afford concerning how changes to the existing social order may be wrought.

References

Adelman, M. L. (1986). *A sporting time: New York City and the rise of modern athletics, 1820-1870.* Urbana: University of Illinois Press.

Bem, S. (1974). The measurement of psychological androgyny. *Journal of Consulting Clinical Psychology, 42,* 155-162.

Bristor, J. M., & Fischer, E. (1993). Feminist thought: Implications for consumer research. *Journal of Consumer Research, 19,* 518-536.

Bryson, L. (1987). Sports and the maintenance of masculine hegemony. *Women's Studies International Forum, 10,* 349-360.

Bryson, L. (1990). Challenges to male hegemony in sports. In M. A. Messner & D. F. Sabo (Eds.), *Sport, men and the gender order: Critical feminist perspectives* (pp. 173-184). Champaign, IL: Human Kinetics.

Connell, R. W. (1990). An iron man: The body and some contradictions of hegemonic masculinity. In M. A. Messner & D. F. Sabo (Eds.), *Sport, men and the gender order: Critical feminist perspectives* (pp. 83-95). Champaign, IL: Human Kinetics.

Crosset, T. (1990). Masculinity, sexuality and the development of early modern sport. In M. A. Messner & D. F. Sabo (Eds.), *Sport, men and the gender order: Critical feminist perspectives* (pp. 45-54). Champaign, IL: Human Kinetics.

Dunning, E. (1986). Sport as a male preserve: Note on the social sources of masculinity and its transformation. *Theory, Culture and Society, 3,* 79-90.

Fasteau, M. (1980). Sports: The training ground. In D. Sabo & R. Runfola (Eds.), *Jock: Sports and male identity* (pp. 44-53). Englewood Cliffs, NJ: Prentice Hall.

Featherstone, M. (1991). *Consumer culture and postmodernism.* Newbury Park, CA: Sage.

Firat, A. F. (1991). Consumption and gender: A common history. In J. A. Costa (Ed.), *Gender and consumer behavior* (pp. 378-386). Salt Lake City: University of Utah Printing Service.

Fischer, E., & Bristor, J. (1993). A feminist poststructural analysis of the rhetoric of marketing relationships. *International Journal of Research in Marketing, 10.*

Fischer, E., & Gainer, B. (1993). Baby showers: A rite of passage in transition. In L. McAlister & M. L. Rothschild (Eds.), *Advances in consumer research* (Vol. 20, pp. 320-324). Provo, UT: Association for Consumer Research.

Gainer, B., & Fischer, E. (1991). To buy or not to buy? That is not the question: Female ritual in home shopping parties. In R. H. Holman & M. R. Solomon (Eds.), *Advances in consumer research* (Vol. 18, pp. 597-604). Provo, UT: Association for Consumer Research.

Gerson, K. (1986). What do women want from men? *American Behavioral Scientist, 29,* 619-634.

Goffman, E. (1959). *The presentation of self in everyday life.* Garden City, NY: Doubleday.

Hoch, P. (1980). School for sexism. In D. Sabo & R. Runfola (Eds.), *Jock: Sports and male identity* (pp. 9-19). Englewood Cliffs, NJ: Prentice Hall.

Kidd, B. (1990). The Men's Cultural Centre: Sports and the dynamic of women's oppression/men's repression. In M. A. Messner & D. F. Sabo (Eds.), *Sport, men and the gender order: Critical feminist perspectives* (pp. 31-44). Champaign, IL: Human Kinetics.

Kimmel, M. (1986). Toward men's studies. *American Behavioral Scientist, 29,* 517-529.

Kimmel, M. (1990). Baseball and the reconstitution of American masculinity, 1880-1920. In M. A. Messner & D. F. Sabo (Eds.), *Sport, men and the gender order: Critical feminist perspectives.* Champaign, IL: Human Kinetics.

Lenskyj, H. (1986). *Out of bounds: Women, sport and sexuality.* Toronto: Women's Press.

Lesbock, S. (1984). *The free women of Petersburg: Status and culture in a southern town, 1784-1860*. New York: Norton.

Majors, R. (1990). Cool pose: Black masculinity and sports. In M. A. Messner & D. F. Sabo (Eds.), *Sport, men and the gender order: Critical feminist perspectives* (pp. 109-114). Champaign, IL: Human Kinetics.

Messner, M. A. (1992). *Power at play*. Boston: Beacon.

Messner, M. A., & Sabo, D. F. (1990). Introduction: Toward a critical feminist reappraisal of sport, men and the gender order. In M. A. Messner & D. F. Sabo (Eds.), *Sport, men and the gender order: Critical feminist perspectives* (pp. 1-16). Champaign, IL: Human Kinetics.

Ogilvie, B., & Tutko, T. (1971, October). Sport: If you want to build character try something else. *Psychology Today*, p. 61.

Pronger, B. (1990). *The arena of masculinity: Sports, homosexuality and the meaning of sex*. Toronto: Summerhill.

Ryan, M. P. (1975). *Womanhood in America*. New York: New Viewpoints.

Sabo, D., & Panepinto, J. (1990). Football ritual and the social reproduction of masculinity. In M. A. Messner & D. F. Sabo (Eds.), *Sport, men and the gender order: Critical feminist perspectives* (pp. 115-126). Champaign, IL: Human Kinetics.

Schaninger, C., & Allen, C. (1981). Wife's occupational status as a consumer behavior construct. *Journal of Consumer Research, 8*, 189-195.

Smith-Rosenburg, C. (1985). *Disorderly conduct: Visions of gender in Victorian America*. New York: Knopf.

Stern, B. B. (1993). Feminist literary criticism and the deconstruction of advertisements: A postmodern view of advertising and consumer responses. *Journal of Consumer Research, 19*, 556-566.

Twin, S. (1979). *Out of the bleachers: Writings on women and sport*. Old Westbury, NY: Feminist Press.

6

The Measurement of Social Comparison to Advertising Models: A Gender Gap Revealed

MARY C. MARTIN

PATRICIA F. KENNEDY

> *So we have the paradox of a man shamed to death because he is only the second pugilist or the second oarsman in the world. That he is able to beat the whole population of the globe minus one is nothing; he has pitted himself to beat that one and as long as he doesn't do that nothing else counts.*
>
> William James, 1892/1984, p. 168

AT the turn of the century, renowned philosopher William James noted the role that self-esteem plays for some individuals. James's definition of self-esteem, one's successes divided by one's pretensions, also highlights social comparison processes by suggesting that aspirations are often defined by comparison with others, often to the detriment of self-esteem. Social comparison theory has central relevance for the dimensions of the self-concept, particularly self-esteem. Comparisons on self-relevant dimensions appear to have special impact on one's self-esteem and feelings (Wood, 1989). The idea that social comparison affects self-esteem was even implicit in Festinger's (1954) original conception of social comparison theory.

But in what ways, and to what extent, do males and females differ in self-esteem? This question has been addressed extensively, with somewhat mixed results. However, recent evidence indicates that females' self-esteem is generally lower than males' self-esteem. For example, Harter (1992, 1993), in a cross-sectional study of third through eleventh graders, found that self-perceptions of physical attractiveness and self-esteem in females appear to decline systematically over time, whereas no such decrease was found in males. Block and Robins (1993), in a longitudinal study of consistency and change in self-esteem, found that males' self-esteem tends to increase and females' self-esteem to decrease from early adolescence (age 14) through late adolescence (age 18) to early adulthood (age 23).

The domain of physical attractiveness consistently appears to be a significant factor in determining both males' and females' levels of self-esteem (Harter, 1992, 1993; Mathes & Kahn, 1975; Rosenberg, 1986). Further, studies suggest that advertising and the mass media may play a part in reinforcing preoccupation with physical attractiveness. For example, Harter (1992, 1993) suggests that contributing to the preoccupation with physical attractiveness is the emphasis that contemporary society places on being beautiful, as demonstrated in movies, television, magazines, music videos, and advertising that glamorize popular role models that both males and females should emulate.

Using social comparison theory, researchers in marketing have begun to determine what effects the beauty of advertising models may have, particularly on preadolescent and adolescent girls and young women (Martin & Kennedy, 1993; Richins, 1991). This represents what Pollay (1986) calls "unintended consequences of advertising." For example, according to Pollay, one of the unintended consequences of advertising is a "sense of inadequacy" instilled in women's self-concepts: "We are all potential victims of the invidious comparisons of reality to the world seen in advertising. Once convinced that the grass is greener elsewhere, one's own life pales in comparison and seems a life half-lived" (p. 27). Pollay also notes:

> It is clearly appropriate for us [the marketing discipline] to take these assertions about advertising's unintended consequences seriously. Despite

the relative lack of data based on research to date, despite the occasional naiveté of some authors with respect to the processes of strategy formulation and advertising execution, and despite the challenge this indictment represents to our own vested interests and ideologies, the charges are much too serious to dismiss cavalierly. The convergence of thought among intellectual leaders of so many diverse disciplines demands our attention and research as allied academics. (p. 31)

On the other hand, Durgee (1986) believes that advertising may *intentionally* play on consumers' self-esteem. For example, according to Durgee, older women represent a group of consumers whose self-esteem "might be lower than average" (p. 26). Consequently, advertisers have developed such copy as "You're not getting older, you're getting better" (for Clairol hair coloring products) for them. Similarly, "You're feeling good about yourself and you're drinking Diet Pepsi—and it shows" may have been purposefully developed for another group of consumers with lower-than-average self-esteem—people trying to lose weight.

It is, therefore, the responsibility of marketers to determine the extent to which today's advertising perpetuates and/or exacerbates its alleged effects, intentional or not, including its contribution to a preoccupation with physical attractiveness and subsequent effects on self-esteem. Whereas most studies have focused on women and suggest that women are particularly susceptible to advertising and media images (Irving, 1990; Martin, 1994; Martin & Kennedy, 1993, 1994; Myers & Biocca, 1992; Richins, 1991; Silverstein, Perdue, Peterson, & Kelly, 1986), the study we discuss below focused on advertising as a basis for comparison of physical attractiveness for both men and women. We investigated whether or not differences exist between men and women in terms of self-esteem, self-perceptions of physical attractiveness, the importance placed on being physically attractive, and susceptibility to the influences of advertising, others around them, and social comparison information.

In exploring these issues, we conducted a scale validation study using male and female college students. Specifically, we developed a scale to measure individuals' comparison of themselves with advertising models. We assessed reliability and employed a multitrait-multimethod analysis (Campbell & Fiske, 1959) to examine whether convergent validity and discriminant validity exist. We undertook a one-way analysis of variance to explore differences between males and females with respect to self-esteem, self-perceptions of physical attractiveness, the importance placed on being physically attractive, and tendencies to compare themselves with models in ads and others and to attend to social comparison information. We further investigated male/female differences with multiple regression.

In the sections that follow, we first highlight findings in the literature concerning self-esteem and the domain of physical attractiveness, and then present the results of the validation study. Finally, we present our conclusions and outline some suggestions for future research directions.

Self-Esteem

For the study, we adopted the definition of self-esteem put forth by Harter (1992): "the level of global regard that one has for the self as a person" (p. 3). Harter (1986, 1992, 1993) presents a conceptualization and operationalization of self-esteem consisting of a competence/importance construct (incorporated from James, 1892/1984). James defines self-esteem as the ratio of one's successes to one's pretensions. Successes are competencies or adequacies in a specific domain of life, whereas pretensions exist in those areas of one's life where one has aspirations to be successful. Thus, if one's successes are at a level equal to or greater than one's pretensions, one would have a high global self-esteem score. Conversely, if one's pretensions toward success exceed one's actual level of success, low self-esteem results. James's formulation implies that a person's lack of success or competence in domains that he or she deems unimportant will not adversely affect that person's self-esteem.

Harter (1986) has translated the constructs of success and pretension into competence or adequacy/importance in 12 specific domains for college students: scholastics, athletics, social acceptance, physical appearance, creativity, intellectual ability, job competence, romantic relationships, close friendships, parent relationships, finding humor in one's life, and morality. As James's formulation implies, two college students may have comparable competencies in any of these domains but have very different global self-esteem scores. For example, Student A, although low in athletic and scholastic competence, may exhibit a high global self-esteem score because he or she can discount the importance of those areas and tout the importance of the other areas in which he or she is doing well. Conversely, Student B, also low in athletic and scholastic competence, may exhibit a very low level of global self-esteem because he or she is unable to discount the importance of those areas. In addition, Harter's (1986) scale measures global self-esteem, indicating how much the individual likes him- or herself as a person overall.

THE DOMAIN OF PHYSICAL ATTRACTIVENESS

Self-esteem may change over time, so it is important to consider changes in the domains that influence self-esteem. Further, even if self-esteem were to remain constant, the domains that shape and form it might change radically. In particular, the domain of *physical attractiveness* consistently appears to be a significant factor in determining both males' and females' levels of global self-esteem (Harter, 1992, 1993; Mathes & Kahn, 1975; Rosenberg, 1986). This appears to be particularly true for females. For example, Lerner, Orlos, and Knapp (1976) found that, in their sample, female college students' self-concepts derived primarily from body attractiveness, whereas males' self-concepts were more strongly related to perceptions of physical instrumental effectiveness. Brenner and Cunningham (1992) found that the women they studied displayed significantly more eating-disordered behavior, lower levels of body satisfaction, and lower levels of self-esteem than men.

Patzer (1985, p. 27) defines *physical attractiveness* as the degree to which a stimulus person is pleasing to observe. A global measure of physical attractiveness has turned the abstract concept into a "powerful research construct." Specifically, a truth-of-consensus method is generally used, in which ratings of physical attractiveness are assigned when agreement is reached among a number of judges. In other words, research shows that people closely agree on overall levels of physical attractiveness (see Patzer, 1985).

However, standards of physical attractiveness vary greatly over time and across cultures. Mazur (1986) writes:

Modern institutions of advertising, retailing, and entertainment now produce vivid notions of beauty that change from year to year, placing stress upon women to conform to the body image currently in vogue. The best known of these beauty standards are the "bosom mania" of the 1950s and 1960s and the current trend toward slenderization. (p. 281)

In the past several decades, the cultural definition of physical attractiveness for women has included thinness, resulting in an evolution toward a thinner standard of beauty for American women. For example, Mazur (1986) has documented decreasing weight among *Playboy* centerfold models and contestants in Miss USA pageants. In the 1983 and 1984 Miss USA contests, 22 finalists averaged 68 inches tall and 120 pounds. In the 1960s, Miss USA contestants also averaged 120 pounds, but with a corresponding height of only 66 inches. Rodin, Silberstein, and Striegel-Moore (1985) report the results of a study in which self-perceptions of weight and body shape constituted the *central* determinants of physical attractiveness in women. Professional models are also affected by this emphasis on thinness. For example, well-known model Beverly Johnson joined Overeaters Anonymous to combat bulimia and anorexia. Johnson says that starvation is "very prevalent" in the modeling business and that "clothes look better on a hanger, so you have to look like a hanger" (quoted in Sporkin, 1993). Percy and Lautman (1987) found a negative exponential decrease in the body shapes of models in advertisements in *McCall's* from 1905 to 1985. Paralleling this emphasis on thinness is an increase in the number of health and weight-loss claims found in food advertisements in women's magazines (Klassen, Wauer, & Cassel, 1990/1991).

PHYSICAL ATTRACTIVENESS IN
ADVERTISING AND THE MASS MEDIA

Downs and Harrison (1985) provide several reasons television advertising may be a primary vehicle for physical attractiveness stereotyping. First, billions of dollars are spent on cosmetics, physical fitness, and weight reduction advertising annually. Second, the increasing popularity of health spas, designer clothing, cosmetics, and similar products hints that appearance-related commercials may be quite effective. Third, stereotypes directed against women, African Americans, and the elderly have been shown to be disseminated by television. Fourth, attractiveness messages may go unchallenged by viewers, especially children, as they tend to accept what appears on television as real. Finally, viewers are exposed to very high numbers of attractiveness-based messages as a result of watching many hours of television. Downs and Harrison (1985) conclude, "Overall, then, there are compelling reasons to suspect that television acts as a salient source of attractiveness-oriented socialization" (p. 10). In fact, in a content analysis of television commercials, these researchers observed some form of attractiveness message in 1 out of every 3.8 commercials.

Silverstein et al. (1986) conducted several content analyses and demonstrated that the standard of physical attractiveness presented on television and in popular magazines is slimmer and more oriented to dieting and staying in shape for women than it is for men. These researchers also demonstrate that the standard of physical attractiveness for women presented in magazines and movies is less curvaceous now than it was in the 1930s.

Irving (1990) examined the effects of the thin beauty standard on the self-evaluations of women exhibiting varying levels of bulimic symptoms. Measures of self- and body-esteem were given to 162 female college students after they were exposed to media images represented by slides of thin, average, and oversize models. Subjects exposed to highly attractive models (thin) gave lower self-evaluations than those exposed to models of average attractiveness (average and oversize). However, contrary to Irving's expectations, women exhibiting high levels of bulimic symptoms did not report lower self-evaluations in response to thin fashion models than did those with few bulimic symptoms, but they did report a greater amount of pressure to be thin coming from media, peers, and family than did those with few bulimic symptoms.

Myers and Biocca (1992) found that watching even 30 minutes of television programming and advertising can alter women's perceptions of body shape. Ideal-body-image commercials lowered body size overestimations and subjects' depression levels, supporting the existence of "an elastic body image." That is, a woman's actual body size is in conflict with a mediated ideal body image, resulting in an unstable self-perceived body image that is responsive to social cues.

Using social comparison theory (Festinger, 1954) as a basis, Richins (1991) examined the effect of "idealized images" (highly attractive models in fashion magazines) on female college students' satisfaction with their own physical attractiveness, and found evidence for the subjects' comparing their own levels of physical attractiveness to that of the models in ads. Richins's results also indicated that exposure to idealized images raised the subjects' comparison standards for physical attractiveness and lowered levels of satisfaction with their own attractiveness. In a similar study, we found evidence that female preadolescents' and adolescents' comparison standards are raised after exposure to advertising models (Martin & Kennedy, 1993).

As the above review indicates, the focus thus far has been on advertising and media effects on women. The question of whether or not men

and women differ in terms of advertising effects needs further exploration. Specifically, our study investigated whether advertising as a basis
for comparison of physical attractiveness for both men and women has
differential effects on men and women. In addition, we explored the
question of whether or not men and women differ in terms of tendencies
to compare themselves with models in ads. First, however, we will
discuss the development and validation of the Comparison to Advertising Models Scale (CAMS).

The Validation Study

The Comparison to Advertising Models Scale is designed to measure
an individual's tendency to compare him- or herself with models in ads
in terms of physical appearance. This construct has received very little
attention in the literature. It has been suggested that consumers compare themselves with images and lifestyles portrayed in ads, but only
our own work (Martin & Kennedy, 1993, 1994) and that of Richins (1991)
has demonstrated empirically that comparison with advertising models does take place. As noted above, Richins (1991) found that "female
college students frequently compare themselves with idealized models
in ads directed toward them" (p. 76). Using the format developed by
Harter (1982), we designed CAMS to minimize social desirability bias
by legitimating either side of a statement or choice. The option of
checking either "sort of true for me" or "really true for me" also
broadens the range of choices over a typical two-choice format. In
addition, none of the choices involves the response "false." Rather, a
subject is first asked to decide which kind of student is most like him
or her (which side of the statement) and then asked whether this is only
sort of true or really true for him or her. Given the sensitivity of these
issues, responses may be particularly susceptible to social desirability,
making this format appealing. The five items that make up CAMS are
listed in Table 6.1.

To employ multitrait-multimethod analysis (Campbell & Fiske, 1959),
we used two similar constructs: the Physical Appearance Comparison
Scale (PACS; Thompson, Heinberg, & Tantleff, 1991); and the Attention
to Social Comparison Information (ATSCI) scale (Bearden & Rose,
1990). The PACS (reliability = .78) measures a person's tendency to
compare him- or herself with other individuals in terms of physical

TABLE 6.1 The Comparison to Advertising Models Scale (CAMS)

Really True for Me	Sort of True for Me				Sort of True for Me	Really True for Me
____	____	Some students don't compare the way they look with models in ads.	BUT	Other students often compare the way they look with models in ads.	____	____
____	____	Some students, when looking through magazines, compare their bodies with the bodies of models in ads.	BUT	Other students do not compare their bodies with the bodies of models in ads when looking through magazines.	____	____
____	____	Some students often compare their physical appearance with models in ads.	BUT	Other students don't often compare their physical appearance with models in ads.	____	____
____	____	Some students don't often compare how good looking they are with models in ads.	BUT	Other students often compare how good looking they are with models in ads.	____	____
____	____	Some students, when watching TV, often compare their height or weight with models in ads.	BUT	Other students don't often compare their height or weight with models in ads when watching TV.	____	____

appearance; it was validated with 80 female college students and found to be strongly related to levels of eating disturbance, body image dissatisfaction, and self-esteem (Thompson et al., 1991). The ATSCI (reliability = .83-.89) measures a person's predisposition to act on available social cues. "Persons scoring high in ATSCI are aware of the reactions of others to their behavior and are concerned about or sensitive to the nature of those reactions. Simply put, such individuals care what other people think about them and look for clues as to the nature of those likely reactions" (Bearden & Rose, 1990, p. 462). Items for these scales were altered to conform to the format used by Harter (1982, 1986).

The alternate measurement method used was Thematic Apperception Test sketches (TATs), representing a projective technique. Rappaport (1942) suggests that respondents, in generating imaginative stories about pictorial stimuli, will reveal unconscious and other hidden aspects of their current concerns, motivations (needs/threats), percep-

Kristi and Amy are hanging out reading magazines.

Figure 6.1. Thematic Apperception Test Sketch for CAMS
NOTE: The TATs reflected the genders of the respondents to whom they were shown.

tions of significant others, and views of the world. The use of projective techniques in marketing research has been revitalized in recent years. For example, Rook (1985) used TATs to investigate the nature of young adults' personal grooming rituals. Most recently, Mick, DeMoss, and Faber (1992) used TATs to investigate the motivations and meanings of self-gifts, and Sherry, McGrath, and Levy (1993) examined negativity and ambivalence in gift exchange with TATs.

Nine TATs were administered—three designed to measure each construct—at the beginning of the survey. A picture with a heading was shown, and the respondent was asked to tell a story about the picture, including what led up to the scene shown in the picture, what is happening at the moment, what the people are thinking and saying, and what will happen next. Sample TATs for CAMS are shown in Figures 6.1 and 6.2. A trained, independent judge coded the TATs for each respondent on a 5-point scale—extremely low, somewhat low,

Dwayne is watching TV.

Figure 6.2. Thematic Apperception Test Sketch for CAMS
NOTE: The TATs reflected the genders of the respondents to whom they were shown.

moderate, somewhat high, and extremely high—with respect to the construct under question.

The TATs were somewhat effective in revealing the extent of comparison with advertising models, comparison with other individuals, and attention to social comparison information. Further refinement of the TATs is needed, however, to ensure that respondents do not stray from the subject at hand—that is, to ensure that they tell stories that concern the construct under question.

The sample consisted of 83 students from a large midwestern university. Eleven surveys were thrown out of the analysis because the respondents filled them out incorrectly (i.e., marked both sides of the items in the Harter [1982, 1986] format) or did not complete the entire survey. For the final analysis, surveys completed by 32 females and 40 males were used, for a total sample size of 72.

TABLE 6.2 Multitrait–Multimethod Matrix

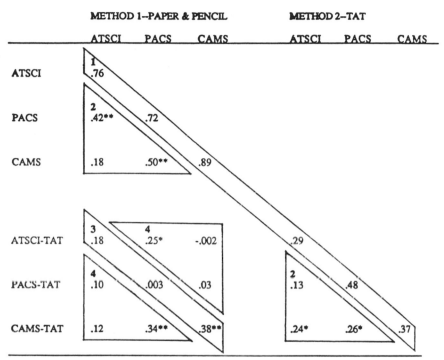

	METHOD 1–PAPER & PENCIL			METHOD 2–TAT		
	ATSCI	PACS	CAMS	ATSCI	PACS	CAMS
ATSCI	**1** .76					
PACS	**2** .42**	.72				
CAMS	.18	.50**	.89			
ATSCI-TAT	**3** .18	**4** .25*	-.002	.29		
PACS-TAT	**4** .10	.003	.03	**2** .13	.48	
CAMS-TAT	.12	.34**	.38**	.24*	.26*	.37

NOTE: ATSCI = Attention to Social Comparison Information Scale; PACS = Physical Appearance Comparison Scale; CAMS = Comparison to Advertising Models Scale.
*Significant at < .05; **significant at ≤ .01 (both two-tailed).

Results

ASSESSMENT OF RELIABILITY AND DIMENSIONALITY

In accordance with Churchill's (1979) recommendation, we assessed the reliability of the scales using coefficient alpha (Cronbach, 1951). Reliabilities are shown in the reliability diagonal (1) of the multitrait-multimethod matrix presented in Table 6.2. Evidence for the reliability of the paper-and-pencil method is quite strong, with coefficient alphas of .89, .72, and .76 for the CAMS, PACS, and ATSCI scales, respectively. However, coefficient alphas are quite low for the TAT method, indicating a lack of reliability. This is most likely caused by a large number of responses that had nothing to do with the construct in question and thus were coded as extremely low with respect to that construct. Item-to-total correlations indicate that no substantial improvement in alpha values would result for any of the constructs or methods.

Despite the lack of evidence for reliability, we believe that TATs may offer a greater depth of insight and be a useful measurement tool in marketing research. Researchers are in the early stages of understanding these processes, and projective techniques can add valuable insight and understanding. We recommend that the TATs used in this study be refined to improve reliabilities by ensuring that respondents tell stories about the subject at hand. For example, refinement of story captions is most likely needed. Some examples of responses among our female subjects to CAMS-TATs include the following:

> Kristi and Amy will fall prey to the demented advertising aimed at young girls, which may cause things such as eating disorders.

> Sue and Teresa will feel inadequate—fat, ugly, disproportionate—after reading this ad.

> These girls are daydreaming about the magazine's models, wishing they could look that gorgeous.

> Couple of girls, doesn't matter the age. They are fantasizing about the girls in the magazine. All women do this.

Male subjects gave similar responses:

> Dwayne is sitting at home in front of the TV—his usual spot almost every night of the week. He just finished eating a bag of chips, some pizza, and a couple of beers. He has recently been putting on a lot of weight and, consequently, has not been able to impress the girl he's after. He becomes very guilty as he watches a Soloflex commercial on TV and wishes he could trade places with the spokesperson. He vows to change his ways and get in shape. But, within a week, Dwayne is back where he was on the chair watching TV, heavy as ever.

> Each of them is saying, "Wow," but thinking, "Holy smokes, how could I ever look that good. I wish I was born taller, had more muscles, better looking. Some people are just lucky."

We examined dimensionality of CAMS using the principal-axis factoring procedure. A one-factor solution resulted, with oblique rotation not executed because of only one factor's being extracted. Thus indications of unidimensionality are present.

ASSESSMENT OF CAMS'S VALIDITY

Face or content validity of CAMS is considered to exist because the scale appears to measure what it is supposed to, and the items appear to capture key facets of the construct. In addition, assessment of the multitrait-multimethod matrix shown in Table 6.2 indicates that CAMS demonstrates convergent validity, as the correlation in the validity diagonal (3) is significantly different from zero (.38). However, evidence for discriminant validity does not exist. As the matrix indicates, the correlations in the validity diagonal (3) are not consistently higher than correlations that occupy the same row and column in the heteromethod block (4) or than the correlations in the heterotrait-monomethod triangles (2). We believe that the lack of discriminant validity for CAMS, PACS, and ATSCI and the lack of convergent validity for PACS and ATSCI are caused in part by the low reliabilities of the TAT methods.

CORRELATIONS BETWEEN CONSTRUCTS AND OTHER VARIABLES

In addition to CAMS, PACS, and ATSCI, we administered Harter's (1986) measures of self-esteem, self-perceptions of physical attractiveness, and the importance placed on physical attractiveness. Correlations among CAMS, PACS, ATSCI, self-esteem, self-perceptions of physical attractiveness, and the importance placed on being physically attractive for all subjects, for females, and for males are shown in Table 6.3. Congruent with others' findings that physical attractiveness is a significant factor in determining self-esteem (Harter, 1992, 1993; Mathes & Kahn, 1975; Rosenberg, 1986), for all subjects self-esteem correlates highly with self-perceptions of physical attractiveness. That is, the higher one's self-perception of physical attractiveness, the higher one's self-esteem. Further, CAMS correlates highly with self-perception of physical attractiveness and self-esteem, indicating that the more one compares oneself with models in ads, the lower one's self-esteem and self-perception of physical attractiveness. The same holds true for PACS and ATSCI. In addition, CAMS and PACS are highly correlated, as are PACS and ATSCI.

Also, the importance placed on physical attractiveness correlates highly with CAMS, PACS, and ATSCI for all subjects. That is, the more

TABLE 6.3 Correlation Matrices

	CAMS	PACS	ATSCI	PA	SE
All Subjects					
PACS	.50**				
ATSCI	.18	.42**			
PA	−.35**	−.58**	−.34**		
SE	−.34**	−.43**	−.29**	.65**	
PAIMP	.35**	.37**	.28*	−.16	−.11
Females					
PACS	.54**				
ATSCI	.25	.51**			
PA	−.35*	−.48**	−.24		
SE	−.37*	−.35*	−.16	.73**	
PAIMP	.67**	.44**	.35*	−.20	−.23
Males					
PACS	.41**				
ATSCI	.02	.27*			
PA	−.25	−.69**	−.40**		
SE	−.32*	−.52**	−.37*	.61**	
PAIMP	.05	.30*	.19	−.07	−.03

NOTE: ATSCI = Attention to Social Comparison Information Scale; PACS = Physical Appearance Comparison Scale; CAMS = Comparison to Advertising Models Scale; PA = self-perception of physical attractiveness; SE = self-esteem; PAIMP = importance placed on being physically attractive.
*Significant at ≤ .05; **significant at ≤ .01.

important physical attractiveness is to one, the more one will compare oneself with models in ads and others and be attentive to social comparison information. Though not as strong, the importance placed on physical attractiveness correlates negatively with self-perception of physical attractiveness and self-esteem. That is, the more important physical attractiveness is to one, the lower one's self-perception of physical attractiveness and self-esteem. Generally, the same relationships hold for both males and females, except for the lower correlations between the importance placed on being physically attractive and CAMS, PACS, and ATSCI for males.

MALE/FEMALE DIFFERENCES

We conducted a one-way analysis of variance to assess whether differences exist between male and female self-esteem, self-perceptions of physical attractiveness, and the importance placed on being physically attractive. Also, we conducted a one-way analysis of variance to assess whether males and females responded differently to the paper-

TABLE 6.4 ANOVA Results and Cell Means

| | ANOVA | | Cell Means | | |
	F	Significance of F	Male	Female	Overall
CAMS	7.49	.01	10.92	13.17	11.91
PACS	2.74	.10	12.53	13.67	13.03
ATSCI	1.67	.20	33.18	34.83	33.91
SE	0.46	.50	18.03	17.42	17.76
PA	3.73	.06	13.74	12.48	13.19
PAIMP	1.95	.17	5.82	6.23	6.00

NOTE: ATSCI = Attention to Social Comparison Information Scale; PACS = Physical Appearance Comparison Scale; CAMS = Comparison to Advertising Models Scale; PA = self-perception of physical attractiveness; SE = self-esteem; PAIMP = importance placed on being physically attractive.

and-pencil CAMS, PACS, and ATSCI. Results of the ANOVA and cell means are shown in Table 6.4. The results indicate that men and women do not differ in terms of self-esteem, self-perceptions of physical attractiveness, and the importance placed on being physically attractive, as none of the main effects of sex was significant. Further, men and women do not differ significantly in terms of comparison of physical attractiveness with others or attention to social comparison information. However, a significant difference was found between men and women in terms of CAMS. That is, women showed greater tendencies to compare themselves with models in ads than did men.

To investigate male/female differences more closely, we conducted stepwise regressions with self-esteem as the dependent variable. Self-perceptions of physical attractiveness, the importance placed on being physically attractive, CAMS, PACS, and ATSCI served as independent variables. The results confirm the notion that self-perception of physical attractiveness contributes greatly to self-esteem, as this was the only independent variable to enter the regression equation for both males and females. However, the high intercorrelations between the independent variables indicate the presence of multicollinearity. Acknowledging the presence of multicollinearity, we dropped self-perception of physical attractiveness from the analysis and conducted stepwise regressions again. For females, CAMS was the only independent variable to enter into the equation. However, this was not the case for males, as PACS was the only independent variable to enter the regression equation. The regression results confirm the notion that women have a greater tendency to compare themselves with models in ads. In addition, the regression results highlight that this tendency by women to compare themselves with models in ads plays a greater role in contributing to women's self-esteem than men's comparing themselves with models contributes to men's self-esteem.

Surprisingly, however, this greater tendency of women to compare themselves with models in ads does not correspond to lower self-esteem or self-perceptions of physical attractiveness than for males. This finding is congruent with Richins's (1991); Richins hypothesized that exposure to advertising with highly attractive models would temporarily lower female college students' self-perceptions of physical attractiveness. Ads from fashion magazines containing highly attractive models were used, with half of the ads showing facial close-ups and the other half showing full-body images of models in revealing sportswear. Richins compared the self-perceptions of physical attractiveness provided by a group of female college students exposed to ads with highly attractive models with those provided by a group exposed to ads with no models. No significant differences were found between the two groups, and the hypothesis, therefore, was not supported. As Richins explains:

> The self-concept includes one's beliefs about the level of one's physical attractiveness, probably developed by examining oneself and comparing one's appearance with others and learning the reactions of others to one's appearance. Even children see ads with very attractive models, and this information is perhaps incorporated in forming a self-perception of attractiveness. By late adolescence, however, the sight of extremely attractive models is "old news" and unlikely to provide new information that might influence self-perception. (p. 74)

Also, by this age, women may realize that unrealistic portrayals exist in advertising, as indicated by one response to a CAMS-TAT:

> Kristi and Amy are laughing at the "beautiful" women in the magazines and discussing how much airbrushing had to be done and how sad it is that society can make some women feel bad about their bodies by portraying airbrushed bodies as the "norm."

Similarly, another respondent indicated:

> The girl is not believing anything that is shown on TV. She is not comfortable with her looks and doesn't believe anything could help her looks. That only works for pretty girls.

Therefore, even though female college students have a greater tendency to compare themselves with models in ads than do male college students, detrimental effects on self-esteem and self-perceptions of physical attractiveness may not necessarily occur, as people's self-concepts may be relatively stable by the time they are in college, and/or they may realize that unrealistic images are often used in advertising.

Conclusion

In this chapter we have presented the results of an attempt to validate the Comparison to Advertising Models Scale. Though we found evidence of reliability for the paper-and-pencil scales employed, the TAT sketches were less successful. We found no evidence for discriminant validity among CAMS, the Physical Appearance Comparison Scale (Thompson et al., 1991), and the Attention to Social Comparison Information Scale (Bearden & Rose, 1990).

Our study focused on male/female differences in self-esteem, specifically in the domain of physical attractiveness. The results of this scale validation study suggest that female and male college students do not differ in terms of self-esteem, self-perceptions of physical attractiveness, and the importance placed on physical attractiveness. However, female college students appear to have greater tendencies than male college students to compare themselves with models in ads. The lack of lower self-perceptions of physical attractiveness and self-esteem accompanying the greater tendency to compare themselves with advertising models in females may occur for several reasons. First, by college age, an individual's self-concept may be relatively stable, and thus the information from comparison may not be incorporated into the notion of the self. Second, female college students may realize that advertising images are unrealistic, and thus do not incorporate the information from comparison into their notions of themselves. Finally, as active audience proponents argue with respect to television viewing, female college students may be able simultaneously to identify with and distance themselves from models in ads (e.g., Fiske, 1987).

Future research should investigate *why* female college students have a greater tendency than males to compare themselves with models in ads. Perhaps male models do not represent a reference group for comparison for males to as great an extent as female models serve as a reference group for females. More simply, perhaps females are more willing than males to admit that they do compare themselves with advertising models.

Another explanation for the greater tendency of females to compare themselves with models in ads may be related to the *motive* for comparison. For example, Wood (1989) and Wood and Taylor (1991) suggest that social comparison occurs for reasons other than self-evaluation. Perhaps female college students compare themselves with models in ads for purposes of self-improvement rather than self-evaluation, hence the greater tendency to compare (Martin, 1994; Martin & Kennedy, 1994). This may also lend understanding as to the lack of evidence for lower self-perceptions of physical attractiveness and self-esteem in females. The existence of different motives for comparison has implications for measurement as well. In this study, we made an effort to keep CAMS motive-free. Future research should attempt to refine these measures to differentiate among motives.

Although we found no evidence in this study of detrimental effects on female college students' self-perceptions of physical attractiveness or self-esteem, future research should also attempt to determine if and when these effects may occur during adolescence, a time when the self-concept is particularly unstable. Recent headlines such as "Women's Best Years End With Puberty" (1993) and "Why It's So Tough to Be a Girl" (Perry, 1992) illustrate the especially difficult plight of females in adolescence. As Perry (1992) notes: "Today's specifications call for blonde and thin—no easy task, since most girls get bigger during adolescence. Many become anorexics or bulimics; a few rich ones get liposuction. We make their focus pleasing other people and physical beauty" (p. 82).

Finally, future research should address the images of women versus the images of men in advertising to determine, for example, whether the physical attractiveness of female models represents a more ideal standard than that of male models and how this affects self-perceptions of physical attractiveness and self-esteem. The marketing discipline has a responsibility to determine the extent of advertising's impact on women because, as Pollay (1986) has put it, "the charges are much too serious to dismiss cavalierly" (p. 31). Only then will advertisers take notice and undertake a widespread attempt to alleviate these problems by de-emphasizing the beauty of advertising models.

References

Bearden, W. O., & Rose, R. L. (1990). Attention to social comparison information: An individual difference factor affecting consumer conformity. *Journal of Consumer Research, 16,* 461-471.

Block, J., & Robins, R. W. (1993). A longitudinal study of consistency and change in self-esteem from early adolescence to early adulthood. *Child Development, 64,* 909-923.

Brenner, J. B., & Cunningham, J. G. (1992). Gender differences in eating attitudes, body concept, and self-esteem among models. *Sex Roles, 27,* 413-437.

Campbell, D. R., & Fiske, D. W. (1959). Convergent and discriminant validation by the multitrait-multimethod matrix. *Psychological Bulletin, 56,* 81-105.

Churchill, G. A., Jr. (1979). A paradigm for developing better measures of marketing constructs. *Journal of Marketing Research, 26,* 64-73.

Cronbach, L. J. (1951). Coefficient alpha and the internal structure of tests. *Psychometrika, 16,* 297-334.

Downs, A. C., & Harrison, S. K. (1985). Embarrassing age spots or just plain ugly? Physical attractiveness stereotyping as an instrument of sexism on American television commercials. *Sex Roles, 13,* 9-19.

Durgee, J. F. (1986). Self-esteem advertising. *Journal of Advertising, 15*(4), 21-27, 42.

Festinger, L. (1954). A theory of social comparison processes. *Human Relations, 7,* 117-140.

Fiske, J. (1987). *Television culture.* London: Methuen.

Harter, S. (1982). The Perceived Competence Scale for children. *Child Development, 53,* 87-97.

Harter, S. (1986). *Manual for the Self-Perception Profile for College Students.* Denver: University of Denver.

Harter, S. (1992). *Visions of self: Beyond the me in the mirror.* Paper presented at the Nebraska Symposium on Motivation, Lincoln.

Harter, S. (1993). Causes and consequences of low self-esteem in children and adolescents. In R. F. Baumeister (Ed.), *Self-esteem: The puzzle of low self-regard* (pp. 87-116). New York: Plenum.

Irving, L. M. (1990). Mirror images: Effects of the standard of beauty on the self- and body-esteem of women exhibiting varying levels of bulimic symptoms. *Journal of Social and Clinical Psychology, 9,* 230-242.

James, W. (1984). *Psychology: The briefer course.* Cambridge, MA: Harvard University Press. (Original work published 1892)

Klassen, M. L., Wauer, S. M., & Cassel, S. (1990/1991). Increases in health and weight loss claims in food advertising in the eighties. *Journal of Advertising Research, 31,* 32-37.

Lerner, R. M., Orlos, J. B., & Knapp, J. R. (1976). Physical attractiveness, physical effectiveness, and self-concept in late adolescence. *Adolescence, 11,* 313-326.

Martin, M. C. (1994). *The influence of the beauty of advertising models on preadolescent self-perceptions, self-esteem, and brand intentions: A longitudinal study* (Working paper). Lincoln: University of Nebraska.

Martin, M. C., & Kennedy, P. F. (1993). Advertising and social comparison: Consequences for female pre-adolescents and adolescents. *Psychology and Marketing, 10,* 513-530.

Martin, M. C., & Kennedy, P. F. (1994). Social comparison and the beauty of advertising models: The role of motives for comparison. In C. T. Allen & D. Roedder John (Eds.), *Advances in consumer research* (Vol. 21, pp. 365-371). Provo, UT: Association for Consumer Research.

Mathes, E. W., & Kahn, A. (1975). Physical attractiveness, happiness, neuroticism, and self-esteem. *Journal of Psychology, 90,* 27-30.

Mazur, A. (1986). U.S. trends in feminine beauty and overadaptation. *Journal of Sex Research, 22,* 281-303.

Mick, D. G., DeMoss, M., & Faber, R. J. (1992). A projective study of motivations and meanings of self-gifts: Implications for retail management. *Journal of Retailing, 68,* 122-144.

Myers, P. N., & Biocca, F. A. (1992). The elastic body image: The effect of television advertising and programming on body image distortions in young women. *Journal of Communication, 42,* 108-133.

Patzer, G. L. (1985). *The physical attractiveness phenomena.* New York: Plenum.

Percy, L., & Lautman, M. R. (1987). *The ideal female figure: From image to eating disorders.* Paper presented at the Conference on Advertising and Consumer Psychology, Chicago.

Perry, N. J. (1992, August 10). Why it's so tough to be a girl. *Fortune,* pp. 82-84.

Pollay, R. W. (1986, April). The distorted mirror: Reflections on the unintended consequences of advertising. *Journal of Marketing, 50,* 18-36.

Rappaport, D. (1942). Principles underlying projective techniques. *Character and Personality, 10,* 213-219.

Richins, M. L. (1991). Social comparison and the idealized images of advertising. *Journal of Consumer Research, 18,* 71-83.

Rodin, J., Silberstein, L. R., & Striegel-Moore, R. (1985). Women and weight: A normative discontent. In T. B. Sonderegger (Ed.), *Psychology and gender: Nebraska Symposium on Motivation 1984* (pp. 267-308). Lincoln: University of Nebraska Press.

Rook, D. W. (1985). The ritual dimension of consumer behavior. *Journal of Consumer Research, 12,* 251-264.

Rosenberg, M. (1986). Self-concept from middle childhood through adolescence. In J. Suls & A. G. Greenwald (Eds.), *Psychological perspectives on the self* (Vol. 3, pp. 107-136). Hillsdale, NJ: Lawrence Erlbaum.

Sherry, J. F., Jr., McGrath, M. A., & Levy, S. J. (1993). The dark side of the gift. *Journal of Business Research, 28,* 225-244.

Silverstein, B., Perdue, L., Peterson, B., & Kelly, E. (1986). The role of the mass media in promoting a thin standard of bodily attractiveness for women. *Sex Roles, 14,* 519-532.

Sporkin, E. (1993, January 11). The body game. *People,* pp. 80-86.

Thompson, J. K., Heinberg, L., & Tantleff, S. (1991). The Physical Appearance Comparison Scale. *Behavior Therapist, 14,* 174.

Woman's best years end with puberty. (1993, March 28). *Lincoln Journal-Star,* p. 1J.

Wood, J. V. (1989). Theory and research concerning social comparisons of personal attributes. *Psychological Bulletin, 106,* 231-248.

Wood, J. V., & Taylor, K. L. (1991). Serving self-relevant goals through social comparison. In J. Suls & T. A. Wills (Eds.), *Social comparison: Contemporary theory and research* (pp. 23-49). Hillsdale, NJ: Lawrence Erlbaum.

7

Division of Financial Responsibility in Baby Boomer Couples: Routine Tasks Versus Investments

GEORGE S. BOBINSKI, Jr.

AMARDEEP ASSAR

THIS chapter examines how couples divide responsibility for routine financial tasks and investment tasks. It has long been recognized that many major consumption decisions are made in the context of the family. Such decisions include those concerning housing, automobiles, higher education, and the management of family finances. Despite this, studies of consumer behavior have tended to focus on the behavior of individuals. The consumer behavior of families remains an area in need of additional descriptive studies, conceptual development, and methodological work. Improved understanding of these issues can have important implications for consumers, marketers, and public policy makers.

AUTHORS' NOTE: The research reported in this chapter was partially funded by the Piaker Endowment for Faculty Development, School of Management, Binghamton University.

Given their potential significance, financial management practices of families have recently been receiving more attention in consumer research. These practices affect families' purchases and can also have important implications for their financial well-being in the long term. Financial management occurs in the context of married couples in the majority of cases. Because of the importance of financial practices, it is likely that they are in turn related to and dependent on factors affecting the relationships of wives and husbands. Such determinants may include societally learned gender roles, wives' participation in the paid labor force, and family characteristics that affect the distribution of power within the relationship.

For the study reported here, routine tasks include making payments and balancing checkbooks, and investment tasks include decisions about when to invest, which investments to make, and how much to invest. Specifically, in this chapter we examine three aspects of financial decisions: (a) whether wives have more responsibility for routine tasks, compared with husbands; (b) whether wives have less responsibility for investment tasks, compared with husbands; and (c) how sex role attitudes and wife's work status are related to this division of tasks. For the wife, our study examined whether being in the paid workforce coupled with the nature of her job has a bearing on responsibility for routine versus investment tasks. For the husband, relationships between sex role attitudes and the same financial tasks were considered.

Our study focused on married baby boomers, that is, those people born between 1946 and 1964. This group is of interest for two important sets of reasons. First, baby boomers grew up during a period that differed from those experienced by previous generations in significant ways. These differences included increased prosperity, greater access to higher education for women and men, and the reality of a strong women's movement that questioned traditional gender roles. In addition, women's participation in the paid labor force grew to unprecedented levels. Two of our hypotheses were concerned with whether these societal changes have altered the traditional division of financial responsibilities within couples.

Second, baby boomers constitute an important market at an aggregate level. In 1991, there were approximately 24 million couples in the 25-44 age group, which amounted to just under half of all married couples. The spending power of this group exceeds $1.1 trillion annually, based on a mean family income of approximately $48,000 for 1990

(U.S. Bureau of the Census, 1991). Finally, many of these couples are now making major financial decisions, such as buying homes and making investments for the future. Thus they are prime targets for marketers of a variety of financial services.

In the next section we examine the distinction between routine and investment tasks, and then review the literature relating these tasks to gender roles as well as wife's work status. We then present the hypotheses examined in our study, followed by the methodology and the findings.

Literature Review

The family is the primary unit for much of consumer decision making, including budgetary allocations, product class purchases, and brand choices. The importance of studying the family has been acknowledged by a number of authors (e.g., Alderson, 1957; Arrow, 1951; Converse, Huegy, & Mitchell, 1958; Samuelson, 1956). Even so, in a significant review paper, Davis (1976) characterizes the field of consumer behavior as having "a preoccupation with consumers as individual decision makers." Davis emphasizes that studies of the consumer behavior of families should examine the extent to which family members have responsibility for particular decisions. Further, he divides decisions into those involving frequently purchased goods and services, durable goods, and financial decisions.

According to Davis and Rigaux (1974), the patterns of responsibility within a couple may vary by (a) type of product, (b) stage in the decision process, (c) type of decision (e.g., budgeting, purchase, or brand choice), and (d) family characteristics. These authors report that decisions may be wife dominated (e.g., for food, kitchenware, and children's clothing), husband dominated (e.g., life insurance, cars), or shared (e.g., housing, vacations). Finally, autonomic decisions are made for oneself (e.g., husband's decisions regarding his own clothing).

FAMILY FINANCIAL DECISIONS

Family financial decisions have received increased attention recently. Researchers have examined relationships between the patterns of relative influence or responsibility and family characteristics in a variety of financial contexts. Examples include determining budgets for different items of expenditures (Schaninger, Buss, & Grover, 1982), implementation of decisions (Rosen & Granbois, 1983), savings decisions (Kim & Lee, 1989; Qualls, 1982), choice of banking institution and credit cards (Douglas & Wind, 1978), and life insurance (Davis & Rigaux, 1974).

The present study distinguished between routine financial tasks and investment tasks. Rosen and Granbois (1983) used principal-components analysis and found that financial decisions can be broken into separate dimensions. One factor was labeled an "implementation dimension," and consisted of bookkeeping tasks such as balancing checkbooks and paying bills. Two other independent dimensions consisted of more significant decisions, such as budgetary aspects and prioritization of payments. Although Rosen and Granbois did not examine investment decisions, their results suggest that specific tasks may be grouped into independent financial dimensions based on analysis of responses. Thus the subjectivity of an a priori classification is avoided.

We now turn to a review of studies of financial decision making, distinguishing between routine tasks and investment tasks. Given the paucity of studies of investments, we decided to include savings decisions in the latter group, because they may be seen as analogous to investment decisions. We conclude our review by relating financial decisions, including the two types of tasks, to sex role attitudes and women's participation in the paid workforce.

ROUTINE VERSUS INVESTMENT DECISIONS

The routine task of paying bills has tended to be the responsibility of wives rather than husbands, or has been performed jointly. In two early surveys, the wife kept track of money and bills in about 40% of the couples, and the husband did this in about one-fourth of the cases (Sharp & Mott, 1956; Wolgast, 1958). Ferber (1973) also found that wives tended to handle money and bills. Finally, Ferber and Lee (1974) found a shift away from joint money management toward the wife's becoming the "family financial officer" for couples who had been married a year.

In contrast, husbands were more likely to have greater responsibility for investment decisions, compared with wives, although in many cases these decisions were made jointly. Douglas and Wind (1978) note that about a third of the couples they surveyed reported that the husband dominated savings and investment decisions, whereas only 11% said these were dominated by the wife. Davis and Rigaux (1974) report savings decisions as falling into the syncretic group, but closer to the husband-dominated end of the scale. However, Wolgast (1958) found that wives in her study were solely responsible for savings decisions in a quarter of the couples, whereas husbands had sole responsibility in about 15% of cases.

SEX ROLE ATTITUDES IN FINANCIAL DECISION MAKING

One variable that has been used in many studies of financial decision making is sex role attitude. Spouses who are traditional are likely to behave in ways consistent with societal mores about distinct areas of responsibility; those who are modern in their sex role attitudes are less likely to behave in accordance with such mores. These spouses may instead choose to divide responsibilities based on factors such as their individual skills, preferences, and time pressures.

For routine implementation tasks, studies of the relationship to sex role attitudes have yielded conflicting findings. Some research shows that these tasks are more likely to be performed by wives when sex roles are traditional (Rosen & Granbois, 1983) and by husbands when roles are modern (Schaninger et al., 1982). Schaninger et al. (1982) developed a scale to relate sex roles to financial decisions, such as paying bills, savings plans, and handling expenses for different areas of expenditures. As hypothesized, sex role modern families showed more husband influence for paying bills, compared with traditional families.

Green and Cunningham (1975) classified homemakers as liberal, moderate, or conservative about women's roles, based on Arnott's Autonomy (Feminism) Scale. They found that women with liberal views reported less joint handling of money and bills than did moderates and conservatives. Finally, Kim and Lee (1989) found no relationship between wife's sex role attitude and financial implementation decisions (e.g., paying bills, balancing checkbooks).

Turning now to savings and investment decisions, the literature suggests that traditional sex roles are associated with husbands having more responsibility. Qualls (1982) found that traditional husbands were more likely than more modern husbands to perceive savings decisions as being their domain, and wives saw these as jointly determined. Similarly, when sex roles were more modern, husbands were found to have less influence for savings (Kim & Lee, 1989; Schaninger et al., 1982) and for investments (Assar & Bobinski, 1991), compared with traditional families. However, in other studies, financial decisions were not found to be related to sex role attitudes (Granbois, Rosen, & Acito, 1986) or specifically to husbands' sex roles (Kim & Lee, 1989).

In summary, although there is some ambiguity, when sex roles are traditional, wives tend to have more responsibility for routine tasks and husbands have more responsibility for savings and investment tasks. As a corollary, when sex roles are modern, husbands may increase their responsibility for routine tasks and wives may increase their responsibility for savings and investments.

WIVES IN THE PAID WORKFORCE

As the number of women in the paid workforce has continued to expand, the implications of this trend have been examined for many areas of consumer behavior. Several studies have considered the wife's work status in examining purchases of durables, convenience foods, and perceived role overload. The earliest studies in this area distinguished between women who worked for pay and those who were homemakers (Anderson, 1972; Strober & Weinberg, 1977, 1980). Other studies categorized wives as nonworking, low occupational status, and high occupational status (Nickols & Fox, 1983; Reilly, 1982; Schaninger & Allen, 1981). These classifications were not particularly useful in discriminating among wives on the behaviors examined. However, using the categories of housewives, nonprofessional working women, and professional working women, Joyce and Guiltinan (1978) found differences in relation to retailing.

Bartos (1977) has proposed a four-way classification based on the annual Yankelovich Monitor Survey. The categories are *stay-at-home* (29%), *plan-to-work* (20%), *just-a-job* (32%), and *career-oriented* (19%). This self-report measure is seen as a composite of employment status and the women's attitudes about the kind of work they do. Bartos (1989) reports that by 1985 the proportions of women falling into these four groups had changed to 22%, 13%, 38%, and 27%, respectively. Thus there were fewer women in the plan-to-work group, and somewhat more in the just-a-job category. Differences were found among these groups of women on demographics, psychographics, and behaviors. Specifically, for families' investments, 10% of wives decided on the amount of money to invest, and 8% decided on the type of investment to make.

For investment tasks, involvement was highest for career women and lowest for stay-at-home wives (Bartos, 1989).

Apart from Bartos's original work, these classifications do not appear to have been used in other studies of the financial decision making of wives and families. However, there is additional evidence that wife's work status and motivations for work may relate to routine versus savings and investment tasks. Rosen and Granbois (1983) found that when the wife is working for financial reasons, prioritization of payments is likely to be done separately by wives and husbands. If the wife's motivation for working is self-fulfillment, employment status does not discriminate on prioritization.

Further, in the sex role scale developed by Schaninger et al. (1982), one dimension is labeled Wife Career Importance. Factor loadings on this dimension for wives were negatively correlated with relative influence for bill payment, and husbands' scores had a marginally significant negative correlation for bill payment and savings decisions. This suggests that when the wife's career is important, she has less responsibility for both bill payment and savings. Thus career women may do less of both routine and investment tasks. Finally, Granbois et al. (1986) conclude that neither wife's work status nor her motivation for working are associated with a set of five family financial decisions. In summary, relatively little research has addressed the possible relationships between wife's work status and financial decisions.

Hypotheses

The findings of the studies cited above suggest that women tend to have more responsibility for routine tasks and less responsibility for investment tasks. However, significant changes have occurred in society in the past two decades, and it is of interest to see whether the traditional gender-based patterns of financial behaviors still persist or have undergone change among baby boomers. Therefore, we propose the following hypotheses regarding the division of responsibility for routine and investment tasks:

H1. Women have greater responsibility for routine financial tasks.

H2. Women have less responsibility for investment tasks.

When wives are not in the paid workforce, they may be seen by their partners as having more time to attend to routine tasks. When they are employed outside the home, they may have less time to deal with such tasks, particularly if they have careers. This is consistent with Schaninger et al.'s (1982) finding that wives' career importance is negatively related to responsibility for bill payment.

On the other hand, the incomes of employed wives may give them enough power in their relationships to be involved in investment tasks, particularly if they have careers as opposed to less remunerative employment. This may underlie Bartos's (1989) finding that for investment tasks, involvement was highest for career women and lowest for stay-at-home wives. Note that our focus is on baby boomers, whereas Bartos examined all families.

Based on these observations, we propose the following hypotheses relating women's employment and attitudes toward their jobs to the allocation of responsibility for financial tasks:

H3.   Women not employed outside the home will have the most responsibility for routine tasks. Of the employed wives, the just-a-job group will have intermediate responsibility, whereas career women will have the least responsibility for routine tasks.

H4.   Women not employed outside the home will have the least responsibility for investment tasks. Of the employed wives, the just-a-job group will have intermediate responsibility, whereas career women will have the most responsibility for investment.

Based on the literature cited previously that relates sex roles to routine versus investment tasks, it appears that more traditional attitudes are associated with husbands' having more responsibility for savings and investment tasks. For the routine tasks the evidence is conflicting, but on balance, research has shown that when husbands' sex roles are modern, they tend to have greater responsibility for routine tasks.

H5.   Men with more traditional sex role attitudes will have more responsibility for investment tasks.

H6.   Men with more modern sex role attitudes will have more responsibility for routine tasks.

Methodology

The data used in this study were collected through a mail survey in a medium-sized city in the northeastern United States. We obtained names of potential participants by contacting a judgment sample of civic and church organizations. Potential participants were first screened to ensure that at least one member of the couple was born between 1946 and 1964. The resulting couples were asked to participate in a study of financial decision making. To encourage participation, we informed each couple that once we received their completed questionnaires, a cash contribution would be made to a charitable organization of their choice, and that they would also have an opportunity to win a prize consisting of U.S. savings bonds.

Each participating couple was mailed two separate surveys, one for the wife and one for the husband, along with a postage-paid return envelope for each. The instructions explicitly requested that each spouse work completely independent of the other. Both surveys were received from approximately three-fourths of the couples who agreed to participate (in two cases, only one member of the couple responded), resulting in a sample of 83 couples. The mean ages of the wives and husbands were 35 years and 36.3 years, respectively, and the median family income of the respondents was $46,500 in 1989, the year these data were collected.

In the first section of the questionnaire the participants were asked to rate their relative responsibility for the various financial tasks associated with those financial products and services that were jointly owned. Later, the sex role attitudes of the respondents were measured using Osmond and Martin's (1975) sex role attitude scale. We modified this scale by dropping items that dealt with stereotypes of male/female nature and behaviors (e.g., "Men should stop appraising women solely on the basis of appearance and sex appeal") and four items that dealt with social change as related to sex roles (e.g., "Unlike the race riots, the battle between the sexes will never involve violence on any large scale"), because we felt that the items omitted had little relationship to the division of financial tasks. In the final section of the questionnaire the wife was asked if she was currently employed for pay outside the home. Women who answered yes to this question were asked to indicate if they felt that this employment was "just a job" or if it was a career

TABLE 7.1 Responsibility for Financial Tasks

Financial Task	Means	
	Wives	Husbands
Responsibility for balancing joint checking account	2.48	2.71
Writes the most checks on joint checking account	2.18	2.44
Decides how much to pay on joint credit card balance	2.59	2.77
Decides when to make investments	3.69	3.68
Decides what types of investments to make	3.69	3.80
Decides how much to invest	3.60	3.63

that was stimulating and challenging. If the wife was not employed, she was asked to indicate if she planned to be employed outside the home in the next five years.

Analysis and Results

Respondents used a 5-point scale to indicate relative responsibility for financial tasks. The original scale categories were *me, me more than my spouse, task shared equally between me and my spouse, my spouse more than me,* and *my spouse.* The responses of the husband were reverse scored, so that for both husband and wife, 1 = wife, 2 = wife more than husband, 3 = task shared equally, 4 = husband more than wife, and 5 = husband.

The study was designed to examine bill payment and investment dimensions rather than to make comparisons across spouses at the level of individual questions. However, the mean responses given by the spouses for the financial tasks are provided in Table 7.1. Both wives' and husbands' responses indicate that the women have more responsibility for check writing, balancing the checking account, and deciding how much to pay on credit card bills, whereas the men have more responsibility for investment decisions.

To examine the appropriateness of classifying check writing, balancing the checking account, and credit card payment decisions as one type of activity and the three investment decisions as another type of activity, we performed principal-component factor analysis using varimax rotation. Responses for the wives and husbands were analyzed separately; these are provided in Table 7.2. For the wives, the first factor accounted

TABLE 7.2 Component Loadings for Relative Responsibility on Financial Tasks

Financial Task	Wife's Responses		Husband's Responses	
	Factor 1	Factor 2	Factor 1	Factor 2
Decides when to make investments	.942		.930	
Decides what types of investments to make	.954		.932	
Decides how much to invest	.921		.871	
Writes most checks on joint checking account		.901		.892
Responsibility for balancing joint checking account		.887		.824
Decides how much to pay on joint credit card balance		.761		.773

NOTE: To facilitate interpretation, loadings of less than .16 are omitted.

for 52% of the variance (eigenvalue = 3.1) and the second accounted for an additional 30% (eigenvalue = 1.8). For the husbands, the first factor accounted for 58% of the variance (eigenvalue = 3.5) and the second for an additional 23% (eigenvalue = 1.4). Thus, for both husbands and wives, the factor analysis indicated that the six tasks could reasonably be grouped into routine tasks and investment tasks.

Given this result, in order to test the hypothesis that wives were more responsible for the routine financial tasks (H1), we averaged the wives' responses for the three routine financial tasks and compared the average with a criterion of 3.0, which indicates an equally shared task. The result supported our hypothesis ($t = -3.63, p < .001$). Additional support was provided for this finding when we utilized the same procedure for the husbands' responses ($t = -2.58, p < .01$).

We tested the hypothesis that wives had less responsibility for investment tasks (H2) in a similar manner. The wives' responses for the three investment tasks were averaged and compared with a criterion of 3.0, which indicated an equally shared task. This test supported the hypothesis ($t = 5.69, p < .001$). Utilizing the same procedure for the husbands' responses, we found additional support for this finding ($t = 6.83, p < .001$).

The data would have allowed an examination of the relationships between responsibility for financial tasks and the four-way classification proposed by Bartos. However, the homogeneity of the plan-to-work group was questionable. Wives who report themselves as being in this category may actually differ from one another in many significant ways. For example, some wives may give up paid employment because they take on primary responsibility for child care for a few years. Others may be unable to find work that is commensurate with their skills, or they may have low levels of skills. Another reason a woman may place herself in this group may be that she believes that planning to work is seen by others as more desirable than choosing not to work for pay. Given these issues, women who planned to work and those categorized as stay-at-home were not expected to differ in the context of financial decision making. The appropriateness of this was verified through a comparison of the factor scores for these two groups; no significant differences were found for either routine ($p > .38$) or investment tasks ($p > .77$). Thus the stay-at-home and plan-to-work categories were combined into one group, and compared with the just-a-job and career-oriented groups. After the groups were combined, the number of wives who classified themselves as not working outside the home was 26. For the just-a-job and career groups the cell sizes were 16 and 26, respectively.

To examine the hypothesis that wife's work status is related to responsibility for routine financial tasks (H3), we performed an ANOVA on the factor scores for the wife's estimate of her relative influence for these tasks. The result was significant ($F = 4.02$, $p < .05$). To examine the relationship between wife's work status and responsibility for routine tasks, we performed post hoc contrasts on the factor scores. The mean factor scores for the nonworking (i.e., not in the paid workforce), just-a-job, and career groups were −0.34, 0.53, and 0.01, respectively (note that lower numbers indicate the wife has more responsibility). Contrasts between the mean factor scores indicated that wives not employed outside the home were doing more of the routine tasks than were those who placed themselves in the just-a-job classification ($t = 3.14$, $p < .01$). In addition, those women who classified themselves as having careers may be doing more of the routine tasks than those in the just-a-job group, although this effect was not significant ($t = -1.65, p < .11$).

We also tested the hypothesis that wife's work status is related to responsibility for investment tasks (H4) by performing an ANOVA on the factor scores for the wife's estimate of her relative influence for these tasks. No significant differences in responsibility for investments were found based on wife's work status.

In testing hypotheses H5 and H6, we used the median on sex role attitude scores as the criterion to classify husbands as traditional ($n = 33$)

or modern ($n = 29$). To examine the hypothesis that men with more traditional sex role attitudes will have more responsibility for investment tasks (H5), we performed an ANOVA on the factor scores for the husband's responses on his relative influence for the investment tasks. The mean factor scores for the modern and traditional groups were −0.30 and 0.26, respectively. This hypothesis was supported ($F = 5.23$, $p < .05$).

The final hypothesis, that men with more modern sex role attitudes will have more responsibility for routine tasks (H6), was examined in a similar fashion. An ANOVA was performed on the factor scores for the husband's responses on his relative influence for the routine tasks. The mean factor scores for the modern and traditional groups were found to be −0.23 and 0.20, respectively, and the difference was not statistically significant ($F = 2.89$, $p < .1$). Thus these results do not support the proposition that husbands with more modern sex role attitudes take more responsibility for routine financial tasks.

Discussion and Future Research

Prior to discussing the findings, we should note some limitations of the present study. Although we sought the cooperation of a wide variety of organizations in developing the sample, certain types of individuals may be over- or underrepresented, as indicated by the relatively high median household income of the respondents. In addition, nonresponse error is also a potential problem.

Although the instructions to the respondents very clearly stated that the surveys should be completed independently by the wife and the husband, in a mail survey it is possible that in some cases spouses may have influenced each other. However, the fact that all of the surveys were returned in separate envelopes, often with spouses' responses arriving on different days, encourages us to believe that such influencing was rare, if it occurred at all. Also, there were often discrepancies within couples in answers to factual questions.

Despite the societal changes of the past few decades, the division of financial responsibility among baby boomers appears to reflect the persistence of gender-specific patterns. In reviewing money and authority patterns in dual-earner couples, Hertz (1992) discusses this persistence and a number of possible explanations, including gender-based expectations and the impact of wife's work status. One of the contributions of the present study is its provision of empirical support for the usefulness of separating financial responsibilities into routine and investment tasks. The results also strongly support our hypotheses that among baby boomers, wives on the average still have more responsibility for routine financial tasks and less responsibility for investment tasks.

Several alternative perspectives can be found in existing research that might explain these findings. In the broader context of the study of couples and power relationships in marriage, Scanzoni and Szinovacz (1980) suggest that the amount of power or influence in decision making may depend on the degree of disparity between husband's and wife's resources. They suggest that such disparities may occur in tangible resources (such as income, occupational status, or experience relevant to the decisions) and also in intangible resources (such as confidence in one's ability). It has also been suggested by Belk and Wallendorf (1990) and Prince (1991) that socialization may be gendered such that women are less likely to view money as a source of power. Based on Davis's (1976) work, another possible explanation may be that spouses could have different levels of personal investment or stake in particular decisions. Wives may not be particularly motivated to influence investment decisions. All of these possibilities merit further inquiry.

Our study also examined how wife's work status and husband's sex role attitudes are related to the division of responsibility in financial decisions. As predicted, women who were not employed were more likely to perform routine tasks compared with the just-a-job group. Although career women were expected to have the least responsibility for these routine tasks, this hypothesis was not supported. Perhaps the women in the just-a-job group are already taxed by the nature of their work outside the home and are less willing to take on routine financial tasks.

The hypothesized relationship between wife's work status and responsibility for investment tasks was also not supported. This is somewhat surprising given Bartos's (1989) finding that for investment tasks, involvement was highest for career women and lowest for stay-at-home wives. In the present study, we hypothesized that women who work outside the home may be expected to have more influence because of their earnings. Apart from the level of earnings, in examining financial decisions, it is also necessary to take into account different patterns of pooling income and access to these resources. These arrangements have been found to differ across couples (Cheal, 1993; Marshall & Woolley, 1993) and may be related to the nature of the wife's workforce participation. Some couples pool all income, with both partners having equal access. In an allowance system, one spouse gives the other an allowance to pay for specific items while retaining control over the balance of his or her income. In a third alternative used by some dual-earner couples, each partner retains control over his or her own earnings and pays for specific shared items. Finally, some career-oriented women may also face greater time pressures. Future research should attempt to investigate how these factors are related to the pattern of influence for investment tasks.

Considering sex role attitudes, as predicted, traditional husbands were found to have greater responsibility for investment tasks. However, husbands with modern sex roles and those with traditional sex roles did not differ in terms of responsibility taken for routine tasks. A recent study by Kim, Laroche, and Zhou (1993) found that husbands with more modern sex roles were more likely to share responsibility for both financial decisions and financial task implementation (i.e., similar to investment and routine tasks). Given that our study found that husbands tended to have greater responsibility for investment tasks and wives had more responsibility for routine tasks, Kim et al.'s findings can be interpreted as consistent with our hypotheses relating husbands' sex roles to performance of investment and routine tasks.

In summary, our study indicates that married women are still more likely to perform routine financial tasks than to handle investment tasks. In addition, the division of responsibility in couples was found to be related to wives' work status and husbands' sex role attitudes. Finally, given the importance of financial decision making in the context of the family, future research should examine some of the other factors that underlie the division of financial responsibility.

References

Alderson, W. (1957). *Marketing behavior and executive action: A functionalist approach to marketing theory.* Homewood, IL: Irwin.

Anderson, B. B. (1972). Working women vs. non-working women: A comparison of shopping behavior. In B. W. Becker & H. Becker (Eds.), *Combined proceedings* (pp. 355-357). Chicago: American Marketing Association.

Arrow, K. J. (1951). Mathematical models in the social sciences. In D. Lerner & H. D. Lasswell (Eds.), *The policy sciences: Recent developments in scope and method.* Stanford, CA: Stanford University Press.

Assar, A., & Bobinski, G. S., Jr. (1991). Financial decision making of babyboomer couples. In R. H. Holman & M. R. Solomon (Eds.), *Advances in consumer research* (Vol. 18, pp. 657-665). Provo, UT: Association for Consumer Research.

Bartos, R. (1977, July). The moving target: The impact of women's employment on consumer behavior. *Journal of Marketing, 41,* 31-37.

Bartos, R. (1989). *Marketing to women around the world.* Boston: Harvard Business School Press.

Belk, R. W., & Wallendorf, M. (1990). The sacred meanings of money. *Journal of Economic Psychology, 11,* 35-67.

Cheal, D. (1993). Changing household financial strategies: Canadian couples today. *Human Ecology, 21,* 197-213.

Converse, P. D., Huegy, H. W., & Mitchell, R. V. (1958). *Elements of marketing* (6th ed.). Englewood Cliffs, NJ: Prentice Hall.

Davis, H. L. (1976). Decision making within the household. *Journal of Consumer Research, 2,* 241-260.

Davis, H. L., & Rigaux, B. P. (1974). Perception of marital roles in decision processes. *Journal of Consumer Research, 1,* 51-62.

Douglas, S. P., & Wind, Y. (1978). Authority patterns: Two methodological issues. *Journal of Marriage and the Family, 40,* 35-47.

Ferber, R. (1973). Family decision making and economic behavior: A review. In F. B. Sheldon (Ed.), *Family economic behavior: Problems and prospects.* Philadelphia: J. B. Lippincott.

Ferber, R., & Lee, L. C. (1974). Husband-wife influence in family purchasing behavior. *Journal of Consumer Research, 1,* 43-50.

Granbois, D. H., Rosen, D. L., & Acito, F. (1986). A developmental study of family financial management practices. In R. J. Lutz (Ed.), *Advances in consumer research* (Vol. 13, pp. 170-174). Provo, UT: Association for Consumer Research.

Green, R., & Cunningham, I. (1975). Feminine role perception and family purchasing decisions. *Journal of Marketing Research, 12,* 325-332.

Hertz, R. (1992). Financial affairs: Money and authority in dual-earner marriage. In S. Lewis, D. N. Izraeli, & H. Hootsmans (Eds.), *Dual-earner families: International perspectives* (pp. 127-150). Newbury Park, CA: Sage.

Joyce, M., & Guiltinan, J. (1978). The professional woman: A potential market segment for retailers. *Journal of Retailing, 54,* 59-70.

Kim, C., Laroche, M., & Zhou, L. (1993). An investigation of ethnicity and sex-role attitude as factors influencing household task sharing behavior. In L. McAlister & M. L. Rothschild (Eds.), *Advances in consumer research* (Vol. 20, pp. 52-58). Provo, UT: Association for Consumer Research.

Kim, C., & Lee, H. (1989). Sex role attitudes of spouses and task sharing behavior. In T. K. Srull (Ed.), *Advances in consumer research* (Vol. 16, pp. 671-679). Provo, UT: Association for Consumer Research.

Marshall, J. J., & Woolley, F. (1993). What's mine is mine and what's yours is ours: Challenging the income pooling assumption. In L. McAlister & M. L. Rothschild (Eds.), *Advances in consumer research* (Vol. 20, pp. 541-546). Provo, UT: Association for Consumer Research.

Nickols, S. Y., & Fox, K. D. (1983). Buying time and saving time: Strategies for managing household production. *Journal of Consumer Research, 10,* 197-208.

Osmond, M. W., & Martin, P. Y. (1975). Sex and sexism: A comparison of male and female sex-role attitudes. *Journal of Marriage and the Family, 37*, 744-758.

Prince, M. (1991). Gender and money attitudes. In J. A. Costa (Ed.), *Gender and consumer behavior* (pp. 284-291). Salt Lake City: University of Utah Printing Service.

Qualls, W. J. (1982). Changing sex roles: Its impact on family decision making. In A. Mitchell (Ed.), *Advances in consumer research* (Vol. 9, pp. 267-270). Ann Arbor, MI: Association for Consumer Research.

Reilly, M. D. (1982). Working wives and convenience consumption. *Journal of Consumer Research, 8*, 407-418.

Rosen, D. L., & Granbois, D. H. (1983). Determinants of role structure in family financial management. *Journal of Consumer Research, 10*, 253-258.

Samuelson, P. A. (1956). Social indifference curves. *Quarterly Journal of Economics, 70*, 1-22.

Scanzoni, J., & Szinovacz, M. (1980). *Family decision-making: A developmental sex role model.* Beverly Hills, CA: Sage.

Schaninger, C. M., & Allen, C. T. (1981). Wife's occupational status as a consumer behavior construct. *Journal of Consumer Research, 8*, 189-196.

Schaninger, C. M., Buss, W. C., & Grover, R. (1982). The effect of sex roles on family finance handling and decision influence. In B. J. Walker, W. O'Bearden, W. R. Darden, P. E. Murphy, J. R. Nevin, J. C. Olson, & B. A. Weitz (Eds.), *An assessment of marketing thought and practice* (Educators' Conference proceedings) (pp. 43-47). Chicago: American Marketing Association.

Sharp, H., & Mott, P. (1956, October). Consumer decisions in the metropolitan family *Journal of Marketing, 21*, 149-156.

Strober, M. H., & Weinberg, C. B. (1977). Working wives and major family expenditures. *Journal of Consumer Research, 4*, 141-147.

Strober, M. H., & Weinberg, C. B. (1980). Strategies used by working and non-working wives to reduce time pressures. *Journal of Consumer Research, 6*, 338-348.

U.S. Bureau of the Census. (1991). *Current population reports: Money income of households, families and persons in the United States: 1990* (Series P-60, No. 174). Washington, DC: Government Printing Office.

Wolgast, E. H. (1958, October). Do husbands or wives make the purchasing decisions? *Journal of Marketing, 22*, 151-158.

8

Children's Apprehension and Comprehension: Gender Influences on Computer Literacy and Attitude Structures Toward Personal Computers

GARY J. BAMOSSY

PAUL G. W. JANSEN

CONSUMER behavior research has long recognized that gender is an important variable in explaining differential outcomes in consumer socialization (Davis, 1970; Moschis, 1987; Qualls, 1987; Ward, 1974), although, as a field of inquiry, this focus has been underrepresented in the literature. More recently, empirical and theoretical research on gender and consumption has focused on a variety of perspectives, ranging from the processes underlying the construction of males' and females' perceptions of the material world, to gender strategies relating to the decision processes inherent in acquiring goods and services for personal use or for gift giving, to consumer disposition (see Costa, 1991).

Although there is a growing body of evidence from both the academic and the popular press on the impacts that changing sex roles and lifestyles have on consumer behavior, a commonly used research perspective has been that of sex role division based on either perceived expertise or culturally mandated sex roles in the buying situation. Thus studies examining the purchase of products such as automobiles, VCRs, and personal computers tend to have predominantly male samples (e.g., Dickerson & Gentry, 1983; Foxall & Bhate, 1991; Venkatesh & Vitalari, 1984). Or, if gender is a research issue, studies tend to report that males initiate and dominate the decision process or have more favorable attitudes toward the product classes under study (Rudell, 1991; Temple & Lips, 1989).

In particular, the consumer behavior literature focusing on the diffusion of innovations and consumer adoption of new technology-based products and services has paid little attention to the role of gender. Although the literature has been systematic in investigating the personal, situational, and product characteristics that encourage or discourage consumer acceptance of innovations, the vast majority of these studies have ignored the possible role of gender differences in attitudes toward technology, or in the adoption of new technology (see Gatignon & Robertson, 1985). Although the study of *innate sex*-based differences in the biological and medical sciences has been and continues to be well funded (Ehrenreich, 1992), other applied disciplines aside from marketing and consumer behavior appear to be equally remiss in their efforts to understand the role that gender plays in the adoption and use of technologically based products. For example, although personal computers are now commonplace in schools, less than 5% of the citations in a recent literature review article on the use of computers in education pay specific attention to the role of gender within the context of computers in the classroom (Krendl & Lieberman, 1990). Likewise, applied studies on personal computers in the workplace tend to focus on constructs such as age, management level, computer experience, efficacy, anxiety, and learning, but not gender (Martocchio & Webster, 1992).

Finally, with few exceptions, the diffusion literature on high-technology products in consumer behavior and the empirical literature from other disciplines tend to draw their samples from adults and college-age students. Given the relative complexity and expense of new high-tech products and the purchasing power that adult status represents, this is an understandable approach. In spite of this "adult" focus, however, there are clear reasons for researching children's attitudes and behaviors toward high-tech products as well. Children born in the past 15 years have grown up in a technological and media-dominated world that is vastly different from anything in previous history. Thus their socialization experiences, attitudes, and understanding of high-tech products are uniquely different from those of previous generations. Also, children of the "high-tech age" will be the future consumers of newer, higher-tech products. An understanding of the development of and changes in their attitudes, knowledge, and belief structures over time will not only be of theoretical interest, but will also provide managerial guidelines for the marketing of these products and services.

The purpose of the study reported in this chapter was to investigate the similarities and differences between boys and girls in their attitude structures, beliefs, learning skills, and perceived "mental models" of the working structure of personal computers—a pervasive high-tech product that is indispensable and unavoidable in their education and upbringing. The study used a variety of measures to examine middle school children who were about to take their first formal computer courses. Thus previous informal computer experiences, potential innate sex-based differences, and other socialization influences were the major alternative explanations for gender differences. In addition to attitude and belief measures, a standardized measure of the children's computer literacy was taken prior to their beginning the formal computer course work. Following the children's 10-week computer course, attitude and computer literacy measures were again taken, and comparisons were made within and between gender groups. By using this test-retest method on first-time computer users, we were able to highlight gender differences regarding attitudes toward and mastery of personal computers.

Literature Review

Within Western industrialized cultures there is the generally held belief that, compared with females, males are more involved with technology, feel more confident and comfortable with it, and derive greater satisfaction from using it (see Kiesler, Sproull, & Eccles, 1985; Rudell, 1991). It has also been well established that at a very early stage, boys and girls seem to "sort out objects and activities and decide which are appropriate for themselves" (Wilder, Mackie, & Cooper, 1985, p. 216). Evidence of this sorting process has been substantiated for personal computers as well, with survey data suggesting that males and females view the use of computers and video games as *male* activities (Wilder et al., 1985).

Empirical studies using computer performance measures offer mixed results on this generally held belief, and sometimes suggest clear differences in opinions between the sexes as well. In a study of 305 Canadian college students, women were just as intrigued by PCs as men were, but felt inhibited from pursuing formal study of computers by uncertainty about their own abilities (Temple & Lips, 1989). These uncertainties were also reinforced by the negative attitudes of their male peers. In a study of British secondary students, males reported more positive attitudes toward computers following a computer course relative to their male classmates who did not take the course, whereas girls who took the course reported a more negative set of attitudes relative to other female classmates who did not take the course (Collis, 1988). In a study of 883 randomly selected Dutch schoolchildren aged 12-14 years, girls were more convinced than boys that men and women had equal capacities in their ability to use computers (Cromhach, 1986). Mandinach and Corno (1985) have reported gender differences in transferring strategic planning skills learned in a computer game to another contest, with girls relying on support from the researcher for feedback, even when it was not needed. However, for high-ability students, these gender differences disappeared.

More often, the literature on computer attitudes and performance has not focused on gender as an independent factor. Dickerson and Gentry (1983) and Venkatesh and Vitalari (1984) examined the decision processes relating to computer acquisition and evaluation, but their samples were predominantly male. Foxall and Bhate (1991) examined the relationship of adaptive and innovative behavior as operationalized by Kirton's Adoption-Innovation Inventory to assess subjects' abilities to sustain innovative behavior with the computer over long periods of time, but, again, the sample consisted of 150 male graduate business students. Finally, as mentioned earlier, empirical studies within other applied social sciences have paid attention to factors relating to the acceptance and use of personal computers, but the focus has tended to be on application, such as using computers for computer-aided instruction (Gist, Schwoerer, & Rosen, 1989; Lieberman, 1985; Martocchio & Webster, 1992), and not on the influences of gender. The perspective and data reported in this chapter focus specifically on gender differences with respect to attitude structures, attitude change, computer mastery, and the students' mental models of computers' working structures.

Methodology

The sampling frame for this study consisted of 17 middle-level schools (equivalent to junior high or middle schools in the United States) from all regions of the Netherlands. Based on an original inventory of 130 schools, these 17 were selected because (a) they used *exclusively* one of two distinct types of computer operating systems for their computer courses (Macintosh or MS-DOS), (b) their courses were of identical lengths (10 weeks, one hour per week), and (c) their course objectives were similar (introduction to the general uses and workings of computers, including operating systems, and the basics of word processing).

A variety of data collection techniques were employed in this study. The principal researchers interviewed instructors from each course to understand their approaches and course goals, and to collect copies of their course handbooks for subsequent content analysis. During the first week of each course, research teams introduced themselves to the students and passed out self-administered questionnaires, which were completed in a 50-minute session and then collected. Measurements included the following:

1. a 33-item battery of attitude questions taken from the Minnesota Computer Literacy and Awareness Assessment Scale (Minnesota Educational Computing Consortium, 1979), a scale that has been translated, adapted, and validated for Dutch students by Crombach (1986)
2. a standardized measure of computer literacy that measures students' conceptual and practical understanding of the computer
3. measures of students' previous experiences with computers before coming to the course, including number of hours on the keyboard and sources of information about computers, such as family, friends, and media
4. demographic information

The Differential Aptitude Test for Spatial Abilities (Fokkema & Dirkzwager, 1960) was administered so we would have some measure of the students' innate abilities with computers; scores on this test were used as covariates in subsequent analyses. Because administration of these measures took the entire 50 minutes, the research teams were invited to stay for additional classes (if any) that were not participating in the study, in order to observe how students interacted with the computer and among themselves while working with the computer.

TEACH-BACK PROTOCOL TASK

In the tenth and final week of the courses, research teams again visited the schools to readminister the attitude battery and the computer literacy test, and asked instructors for grades of students' performance in the classes, using a 10-point scale (the common grading measure in the Netherlands). In addition, as a method of assessing students' mental models of computers and how they work, students were asked to perform a teach-back protocol. This protocol task was presented to the students as follows:

> We would like to know how you imagine the computer system you've been working with the past 10 weeks. Therefore, we'd like to ask you the following question:
>   Explain to a friend who did not take the computer class how you would (1) look for a text that is present on one of the disks, (2) display this on the screen, (3) make a copy of the text on another disk, and (4) send a copy of the text to the printer. Use whatever you like: words, drawings, or schemes. If needed, you may continue on the following page.

The instructions were read aloud and were also printed on the top of an otherwise blank page. In some cases, students needed individual encouragement to get started, which the research teams provided in a way that did not bias the actual direction of task completion. The teach-back protocols were subsequently scored by two independent raters following the procedures formulated by van der Veer (1989). All scores that showed a difference between the two raters were discussed by them, and a common decision was made regarding the final interpretation of the protocol.

During the first week, 655 questionnaires were completed in 29 classes at the 17 different schools. Owing to dropouts and illness during the day of data collection in the tenth week, a total of 607 students remained in the study. In the majority of data collection sessions, the research team was composed of one male and one female researcher, so the potential bias of interviewer-interviewee interactions based on gender should have been minimal.

Results

As is always the case in studies where socialization processes are believed to be critical to attitudes and behavior, subjects do not come to studies as tabulae rasae. This field study of Dutch students was no different in that regard, especially with respect to gender. Although the course work was the students' first formal introduction to the computer, 55% of them reported having had at least one experience with a personal computer in the past. Although there were no gender differences in having had at least one experience with a PC, boys were significantly higher in self-reporting the number of hours on the keyboard. Subsequent questions relating to types of programs used (word processors, databases, math programs) showed extremely low usage rates for the entire sample, and no differences between boys and girls on these types of applications. The major explanation for differences between boys and girls in computer experiences comes from playing computer games.

Boys self-reported a higher incidence of having a PC at home (60% for boys versus 45% for girls) and having family discussions about the possibility of getting a PC for the home. Boys also self-reported a higher incidence of reading books and magazines that specialize in computers relative to girls. In more general terms, there are also gender differences in preferences for school subjects, with boys reporting higher preferences for math and "hard" sciences and girls reporting higher preferences for language courses, drawing, and music (all differences at $p \leq$ .05). Finally, boys scored on average about 10% higher on the spatial abilities test ($t = 2.72, p \leq .01$), a common finding for subjects in this age group. Given the large range in the number of hours on the keyboard, and the individuals' innate differences in spatial ability, both of these variables are used as covariates in all subsequent analyses. Partialing out the effects of prior computer experience and innate spatial ability differences in subjects will allow for more confidence in discussing the results within the context of gender differences. The final sample comprised 326 boys and 281 girls from all regions of the country, with an average age of 14.3 years ($SD = 2.2$ years).

ATTITUDE STRUCTURE AND CHANGE

In order to assess the dimensions of the students' attitude structure toward computers prior to the course work, we conducted principal-components factor analysis with varimax rotation on the 33 attitude questions. This resulted in five significant factors, accounting for 40% of the variance in the data set. Factor loadings and Cronbach's alphas for the attitude items are given in Table 8.1. In order of explained variance, the five factors comprised items that could be described as the dimensions of fear, self-efficacy, negative affect, positive affect, and utility beliefs. Four of the five factors are similar in dimensions to those found in Crombach's (1986) study, and the additional factor in these data is explained by the two dimensions of affect, as opposed to Crombach's one affective dimension.

Although it might be tempting to view affect as one dimension along a continuum ranging from positive to negative, Watson and Tellegen's (1985) mood models offer consistent evidence of positive affect and negative affect as independent orthogonal dimensions that emerge in factor analysis after a varimax rotation (see also Meyer & Shack, 1989). In describing these dimensions, the high negative affect continuum is characterized by terms such as "distressed," "fearful," "jittery," "nervous," "hostile," and "scornful"; the low negative affect continuum is characterized by terms such as "at rest," "placid," "calm," and "relaxed." The high positive affect continuum loads strongly on items such as "excited," "active," "elated," "enthusiastic," "peppy," and "strong," whereas low positive affect is described as "drowsy," "dull," "sleepy," and "sluggish" (Meyer & Shack, 1989, p. 693). Within the context of the two affective factors derived from the personal computer attitude items in this study, each could be interpreted as being on the "high" affective end of Watson and Tellegen's mood model. These dominant dimensions of positive affect and negative affect have been empirically tested on American subjects, but there is also evidence of the positive and negative affect structures across cultures (Watson, Clark, & Tellegen, 1984) and across differing response formats (Watson, 1988).

Table 8.2 displays results on differences in attitudes and computer literacy test scores between boys and girls both prior to and following the 10-week courses. Both prior to and following the courses, girls had significantly higher scores on the fear and negative affect constructs relative to boys, whereas boys were significantly higher on measures of

TABLE 8.1 Factor Structures on Computer Attitudes

	Factor Loading
Items in Factor 1 (Fear)	
The strange words and symbols used in computers frighten me.	.62
I feel nervous when I'm sitting in front of a computer.	.70
Computers remain a mysterious thing to me.	.59
I'm afraid to push a wrong key on the computer.	.68
Computers frighten me.	.49
I get nervous if I see a computer.	.56
% of variance explained	9
Cronbach's alpha	.74
Items in Factor 2 (Self-Efficacy)	
I think I'll learn quickly how to use a computer.	.76
I'll easily learn how to use a computer.	.81
I think I'll get a good grade in my computer class.	.40
I feel ready to use computers.	.44
% of variance explained	8
Cronbach's alpha	.74
Items in Factor 3 (Negative Affect)	
I don't want to take computer lessons at school.	.70
I'm not prepared to work with a computer.	.55
I've got something against computers.	.63
Computers have very little use to me.	.60
I think it will be boring to use a computer in class.	.60
% of variance explained	8
Cronbach's alpha	.76
Items in Factor 4 (Positive Affect)	
I always stop in front of a store window displaying computers.	.71
I'd like to take a computer class in my free time.	.60
I feel relaxed in using a computer.	.54
I like to read about computers.	.71
% of variance explained	8
Cronbach's alpha	.74
Items in Factor 5 (Utility Beliefs)	
Computers play an important role in our daily lives.	.53
I think it's important for everyone to know about computers.	.61
All students should know what roles computers play in our world.	.59
Computers have more disadvantages than advantages.	.53
Learning how to get on with computers is important for my future.	.64
% of variance explained	7
Cronbach's alpha	.62

self-efficacy, positive affect, and beliefs regarding the utilities of computers. By far the largest gender difference was on the positive affect construct (F value > 50). In terms of computer literacy, the boys scored

TABLE 8.2 Pre-Post Measures on Attitudes and Computer Literacy Test Scores

	Significant Differences Between Groups	*F Value*
Precourse measures		
attitudes		
fear	girls > boys	13.02
self-efficacy	boys > girls	10.09
negative affect	girls > boys	3.99
positive affect	boys > girls	51.35
utility beliefs	boys > girls	12.40
computer literacy		
conceptual	boys > girls	20.63
practical	boys > girls	2.22 (n.s.)
spatial ability test	boys > girls	2.72 (t)
Postcourse measures		
attitudes		
fear	girls > boys	28.79
self-efficacy	boys > girls	25.16
negative affect	girls > boys	11.26
positive affect	boys > girls	50.20
utility beliefs	boys > girls	7.58
computer literacy		
conceptual	boys > girls	9.51
practical	boys > girls	11.54

significantly higher on their conceptual understanding of the computer both prior to and following the course work, and significantly higher on the practical understanding of the computer in the postcourse measurement. This additional significant difference in gained practical knowledge suggests that boys profit more than girls from taking computer lessons.

Although the main focus of this study is an examination of gender differences with respect to attitudes and learning about personal computers, it should be noted that there is an extensive body of theoretical literature and empirical evidence suggesting that anxiety inhibits motivation and performance within the context of learning about computers (Eason & Damodaran, 1981; Glass, Knight, & Baggett, 1985; Schneiderman, 1979; Weinberg & Fuerst, 1984). Table 8.3 shows results of shifts in attitude and learning constructs over the 10-week computer courses. In addition to being examined for within-group gender differences, the data were analyzed by level of fear, by taking the median split for each gender's distribution of precourse fear scores separately to form "high" and "low" within-gender fear groups. Not only are there main effects for gender, as shown in Table 8.2,

TABLE 8.3 Gender and Fear: Within-Group Differences on Pre-Post Attitude
Measures and Computer Literacy Test Scores

Construct	Girls			Boys		
	High Fear	Low Fear	Total	High Fear	Low Fear	Total
Self-efficacy	n.s.	n.s.	n.s.	n.s.	+	+
Negative affect	n.s.	n.s.	n.s.	+	n.s.	+
Positive affect	n.s.	n.s.	n.s.	n.s.	+	+
Utility	n.s.	+	+	+	n.s.	+
Computer literacy, concept	+	+	+	+	+	+
Computer literacy, practical	+	n.s.	+	+	+	+

NOTE: Cells report within gender analyses. A "+" indicates a significant, positive shift within group at $p < .05$. Cells with n.s. are non-significant differences.

but there is also evidence for some main effects owing to level of fear, with low-fear groups making more improvements than high-fear groups, although this was more the case for boys than for girls.

Computer lessons also seem to reduce the effect of fear on practical knowledge of computers. Prior to the lessons, the high-fear groups were significantly lower on practical knowledge of the PC than the low-fear groups, whereas in the postcourse measures these differences disappeared. For girls, the pattern of results suggests that the effect of level of fear was influential only on the learning constructs of conceptual and practical uses of the personal computer, and an increase in the sense of utility for the low-fear girls. In contrast, high-fear boys made significant improvements in terms of their negative affect and utility scores as well as in their practical and conceptual understanding, whereas low-fear boys had significant increases in self-efficacy, positive affect, and both computer literacy scores. Generally, the within-gender analysis suggests that boys made significant, positive shifts in all difference scores, whereas girls improved in beliefs about utilities and computer literacy scores, but had no changes in self-efficacy or positive or negative affect, regardless of the intervening level of fear they brought to the classroom.

MENTAL MODEL REPRESENTATIONS OF THE PC

Table 8.4 provides an overview of the distribution of scores that were assigned in the different scoring categories, as well as some comments

TABLE 8.4 Distribution of Mental Model Scores Based on Teach-Back Protocol

Area of Representation	Percentage of Protocols (n = 607)
Style (scored 0-1)	
verbal description	91
visual-spatial image	25
use of icons	28
set of production rules	6
program	34
Level (scored 0-1)	
task	8
semantics	30
syntax	49
keystroke	78
Completeness	
4 (all aspects mentioned)	22
3	27
2	19
1	16
0 (no aspects mentioned)	17
Correctness	
correct	9
partially correct	41
incorrect	51

regarding the analyses of selected protocols. The appendix to this chapter offers some representative examples of the students' mental models of the computer's working structure.

Style of representation. Most of the protocols contained verbal elements (descriptions of the system or of interaction with the system in the form of sentences, however fragmentary). One-fourth of all protocols consisted at least partially of visual-spatial images, representing structural relations in the system, structural aspects of interaction, or structural relations of the information processed (e.g., files in directories or folders, or the relative position of objects on the screen). More than one-fourth of all protocols contained elements of iconic character, small and simple images indicating objects, user actions (keystrokes or mouse clicks), or elements in a program, such as the printing phase. Representations often had a programlike structure, indicating causal or temporal relations between events. Both *style* of representation and *level* of representation may be scored in more than one category, but by definition a program cannot be a set of production rules. A production rule structure was a rare feature in this group of protocols.

Level of representation. A representation of knowledge at task level was only rarely found in these teach-back protocols, and semantic knowledge showed in less than one-third of the cases. Students normally described the system and the interaction either by rather pure keystroke representations (literally listing what they think has to be typed, or where to point and click the mouse) or by an integration of syntax and keystroke indications.

Completeness. In these data, all levels of completeness occurred in about equal proportions. One-fifth of all students at least implicitly mentioned all aspects asked for in the teach-back instruction, whereas slightly less than this proportion did not mention any of these at all. This variable was perhaps the most difficult to score, because raters often had to deduce from the description of an action or of a system characteristic which of the elements of the question was intended to be described, whereas the description itself was often at least partly incorrect.

Correctness. Totally correct representations were rare. Students had just completed a 10-week course, mainly exploring activities of the system, and learning for the first time the structure of working relationships of the computer. Half of the protocols contained many incorrect representations, and students were often unable to generalize from knowledge of one basic task (e.g., copying a file) to another (e.g., printing a file).

Both correctness and completeness of the representation of the system knowledge asked for may be considered an indication of students' understanding and abilities to work the computer. In fact, correctness and completeness are theoretically related, and both aspects will be strongly dependent on the teacher's knowledge and effectiveness and on the teaching materials used. In order to get an idea of the relationship between these two aspects, we calculated Spearman rank correlation coefficients for each class group on correctness and completeness, correcting for ties. Groups differed in size from 8 to 37, and the correlations were positive for all but five groups, although there was considerable variation in strength.

In terms of testing for gender differences in mental model representations, chi-square analyses on these dichotomous and ordinal data were performed with the median split of spatial abilities scores used to divide boys and girls into high and low groups and to serve as a controlling variable. Significant differences were found only within the high spatial abilities groups, with boys having greater semantic knowledge of the systems' relationships ($\chi^2 = 5.5, p < .01$); boys were also four times as likely as girls to have scores of being completely correct on the correctness variable ($\chi^2 = 19.4, p < .01$).

Discussion

Results from this field study clearly suggest the influence of gender socialization with respect to attitudes toward computers in young Dutch students. Controlling for differential spatial ability and prior experience with personal computers does not completely clear up other potentially confounding effects in the data, but it does allow for more confidence in interpreting the results. A reasonable conclusion here is that boys have less fear, greater self-confidence, more positive attitudes, and stronger beliefs regarding the uses of computers than do girls prior to ever having any formal computer training, and these differences are caused by socialization influences. Furthermore, the "gains" of the boys in this study in computer literacy and positive attitude shift were significantly higher on all constructs relative to girls following the 10-week courses. Finally, boys in the high spatial abilities group were much more likely than girls with high spatial ability to offer a higher level of semantic representation of the computer's working relationships, and four times as likely to offer correct representations of the protocol tasks. This finding in particular is highly consistent with the statistical differences found between boys and girls based on the other scale measures.

Although both sexes' fear levels dropped and beliefs in the utility of computers increased following the training, a within-group analysis shows that only the boys had significant shifts in attitudes and confidence measures following the computer courses. Boys were more self-confident and more positive in attitude than were girls, both coming into and after finishing the courses. These results raise questions as to why girls did not have any shifts with respect to self-efficacy or attitudes following the courses. One potential explanation for these findings comes from Fujita, Diener, and Sandvik (1991), who provide evidence suggesting that women are more affectively intense than men. Measuring positive and negative affect intensity in four different ways, these researchers obtained results that offer support for the idea that women in the United States experience emotion more strongly than do men, and that women differ in their intensity of both positive and negative emotions. One possible explanation for the lack of shift in self-efficacy and attitudes for girls in this study might well be that a 10-week course in personal computers was an insufficiently strong stimulus to move them in either a positive or a negative direction. An alternative explanation may be that boys in this age group, compared with girls, have a tendency to exaggerate their behaviors and self-reported attitudes. Thus the significantly different results both coming into and at the end of the courses may be partially accounted for by gender differences in self-reporting. This would not account for the shifts within gender groups, however.

Participant observation during the data collection sessions yielded an alternative explanation for the lack of shift among girls. Research teams attended a number of introductory computer classes during the first and last weeks of the study, simply to observe the human-machine interactions of students and teachers and the interactions among the students themselves. In all classes except one, students were paired at computers for the lessons. In some cases the teachers assigned the pairs; in others, the students self-selected their partners. Regardless of the pairing process, almost all pairs were same sex.

There were easily observable differences between pairs of boys and pairs of girls with respect to the use of the computer. Generally, boys were more animated and more willing to experiment with the computer. Their responses at completing a task successfully, or first, were often accompanied by loud exclamations, and those successful pairs would often offer assistance (or ridicule) to other pairs of boys and girls who were having less success. Generally speaking, boys seemed to "have fun," and their enthusiasm was visible, shared, and infectious. This type of behavior was also present among girl pairs, although with much less frequency.

Girls more typically had looks of concern, confusion, and stress on their faces, and talked quietly with their partners about what they should be doing. They were more likely to ask the teacher or other girl pairs for support, relative to boy pairs. There was high interjudge agreement among the four field researchers regarding these patterns of behavior. These in-class observations were also supported by data gathered in the tenth week that concerned students' self-reported behaviors of how they dealt with computer problems. Girls self-reported that computer crashes or computer execution problems were significantly more annoying to them, relative to boys' self-reporting, and reported greater frequency in asking the (usually male) teacher for help. Finally, girls were more likely to agree with the postcourse evaluation that "working with the computer was more fun at the *beginning* of the course than at the *end*," and agreed less with the statement that "learning with the computer is better and easier in comparison with regular lessons with a teacher" (all differences at $p < .01$). Clearly, the 10-week course itself was an exercise in gender socialization with respect to personal computers.

Conclusions and Directions for Further Research

The study reported here offers results that support the general findings in the literature regarding gender socialization with respect to high-technology products. That males have greater self-efficacy and more positive attitudes regarding high-tech products relative to females is in itself no new contribution to knowledge, apart from the context of the sample, which involves boys and girls rather than adults. This study offers additional understanding of attitude structures and mental model representations held by children toward personal computers. Based on the ordering of attitude dimensions in the factor analysis, it seems that children come to the computer with a sense of fear, confidence, separate dimensions of positive and negative affect, and beliefs about the usefulness of the computer.

Approaches to understanding gender differences with respect to computers can and should come from other measures besides self-efficacy and attitudes. One perspective with promise is the teach-back protocol method, which allows for a different type of cognitive elaboration to express understanding of the workings of a computer. Comparing interpretations of this more qualitative type of data will offer new and different insights into gender differences.

Another perspective for understanding gender differences comes from investigating differential responses to the type of operating system with which the new student is confronted. Generally speaking, two types of systems are widely available. Both systems have comparable functionality and hardware elements for most of the tasks carried out by the operating system. They differ strongly, however, in terms of syntax and interaction style of the user interface. One type suggests metaphors for the conceptual level of the system and its applications, whereas the other leaves the development of the student's "mental model" of the computer and its operating system to the teacher's skill and the student's previous knowledge of that system.

The Macintosh interface (and, to a lesser extent, Windows) may be characterized as "more intuitive" than MS-DOS because of its strong reference to the spatial relations of the semantics of the system by means of a desktop metaphor. The Macintosh operating system involves a collection of iconic elements in the lexicon and an interaction style that is a mixture of menu selection and object manipulation. The use of a mouse strongly determines the physical basis for interaction and for supplying the computer with system commands. Alternatively, the MS-DOS interface is based on a typewriter metaphor, a written lexicon, and an interaction style that is primarily command-language oriented. This type of interface does not refer to the spatial relations of the system's semantics, and is less "intuitive" and metaphor based. These widely different approaches to learning how to operate and interact with the computer may be subject to differential responses based on gender, given females' greater abilities to deal with metaphorical representations and their different sense of intuition (see Silverman & Eals, 1992).

Finally, research examining the cognitive and socialization interactions that shed light on the threshold levels at which attitudes and learning changes take place will offer a clearer understanding of gender-related differences in the use of high-technology products. For example, in spite of the gender differences found in the pre-post measures in this study, it is not clearly established that true shifts in attitudes and learning have a linear character. Given the body of evidence on computer phobia cited earlier, one should not rule out the construct of fear as an intervening or inhibiting variable that is strongly related to gender, where perhaps a threshold level has to be crossed before real gains in learning and attitudes can take place. Models that attempt to assess how dominant the influence of fear or apprehension is in the process of attitude formation, attitude change, and learning to use high-technology products can clearly benefit from using gender as an exogenous variable. The insights gained will be of theoretical and practical interest to social scientists, teachers, and trainers, and of design interest to engineers working in cognitive ergonomics.

Appendix:
Comments on Analyses of Protocols

- *Protocol 217 (12-year-old girl):* This example shows a representation that is characterized by a variety of styles. It contains fragments of a verbal program, icons (i.e., indicating the return key), and various images (the screen with a directory listing, the configuration of the cursor keys). There are clear fragments of keystroke and syntax representation, and some hints of semantics.

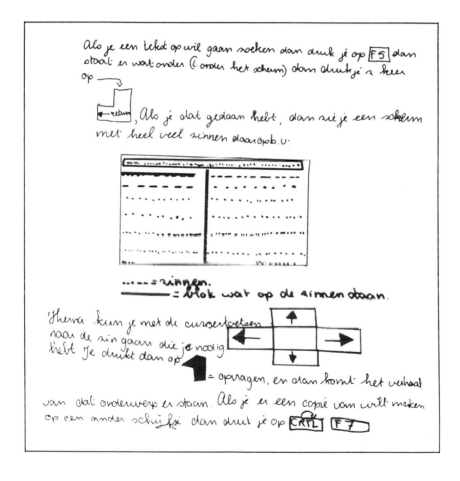

Protocol 217, part 1 (originally in several colors)

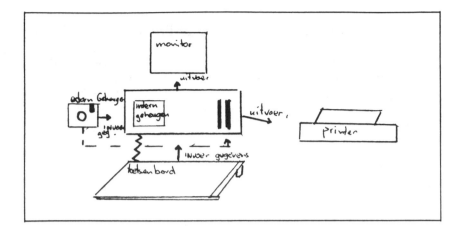

Fragment of Protocol 349

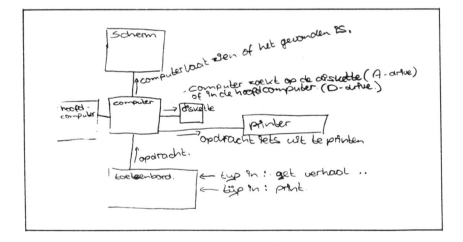

Fragment of Protocol 010

- *Protocol 349 (12-year-old boy) and Protocol 010 (14-year-old girl):* Protocol 349 shows the relation of system components indicating the transport of information. In this protocol, system elements are indicated by simple icons. *Geheugen* means memory, *Toetensbord* is keyboard, and *invoer* and *uitvoer* indicate input and output, respectively. The representation found in Protocol 010 is of the same character, but the system components are

Fragment of Protocol 189

Fragment of Protocol 612

represented by abstract labels in boxes without any iconic value, and the transport of information is verbally described.

- *Protocol 189 (12-year-old boy) and Protocol 612 (13-year-old boy):* These two protocols work heavily with icons. Protocol 189 contains icons representing keys, although the key functions are mostly irrelevant to the task described in the study's methodology. Protocol 612 shows some examples of icons indicating pieces of hardware, such as the mouse, a disk, the keyboard. The text describes sequences of actions relating to the task, although they are incomplete.

References

Collis, B. (1988). Secondary school females and computers: Implications of attitudes for teaching and learning. In N. Beishuizen et al. (Eds.), *The use of the microcomputer in teaching and learning* (pp. 83-91). Lisse, Netherlands: Swets & Zeitlinger.

Costa, J. A. (Ed.). (1991). *Gender and consumer behavior.* Salt Lake City: University of Utah Printing Service.

Crombach, M. J. (1986). Ontwikkeling en Validering van een Computer-Attitudeschaal [Development and validation of a computer attitude scale]. In R. van der Linden & W. Wijnstra (Eds.), *Ontwikkelingen in de Methodologie van het Onderwijsonderzoek* [Developments in the methodology of educational research]. Lisse, Netherlands: Swets & Zeitlinger.

Davis, H. (1970). Dimensions of marital roles in consumer decision making. *Journal of Marketing Research, 7,* 168-177.

Dickerson, M. L., & Gentry, J. W. (1983). Characteristics of adopters and non-adopters of home computers. *Journal of Consumer Research, 10,* 225-235.

Eason, K. D., & Damodaran, L. (1981). The needs of the commercial user. In H. Coombs & E. Alty (Eds.), *Computing skills and the user interface* (pp. 115-139). New York: Academic Press.

Ehrenreich, B. (1992, January 20). Making sense of la différence. *Time,* p. 43.

Fokkema, S. D., & Dirkzwager, A. (1960). *Differential Aptitude Test for Spatial Abilities* (Dutch translation). Amsterdam: Swets & Zeitlinger.

Foxall, G. R., & Bhate, S. (1991). *Extent of computer use: Relationships with adaptive-innovative cognitive style and personal involvement in computing* (Working paper). Birmingham, England: Birmingham Business School, Department of Commerce, Consumer Research Unit.

Fujita, F., Diener, E., & Sandvik, E. (1991). Gender differences in negative affect and well-being: The case for emotional intensity. *Journal of Personality and Social Psychology, 61,* 427-434.

Gatignon, H., & Robertson, T. (1985). A propositional inventory for new diffusion research. *Journal of Consumer Research, 11,* 849-867.

Gist, M. E., Schwoerer, C., & Rosen, B. (1989). Effects of alternative training methods on self-efficacy and performance in computer software training. *Journal of Applied Psychology, 74,* 884-891.

Glass, C. R., Knight, L. A., & Baggett, H. L. (1985). Bibliography on computing anxiety and psychological aspects of computing use. *Psychological Documents, 15,* 25 (Ms. 2723).

Kiesler, S., Sproull, L., & Eccles, J. (1985). Poolhalls, chips, and war games: Women in the culture of computing. *Psychology of Women Quarterly, 9,* 451-462.

Krendl, K., & Lieberman, D. (1990). *Computers and learning: A review of recent research* (Working paper). Bloomington: Indiana University, Department of Telecommunications.

Lieberman, D. (1985). Research on children and microcomputers: A review of utilization and effects studies. In M. Chen & W. Paisley (Eds.), *Children and microcomputers: Research on the newest medium.* Beverly Hills, CA: Sage.

Mandinach, E. B., & Corno, L. (1985). Cognitive engagement variations among students of different ability level and sex in a computer problem solving game. *Sex Roles, 13,* 241-251.

Martocchio, J. J., & Webster, J. (1992). Effects of feedback and cognitive playfulness on performance in microcomputer software training. *Personnel Psychology, 45,* 553-578.

Meyer, G. J., & Shack, J. R. (1989). Structural convergence of mood and personality: Evidence for old and new directions. *Journal of Personality and Social Psychology, 57*, 691-706.

Minnesota Educational Computing Consortium. (1979) *Minnesota Computer Literacy and Awareness Assessment*. St. Paul: Author.

Moschis, G. P. (1987). *Acquisition of the consumer role by adolescents* (Research Monograph No. 82). Atlanta: Georgia State University.

Qualls, W. (1987). Household decision behavior: The impact of husbands' and wives' sex role orientation. *Journal of Consumer Research, 14*, 264-279.

Rudell, F. (1991). Boys' toys and girls' tools? An exploration of gender differences in consumer decision-making for high-tech products. In J. A. Costa (Ed.), *Gender and consumer behavior* (pp. 187-198). Salt Lake City: University of Utah Printing Service.

Schneiderman, B. (1979). Human factors experiments in designing interactive systems. *Computer, 12*, 9-24.

Silverman, I., & Eals, M. (1992, January 20). Sizing up the sexes: Interview with J. Madeleine Nash in Gorman. *Time International*, p. 40.

Temple, L., & Lips, H. M. (1989). Gender differences and similarities in attitudes toward computers. *Computers in Human Behavior, 5*, 215-226.

van der Veer, G. (1989). Users' representation of systems: Variety as function of user interface, culture, and individual style. In F. Klix, N. A. Streitz, Y. Waern, & H. Wandke (Eds.), *Human computer interaction: Psychonomic aspects*. Heidelberg: Springer Verlag.

Venkatesh, A., & Vitalari, N. (1984). Households and technology: The case of home computers some conceptual and theoretical issues. In J. Roberts & L. Wortzel (Eds.), *Marketing to the changing household: Management and research perspectives* (pp. 187-203). Cambridge, MA: Ballinger.

Ward, S. (1974). Consumer socialization. *Journal of Consumer Research, 1*, 1-13.

Watson, D. (1988). The vicissitudes of mood measurement: Effects of varying descriptors, time frames, and response formats on measure of positive and negative affect. *Journal of Personality and Social Psychology, 55*, 128-141.

Watson, D., Clark, L. A., & Tellegen, A. (1984). Cross-cultural convergence in the structure of mood: A Japanese replication and a comparison with U.S. findings. *Journal of Personality and Social Psychology, 47*, 127-144.

Watson, D., & Tellegen, A. (1985). Toward a consensual structure of mood. *Psychological Bulletin, 98*, 219-235.

Weinberg, S. B., & Fuerst, M. (1984). *Computer phobia*. Effingham, IL: Banbury.

Wilder, G., Mackie, D., & Cooper, J. (1985). Gender and computers: Two surveys of computer related attitudes. *Sex Roles, 13*, 215-228.

9

Construction of a Meaningful Wedding: Differences in the Priorities of Brides and Grooms

TINA M. LOWREY

CELE OTNES

IN recent years, researchers in consumer behavior have begun to focus their attention on the types of purchases associated with ritual occasions in American culture, such as Christmas (e.g., Belk, 1989; Fischer & Arnold, 1990; Hirschman & LaBarbera, 1989; Otnes, Lowrey, & Kim, 1993; Sherry & McGrath, 1989) and Thanksgiving (Wallendorf & Arnould, 1991). As Rook (1985) notes, these occasions are worthy of study because consumers often devote much time and effort to the purchase of goods and services that enable them to partake fully in events surrounding these occasions.

AUTHORS' NOTE: We would like to thank L. J. Shrum for his insightful comments on this chapter. In addition, we wish to thank the Summer Research Opportunities Fund and the James Webb Young Fund at the University of Illinois for help with financial support for the study reported here.

164

One special occasion that has received only limited attention within consumer behavior is the wedding (McGrath, 1993; Otnes & Lowrey, 1993). This is surprising, given that purchases of wedding-related goods and services generate more than $30 billion in annual sales for American retailers, for an average cost of about $19,000 per wedding (Chapman, 1993). Given that weddings are one of the few rites of passage in Western cultures (Cheal, 1988), these events will probably remain salient even in the face of high divorce rates in this country (Glick, 1982). Although bridal showers have been studied (Casparis, 1979; Cheal, 1988), actual wedding ceremonies have been somewhat overlooked, with the exception of studies of weddings in other cultures (Barker, 1978; Kendall, 1989; Wilson, 1972). Clearly, however, the American wedding has remained a highly significant cultural ritual and, as such, deserves further study.

In addition to their obvious sociological and economic significance, weddings should be of interest to consumer researchers for a number of reasons. Weddings are often elaborate and require a long period of planning (Gilbert, 1983). Therefore, examining these occasions affords researchers an opportunity to learn how consumers coordinate the purchase of goods and services for one of the most important days of their lives. As Greenblat and Cottle (1980) note, "The period from the engagement to the wedding, which is so important psychologically, socially and economically, has been ignored in the literature" (p. 2).

More important, studying the expensive and often highly public ceremony celebrating the union of a man and woman provides an interesting and natural context in which to examine how the different genders engage in ritual-related consumption. Such exploration would expand on research that has examined gendered participation in other occasions (e.g., Caplow, 1982; Cheal, 1987; Fischer & Arnold, 1990; McGrath & Otnes, 1993; Otnes, Kim, & Kim, in press; Otnes, Ruth, & Milbourne, 1993; Sherry & McGrath, 1989; Wolfinbarger & Gilly, 1991). These previous studies have primarily explored gender differences that emerge during the rituals of gift exchange. Most findings support the assertions of Caplow (1982) and Cheal (1987) that women are delegated the gift-exchange activities primarily because their role in the North American family has included nurturance of kinship ties and other social relations. Moreover, women simply seem to hold more positive attitudes about gift giving than do men (Fischer & Arnold, 1990; Wolfinbarger & Gilly, 1991), and also appear to plan and execute their gift-selection activities in a more deliberate manner (Sherry & McGrath, 1989). Moreover, gender differences appear to interact with personality variables, such as level of self-acceptance, in determining how much an individual participates in a gift-exchange occasion (Otnes, Ruth, & Milbourne, 1993).

The few studies that have focused on gender differences within the broader scope of actual ritual celebration have actually examined these differences among children. For example, Otnes et al. (in press) analyzed children's letters to Santa Claus, and found that boys typically were much more direct in communicating their desires for toys than were girls. McGrath and Otnes (1993) applied Rook's (1985) framework of ritualistic elements to the study of how boys and girls experience birthday parties and found evidence that girls are much more aware of the types of "ritual artifacts" required at a birthday party than are boys. In addition, girls and boys seem to favor different scripted activities at parties, with boys anticipating outdoor play and girls' descriptions centering on eating and indoor games as preferred activities.

Given that studies of gender differences within ritualistic contexts have focused on the areas described above, the purpose of this chapter is to begin exploring the gender differences that may exist during the process of wedding planning. We employ Rook's (1985) framework of ritualistic elements. Rook discusses four such elements: ritual artifacts, scripts, performance roles, and the audience. According to Rook, *ritual artifacts* are "consumer products . . . that accompany or are consumed in a ritual setting" (p. 253). *Scripts* are formal or informal guidelines that determine the use of various artifactual materials. *Performance roles* of the individuals actively participating in the ritual can be, but are not always, explicitly scripted. Finally, the *audience* typically consists of those individuals who do not have specified performance roles, but whose observation of the ritual provides both a public element and added drama to the event.

In this chapter we focus specifically on whether gender differences emerge with respect to the ritual artifacts, or goods and services, used in the American wedding. We have chosen to include services (in particular, those that a minister provides) in our conceptualization of ritual artifacts. Although technically occupying what Rook (1985) would describe as a ritual performance role, ministers (and the services that they provide) can be viewed as artifacts because they are "purchased" with an honorarium or fee. In addition, the services provided by a minister are often accompanied by tangible items essential to the wedding ritual. For example, the minister's services are commonly included with the rental of the church and normally include an official, signed wedding certificate.

To begin exploring gender differences in wedding-related consumption, we focus on three research questions:

1. What types of ritual artifacts do women deem the most important for use in their weddings and receptions?
2. What types of ritual artifacts do men deem the most important for use in their weddings and receptions?
3. Is the emphasis on artifacts different across genders, and, if so, what reasons could account for these differences?

Method

During the summer of 1991, separate focus groups were conducted with brides and grooms in a midwestern city (population approximately 100,000). Participants included 19 brides and 14 grooms. As part of a larger study, a segment of each focus group was devoted to examining the ritual artifacts that brides and grooms deem most important when planning their weddings.

Each focus group involved a small number of participants (6 to 10) in accordance with existing recommendations (Krueger, 1988; Morgan, 1988). Participants ranged in age from their early 20s to their mid-30s and represented a blend of undergraduate and graduate students from the local university and working adults not associated with the university. Participants were recruited through newspaper ads and through notices placed in bridal shops throughout the city. Sessions lasted from 60 to 90 minutes, and participants were paid $25 each. The focus groups were videotaped, and these tapes were transcribed, yielding more than 150 pages of text. We addressed the trustworthiness of the data (Wallendorf & Belk, 1989) by assuring anonymity when reporting results, and by using techniques recommended by skilled focus group moderators (Krueger, 1988).

Although the group moderators followed an interview schedule, informants were allowed to discuss other aspects of wedding planning that were important to them personally. The interview schedules for subsequent focus groups were then modified to include questions relating to these issues.

Our analysis was interpretive in nature (see Hirschman & Holbrook, 1992). That is, we sought patterns in the text that would enable us to discern whether gender differences existed with respect to artifact preferences. We created our final interpretation by a process of negotiation among authors, arriving at an agreed-on synthesis of our individual interpretations (see Belk, Wallendorf, & Sherry, 1989; Otnes, Lowrey, & Kim, 1993).

Findings

Given that clear gender differences have emerged in studies examining other types of ritual consumption (e.g., Fischer & Arnold, 1990; Sherry & McGrath, 1989), we believed that the wedding is a natural context in which to explore whether gender differences exist with regard to artifact preferences. We discuss below the preferences observed among each gender, and then provide our interpretations of why some differences exist.

ARTIFACTS PREFERRED BY BRIDES

Brides often regard a select group of artifacts as important as they assemble goods and services to help create their weddings (Otnes & Lowrey, 1993). Indeed, every bride in our focus groups named at least one wedding-related artifact that she regarded as crucial for inclusion in her wedding, and many mentioned several. In addition, the brides often spoke about these artifacts with anticipation, rhapsody, or reverence in their voices. This suggests that the brides viewed many of these wedding-related artifacts as "sacred" items, or items that are "more significant, powerful and extraordinary than the self" (Belk et al., 1989, p. 13). In the following paragraphs we discuss the most prevalent items described in this manner.

The wedding dress and related accessories. The wedding dress and related accessories are by far the items most commonly regarded as important or sacred by brides (Otnes & Lowrey, 1993). Furthermore, these items of clothing are often acquired through "hierophany," a process described by Belk et al. (1989) in which the "right" or "perfect" item appears to be revealed almost magically. Several brides in our groups described the hierophanies that occurred when they found their dresses, particularly Jenny:

> When I found that dress, I mean I put it on . . . I started crying, 'cause I was like, "Lisa, this is my dress!" . . . and the whole thing seemed so much more real; that we were really getting married, and that this was going to happen, and it just, it just was a really overwhelming, I guess, type of feeling.

Given the fact that so many of our brides described the revelations of their dresses through hierophany, it appears these dresses were the most salient symbols of the wedding—and of the rite of passage (van Gennep, 1960) that the bride was soon to experience. Furthermore, the significance of a singular and expensive dress no doubt helped the bride to separate herself from the ordinary world, and to position herself as the center of attention on her wedding day.

Wedding dresses were sacralized in other ways as well (see Belk et al., 1989). For example, many of the brides described fantasies or visions of how they had always wanted to look in their dresses. For example, Elaine remarked: "I always imagined myself, ever since I was little, in, you know, the perfect huge white gown. . . . It's not something that I could settle for, it had to be the one."

Items that were imbued with tradition also attained sacred status. Many of the brides' dresses, veils, handkerchiefs, and other accessories were sacralized in this manner. Jody, in particular, had a special accessory for her wedding:

> I'm carrying my grandmother's prayer book that she carried when she was married. That was, you know, no question of whether I wouldn't or would . . . that she carried in 1908 and all of her sisters, my mom's sisters have carried, and that all of their kids have carried.

Tradition as a sacralization process was most common for dresses and accessories that had been used in the weddings of relatives, or that had been made by loved ones especially for the bride.

The minister and the church. Brides tended to place a great deal of importance on the selection of the ministers for their weddings, because of the ability of the minister to "contaminate" the wedding with sacredness (Belk et al., 1989). Many of the choices made also seemed to be related to the sacralization process of tradition. For example, Jody had to compromise on her wedding site to ensure the availability of her childhood priest:

> I wanted this priest who I had known from childhood to do it. . . . You decide what's negotiable and what's not. And the place was negotiable at that point. He wasn't negotiable. I wanted him, so that's the way that worked out.

Not surprisingly, the brides also regarded the church as a wedding artifact that could "contaminate" the entire wedding with sacredness (Otnes & Lowrey, 1993). Even when the wedding did not take place in a church invested with personal importance (e.g., a childhood parish or a church currently being attended), some brides still considered a "church wedding" important. Sue explained:

> To me it's important to have it in church because it feels more like it's blessed. . . . It just doesn't seem married unless it's in the church. . . . If I was just up at the courthouse, you know, it would be . . . I don't know . . . like it wasn't really happening, like it was practice or pretend. . . . Yeah, just like when you're little kids, that kind of thing.

Thus the inherent sacredness of the minister and/or the church was viewed by many of our brides as ensuring that their wedding ceremonies were blessed.

Other artifacts. Other items brides mentioned included the music selected for the wedding ceremony, decorations (for the ceremony, not the reception), photographs of the wedding, and rings. Decorations, particularly flowers, helped fulfill some brides' fantasies, in a manner similar to their wedding attire. For instance, Lynn stated, "I think that is going to be the most important part, as far as building the atmosphere, of the whole ceremony."

Other artifacts were perceived as sacred because of their strong communicative power. Music, in particular, was important to some of our brides, especially Lynn: "I would like to have people really pay close attention to the wording of the songs, and you know, the timing of them. . . . I want people to remember . . . the song that was sung when we lit the candles." Music was seen as a way to communicate the personal values of the bride and groom on their wedding day. Photographs and rings, on the other hand, "were considered sacred for their power to communicate long after the wedding was over" (Otnes & Lowrey, 1993, p. 327).

In summary, brides mentioned several items that were significant to them on their wedding days. Furthermore, most of these items were designed to be used during the actual wedding ceremony itself. Finally, these artifacts were sacralized by brides through a number of processes.

ARTIFACTS PREFERRED BY GROOMS

In comparing the importance of wedding-related artifacts among brides and grooms, a major difference becomes immediately evident. That is, most of the grooms in our focus groups did not articulate a single item related to the wedding *ceremony* that they believed to be significant. Rather, when grooms mentioned artifacts that were salient to them personally, they tended to focus on two types of items: those that would enhance the reception, and photographs. In addition, compared with the brides, the grooms expressed less excitement and enthusiasm when discussing these items.

Items for the reception. Most important to our grooms were artifacts contributing to the creation of the reception. For example, when asked whether he had seen anything that he had to have for his wedding, Stan responded, "Nothing we saw. I just wanna make sure we have some good music and good food." Similarly, Brian said he cared about having "a reception for everybody." And Pete reported that he was "actively involved" in selecting the German restaurant where his reception would be held.

In addition, many described how important it was to have the reception in a comfortable and convenient place. Al said:

> I wanted to make sure there was nothing pretentious about it, that it is casual and hearty, tasteful but just trying to pick out the most sensible good things to put together. So everyone was real happy, relaxed.

Mike, whose wedding had already taken place, mentioned the importance of the location of the reception "because most people were traveling by car and it was important that we had it right there and that nobody had to leave. . . . It made everything easier for everybody else."

Some grooms mentioned how the reception hall had to have the "right" kind of atmosphere. For example, Greg explained how important this issue was for him and his fiancée:

> We probably looked at 15 or 20 places and then we found this one that we saw, and said, "This is the one that fits our personality. This is the one that we'd better have." And that was really the only thing that once we saw, we said, "We just have to have this." . . . We would have gotten it no matter how much it would have been.

Greg's experience revealed that hierophany appeared to dictate his selection of a reception hall, and other grooms mentioned similar experiences as well. In contrast, the brides most often experienced hierophany when selecting dresses and other attire. Thus it appears that the grooms wanted to communicate fellowship at the reception, a special social occasion, whereas the brides wanted to communicate their place in the spotlight during the actual ceremony.

Photographs. There was some overlap across genders with respect to the importance of a few items, including photographs. However, the grooms appeared much more concerned with photos than did the brides. In response to the question, "If you could only have one item for your wedding, what would it be?" Pete said, "Well, since this is gonna be very small I'd say I'd have a picture of the whole group." Similarly, Stan responded:

> I don't think there's any one thing I could own that would, I don't know, memorabilia of the wedding, other than, y'know, pictures. And just have all the memories attached to it.

Likewise, Ben emphasized how important it was to select a photographer who would best communicate the spirit of the wedding for years to come:

> We found that every photographer . . . [their] personality shows up in their photography. And we were looking [for the cheapest, but] we both decided that the photographs would be the kind of thing to stay with us

down the line. . . . The kind of creativity [we were after] we were willing to pay for it, whatever the price.

Thus, as with the brides, grooms valued photographs for their long-term communicative power.

Other artifacts. A few grooms mentioned the importance of ritual artifacts that had specific meaning for their own wedding ceremonies. For example, Joe, who was marrying a Japanese woman, considered a symbolic bottle of sake wine to be an important part of their ceremony:

> So I'm gonna get a really nice bottle of sake. . . . I really like the symbolism. There's a part of that sharing . . . the way that it has to be poured, that, just, there's something about . . . the ritual involved in that, that I just find to be extremely important.

Similarly, Wayne, who is of the Quaker faith, had this to say about an artifact that he considered sacred:

> In the Quaker wedding, what happens is the bride and groom sign a certificate that sort of states . . . that you got married, and then all the people who had been invited to the wedding sign as witnesses. . . . It's a really nice, ornamental thing. And so that's probably what we'll spend most of our money on.

Both of these examples typify sacred artifacts that were imbued with tradition, yet it is worth noting that very few items mentioned by the grooms attained sacred status in this manner.

Finally, some grooms felt that the most important artifacts for their weddings were those that held particular significance for their brides. When asked what one item he would want for his wedding, Doug responded, "Her dress. . . . I know what it means to her. And that's just the most important thing." Similarly, Randy said, "I don't really know, but probably the pictures, but I defer this question to her, whatever would make her happy."

In summary, whereas brides mentioned many artifacts that attained sacred status in a number of ways, the artifacts discussed by grooms were not only fewer in number, but sacralized in fewer ways. In addition, most of the grooms tended to focus on the reception rather than the wedding ceremony.

Interpretation

We interpret the reasons for the gender differences noted above in artifact preference to be attributable to at least three factors. First, we believe that by far the most important reason is the traditional view of a wedding as "the bride's day." Several grooms mentioned that "their" wedding was really "her" wedding. For example, when explaining his role in the planning process, Doug had this to say:

> I have taken a very active interest in agreeing with everything she does. . . . This is her show. . . . It's . . . an overwhelming realization of what all is gonna go into this. . . . Once you realize that you're basically organizing a coronation, then it's okay.

However, perhaps Mike made the most succinct observation as to "whose wedding" it would be in the following interchange:

Mike: What was the name of that [recent TV] show that was on? Because I watched part of it.
Moderator: It was *Brides: A Tale of Two Weddings.*
Mike: Right. Right. Not *Grooms: A Tale of Two Weddings.*

Furthermore, both brides and grooms seemed to recognize that socialization often leads to the wedding day's being regarded as "for the bride." For example, Doug noted:

> The U.S. definitely gives women the image that your day to shine is very much a part of joining society. . . . In the [supermarket] checkout line, any number of magazines are gonna have a wedding article. And those are women's magazines. . . . The men's side doesn't have that.

Likewise, Josh observed that in grade school "you see all these little girls and they're always playing wedding. . . . You never see little boys playing it." One bride, Jody, agreed: "Every little girl thinks about her wedding." In fact, the majority of our brides could readily articulate visions of their wedding days, whereas no grooms could do so.

There are, of course, sociological reasons for this emphasis on the bride. Historically, in patriarchal societies, a woman's role was to marry and serve her husband and children, rather than to participate independently in the workplace. Furthermore, women were encouraged to "find a husband who would pull them into a higher social class position. In many instances, marriage was (and is) for women the only means of upward mobility" (Greenblat & Cottle, 1980, p. 48). Thus, although getting married is a significant rite of passage for both men and women, it traditionally has been a more critical one for women. These views of the proper place for women undoubtedly contributed to the tradition of a wedding as an opportunity for a father to "give away" his daughter to another man.

The second reason brides may place more emphasis on the selection of artifacts is that being concerned about material goods related to the wedding may be typed as a feminine or, more pointedly, an unmasculine activity. For example, Lynn noted: "What happened was, [my fiancé] went to the bridal show. . . . Well, bad mistake, cause his friends found out he went with me, and they kinda rubbed it in, like 'You don't do those kinds of things.' "

Furthermore, even though many grooms described themselves as being involved in the final selection of items, often this involvement stemmed more from a motivation to keep the bride happy than from any real interest in the items being selected. For example, Pete explained how unconcerned he was about the flowers:

> My fiancée's real concerned about the meaning of different types of flowers. . . . I honestly don't care. . . . And she picked some rather odd ones that are really hard to get. I keep telling her, "Those florists don't carry those darn flowers." So, I guess my honest opinion is I'm not too excited about that.

Similarly, when asked if there was anything that he didn't care about, Randy replied, "Just like the flowers, uh, the bridal registry, the plates, the forks." Thus attention to the artifacts used in the wedding may still be perceived as falling within the domestic (i.e., "feminine") sphere of existence. Of course, this is very closely tied to the sociological underpinnings of the first reason discussed, that of the wedding being "for the bride."

The third reason brides and grooms may have completely different attitudes toward artifacts may stem from the issues of power and control that are tied to the source of money for the wedding. In most traditional weddings, the bride's parents pay for the majority of purchases, with few exceptions. Several of the brides and grooms mentioned they were following this tradition. This situation has many implications for the planning of the wedding—specifically, who has the authority to make decisions and who takes on the task of wedding planning. Indeed, in the "traditional" system of payment, the bride and her mother usually exert most of the control and bear most of the burden of wedding planning. Yet our findings indicate that even when the bride's family was paying, some grooms implied they would object if they felt certain aspects of the wedding were unacceptable. For example, Randy stated, "If she told me something and I didn't like it, I'd put my foot down."

In summary, it appears that the three major reasons our brides and grooms differed when discussing important artifacts all center on the types of gender roles being expressed. In other words, the traditional wedding focuses on the bride, with funding by the bride's family and limited participation by the groom in terms of the actual planning. Yet, in addition to this relatively traditional approach to weddings, there were several couples who were trying to create more contemporary weddings, in terms of the gender roles expressed. Often, these couples were either helping to pay for the wedding or paying for it entirely, although this was not always the case.

What differentiated these couples' weddings from the more traditional ones was the degree to which the bride and groom shared in the planning. And, interestingly, the more they shared in the planning, the more they agreed on which artifacts were sacred to them. In other words, the gender roles expressed by the couple seemed to be the strongest determinants of how they approached this significant rite of passage. To illustrate these differing approaches to wedding planning, we offer two case studies of couples—all of whom participated in the separate-gender focus groups—who adopted two different approaches to the planning of their weddings.

CASE STUDY 1:
TRADITIONAL GENDER ROLES—STAN AND KIM

Stan and Kim, a couple in their early 20s, had been dating for one and a half years. Kim had recently completed an undergraduate degree at the university, and was a public relations representative in a large city. Stan was completing his senior year in the undergraduate advertising curriculum at the university. Their wedding was to be held in Kim's hometown, in a Lutheran church that she had attended all of her life

(Stan was also Lutheran). Both described their wedding as very traditional. Kim and Stan represented the type of couple whose wedding was being paid for by the bride's parents, and Kim and her mother were responsible for the majority of the wedding planning. Because of this, Kim recognized that Stan had been left out of the planning process:

> I grew up with my church. I know what works, what is too much, what looks kind of silly over there. . . . He feels a little left out now but I keep telling him that, you know, I know what can work and he says, "Well maybe this," and I say, "No, that won't work."

Interestingly, she went on to explain that even though Stan didn't really know much about wedding details, he did have some influence:

> He basically is clueless when it comes to these kinds of things. And he'd have more to say about if it were his family who's paying for it, but since it's my family he said that it's basically up to us. Of course he will, you know, put limits on what we do, but it's my mother and my best friend that are helping me.

In a grooms' focus group, Stan noted that he basically saw things the same way:

> She has more interest in how it goes and everything. I mean I'll say if I don't like this or I don't like that. And I'll probably pick out the tux myself. Y'know, at the end, I'll just approve everything. . . . For me, it's more her wedding . . . um, she's really into the details. . . . I just see myself as making sure everything is cool. And, I mean, if I see something really idiotic or stupid, I'll say something. But that's the only way I'll feel left out of the process, if they go ahead and do something that's really goofy.

As a result of this traditional approach, Stan and Kim differed greatly in terms of the artifacts that were of importance to them. Kim's most sacred artifact was her wedding dress. In fact, her mother had told her that the family wanted to concentrate on Kim being the center of attention:

> People have already talked about my wedding since I was like 5 . . . and my mom said, "Oh, you're gonna have the most beautiful gown and price is not an object." . . . And so that's—I just keep imagining like everyone glowing—staring at us, you know, or just smiling at me. But it's basically she just said, "I want you to be the most beautiful bride they've ever seen."

On the other hand, Stan (like many grooms) stated that the only material items that concerned him were good music and food at the reception, and photographs.

Another factor that contributed to Stan and Kim's traditional approach to wedding planning appeared to be Kim's greater experience with weddings. Stan observed that Kim "went to a lot of weddings, growing up, and I've been to like two in my life. . . . So I really don't have a good picture of what it should be like." Kim's interest in, and expertise, regarding the wedding was also evident in Stan's comment that "we were going out six months and she was already buying brides' magazines and saying, 'This is what the best man has to buy. This is what the groom has to do.' "

Thus the traditional gender roles being expressed by Kim and Stan seemed to be reinforced by a number of factors: the desire of Kim's mother for the wedding to be "Kim's day," Stan's neutrality toward many decisions, Kim's expertise, and, perhaps, the cues Kim had acquired through the media.

CASE STUDY 2:
MODERN GENDER ROLES—JIM AND HEATHER

Jim and Heather were a couple in their mid-20s. Both were enrolled in graduate programs at the university—she in plant science and he in biochemistry. They had lived together for five years, and Jim remarked that he was not convinced of the value of marriage until about five months prior to their engagement. Their wedding was to be held at a historical museum in the city where they attended college. For this reason, they described their wedding as more modern than traditional. Indeed, the only traditional touch, in their collective opinion, was the fact that they would be wearing wedding attire that had been worn by Jim's parents, including the "white dress."

The couple was basically responsible for creating their own ceremony, despite "traditional" funding by Heather's parents. Jim explained:

> Heather and I are basically doing everything ourselves. Her parents are in Chicago and they've been completely hands-off. Even Heather's parents are paying for it, and that's unusual, they, I didn't want them to really have that much input. . . . They're happy that we're doing it all ourselves. . . . We're trying to keep it simple. There's only a few things we're paying

attention to. And, uh, we're not going through a lot of the traditional steps that you go through. Um, so since it's just Heather and I to negotiate who does what, it's been pretty democratic.

In the bride's focus group, Heather agreed:

Jim and I are doing most of the planning. And the parents have taken all of this into consideration, so they're impressed that we're taking on some of the responsibility. . . . We wanted to have control over the process.

Furthermore, when asked what her vision had been for her wedding, Heather indicated that she and Jim had created their vision together:

Yeah, my vision. I don't think I really had one before Jim and I started talking about marriage. And we wanted something small, with just close friends and family . . . and, um, we never envisioned a church wedding, so we're having the wedding and reception in the same place. It'll just be like a party.

Although Jim and Heather could be described as a couple who were not truly materialistic in nature, they nevertheless regarded the same wedding artifacts as important, unlike Stan and Kim. For example, Jim noted that he enjoyed working on the design of their rings, and Heather stated that she thought the ring was important because "we kind of designed it ourselves." Furthermore, both considered the location of their wedding to be important. Finally, Jim mentioned that he was pleased Heather was wearing the wedding dress worn by his mother, and Heather related the following:

I felt something really positive when we were joking with Jim's parents about a wedding dress and the groom's outfit, and they pulled them out of the closet and we showed a lot of preference toward them, and we tried them on and they fit.

These findings suggest that when brides and grooms plan their weddings together, they place similar values on artifacts, rather than emphasizing different aspects as important. Furthermore, Jim and Heather's case illustrates that even though Heather's parents were paying for the wedding, it may be the attitudes of the bride and groom toward gender roles in general that affect the gender roles enacted in planning a wedding, rather than the attitudes of those footing the bill. Although these gender roles can be challenged by other members of the family, and often are, the fact that Heather's mother had given the couple free rein in planning their wedding helped reinforce the roles Heather and Jim wished to enact.

Summary and Implications

This study is unique in its comparison of the emphases that brides and grooms place on artifacts selected for use in their weddings and receptions. Our findings indicate that the brides participating in our focus groups had no difficulty describing artifacts that were important to them. For instance, the brides typically described their wedding dresses and related accessories, the minister, the church, music, decorations, photographs, and rings as important. In addition, the ways in which these artifacts attained sacred status varied greatly.

In contrast, grooms had greater difficulty naming items they believed were important, and those items they did mention tended to be related to the reception (food, drink, and the reception hall) or were photographs. And, as opposed to the brides' artifacts, these items attained sacred status mainly because of their communicative power (and to a limited extent because they were attained through hierophany).

Furthermore, our case studies suggest that the emergence of traditional or modern gender roles in wedding planning is partially determined by the attitudes of the bride and groom toward these roles. In addition, other factors, such as parental interest in control over the wedding and the bride's prior experience with weddings, are also salient in determining the types of gender roles that will be portrayed.

We believe this study has several implications for researchers interested in wedding planning in particular, and ritualistic consumption in general. For example, even though we observed more participation by grooms than we anticipated, the tasks involved in wedding planning still seem to be divided by gender to some extent. This is consistent with findings of gendered participation in other consumption rituals (Fischer & Arnold, 1990; Sherry & McGrath, 1989).

To gain a greater understanding of the dynamics of the wedding ritual, it is important to examine how men and women are socialized into their respective gender roles. Such knowledge could be acquired by exploring attitudes toward weddings among younger respondents, to determine how children and adolescents perceive the roles in wedding planning to evolve. This would provide researchers interested in wedding-related consumption with greater insights into the roots of the gender differences that have been reported here.

From a broader perspective, it is important to examine whether gendered participation in rituals is static or dynamic. In other words, it is possible that men's roles in creating rituals may change in American culture given increases in single-parent families and nontraditional households. For example, although men generally participate in rituals to a lesser extent than women, will the rise of households headed by single men contribute to an increased level of participation in rituals by single fathers? Single or working mothers, on the other hand, may decrease ritualistic participation from levels demonstrated by stay-at-home mothers. Perhaps rituals will become less important in this culture as a result of these demographic trends. Alternatively, as gender roles evolve, the patterns of ritualistic consumption may become more complex.

We have explored in this chapter the extent to which gender differences exist in the selection of significant artifacts for one of the most salient American consumption rituals, the wedding. We believe that exploring the issue of male and female participation in this occasion—as well as how gender roles may affect participation in other rituals—would contribute greatly to our understanding of consumer rituals in American culture.

References

Barker, D. L. (1978). A proper wedding. In M. Corbin (Ed.), *The couple* (pp. 56-77). New York: Penguin.

Belk, R. W. (1989). Materialism and the modern U.S. Christmas. In E. C. Hirschman (Ed.), *Interpretive consumer research*. Provo, UT: Association for Consumer Research.

Belk, R. W., Wallendorf, M., & Sherry, J. F. (1989). The sacred and the profane in consumer behavior: Theodicy on the odyssey. *Journal of Consumer Research, 16,* 1-38.

Caplow, T. (1982). Christmas gifts and kin networks. *American Sociological Review, 47,* 383-392.

Casparis, J. (1979). The bridal shower: An American rite of passage. *Indian Journal of Social Research, 20*(1), 11-21.

Chapman, F. (1993, May 18). Cost of average wedding now up to mere $19,000. *Champaign-Urbana News Gazette,* p. T-7.

Cheal, D. (1987). Showing them you love them: Gift-giving and the dialectic of intimacy. *Sociological Review, 35,* 150-169.

Cheal, D. (1988). Relationships in time: Ritual, social structure, and the life course. In N. K. Denzin (Ed.), *Studies in symbolic interaction* (pp. 83-109). Greenwich, CT: JAI.

Fischer, E., & Arnold, S. F. (1990). More than a labor of love: Gender roles and Christmas gift shopping. *Journal of Consumer Research, 17,* 333-345.

Gilbert, E. (1983). *The complete wedding planner: A practical guide for the bride and groom.* New York: Frederick Fell.

Glick, P. (1982). Marriage, divorce, and living arrangements: Prospective changes. *Journal of Family Issues, 5,* 7-26.

Greenblat, C. S., & Cottle, T. J. (1980). *Getting married.* New York: McGraw-Hill.

Hirschman, E. C., & Holbrook, M. B. (1992). *Postmodern consumer research: The study of consumption as text.* Newbury Park, CA: Sage.

Hirschman, E. C., & LaBarbera, P. (1989). The meaning of Christmas. In E. C. Hirschman (Ed.), *Interpretive consumer research* (pp. 136-147). Provo, UT: Association for Consumer Research.

Kendall, L. (1989). A noisy and bothersome new custom: Delivering a gift box to a Korean bride. *Journal of Ritual Studies, 3,* 185-202.

Krueger, R. A. (1988). *Focus groups: A practical guide for applied research.* Newbury Park, CA: Sage.

McGrath, M. A. (1993, February). *Communal exchange in the context of intergenerational giving of wedding gifts.* Paper presented at the American Marketing Association Winter Educators' Conference, Newport Beach, CA.

McGrath, M. A., & Otnes, C. (1993, June). *Children's understanding of birthday parties: A study of gender differences.* Paper presented at the Second Conference on Gender and Consumer Behavior, Salt Lake City.

Morgan, D. L. (1988). *Focus groups as qualitative research.* Newbury Park, CA: Sage.

Otnes, C., Kim, K., & Kim, Y. C. (in press). Yes, Virginia, there is a gender difference: Analyzing children's requests to Santa Claus. *Journal of Popular Culture.*

Otnes, C., & Lowrey, T. M. (1993). 'Til debt do us part: The selection and meaning of artifacts in the American wedding. In L. McAlister & M. L. Rothschild (Eds.), *Advances in consumer research* (Vol. 20, pp. 325-329). Provo, UT: Association for Consumer Research.

Otnes, C., Lowrey, T. M., & Kim, Y. C. (1993, September). Gift selection for "easy" and "difficult" recipients: A social roles interpretation. *Journal of Consumer Research, 20,* 229-244.

Otnes, C., Ruth, J. M., & Milbourne, C. C. (1993, February). *I like you, I like me: The influence of gender, romantic involvement and self-acceptance on Valentine's Day exchange.* Paper presented at the American Marketing Association Winter Educators' Conference, Newport Beach, CA.

Rook, D. (1985). The ritual dimension of consumer behavior. *Journal of Consumer Research, 12,* 252-264.

Sherry, J. F., Jr., & McGrath, M. A. (1989). Unpacking the holiday presence: A comparative ethnography of two gift stores. In E. C. Hirschman (Ed.), *Interpretive consumer research* (pp. 148-167). Provo, UT: Association for Consumer Research.

van Gennep, A. (1960). *The rites of passage.* Chicago: University of Chicago Press.

Wallendorf, M., & Arnould, E. (1991). We gather together: Consumption rituals of Thanksgiving Day. *Journal of Consumer Research, 18,* 13-31.

Wallendorf, M., & Belk, R. W. (1989). Assessing trustworthiness in naturalistic consumer research. In E. C. Hirschman (Ed.), *Interpretive consumer research* (pp. 69-84). Provo, UT: Association for Consumer Research.

Wilson, M. (1972). The wedding cakes: A study of ritual change. In J. S. LaFontaine (Ed.), *The interpretation of ritual*. London: Tavistock.

Wolfinbarger, M. F., & Gilly, M. C. (1991). The relationship of gender to gift-giving attitudes (or, Are men insensitive clods?). In J. A. Costa (Ed.), *Gender and consumer behavior* (pp. 223-233). Salt Lake City: University of Utah Printing Service.

10

Gender Dimensions of the Alphabetic Characters With Implications for Branding

TERESA M. PAVIA

JANEEN ARNOLD COSTA

ALTHOUGH some may claim that "a rose by any other name would smell as sweet," there is substantial research that suggests that listeners and readers endow certain words with meanings that extend beyond the words' literal definitions. Research in this field, referred to as phonetic symbolism, has generally investigated inferences that people make based on the sounds or appearances of nonsense words. One of the essential qualities of a word or a sound that informants appear to use for their evaluation is visual or aural sharpness, harshness, or percussiveness. In more general settings, qualities of angularity, sharpness, roundedness, and softness have been associated with gender. However, very few phonetic symbolism studies have focused on the degree to which certain words are perceived as masculine or feminine beyond their literal meanings. The meaning a word may have beyond its literal definition is often referred to as its *excess meaning.*

184

The excess gender symbolism that words may have is one of the gaps in the broad array of topics covered by existing research. A second area that has not received adequate research is the excess meaning the letters of the alphabet themselves may have. This second area is important because a number of brand names now use letters or sequences of letters that are not rightfully words, for example, J-H-L fragrance and WD-40. Previous research has shown that consumers do infer qualities about a product based solely on its brand name. Consequently, in this chapter we will focus on two questions: Do individuals endow the letters of the alphabet with excess meaning or dimensions of gender? And if consumers do endow letters of the alphabet with excess meaning or gender dimensions, do nonword sequences of letters in a brand name for a product influence consumer beliefs about the product?

The Gender Dichotomy

The dualism that is used within American culture to endow concepts with gender distinctions is widespread. The home is classically the female's domain, and outside the home is the male's domain (Sanday, 1981; Schneider, 1968). Reason, rationality, science, and individual goals are frequently associated with masculinity, whereas passion, intuition, nature, and communal goals are frequently associated with femininity (Easlea, 1986; Keller, 1983; Meyers-Levy, 1988; Weinreich-Haste, 1986). Further dimensions of gender duality may be found in one of the instruments used to ascertain the level of sex typing an individual exhibits, the Bem Sex Role Inventory (BSRI). Among the 20 personality characteristics the BSRI classifies as masculine are aggressive, analytical, competitive, *forceful,* independent, individualistic, self-reliant, and self-sufficient; among the feminine personality traits are cheerful, childlike, *does not use harsh language, gentle, soft-spoken,* sympathetic, understanding, warm, and yielding (Bem, 1974; emphasis added).

Angularity, sharpness, and minimalist design are also considered masculine characteristics, whereas roundness, softness, and refined design are seen as more feminine. These classifications appear to hold true whether perceived in product packaging (Schmitt, Leclerc, & Dube-Rioux, 1988) or in plain geometric figures. To test the gender associations of geometric figures, cross-cultural researchers have asked respondents to identify stick figures with round and square heads as

either male or female. The round-headed figure was generally designated the female and the square-headed figure the male (Davis, 1961).
One explanation of this came from Black Elk, an Oglala Sioux elder, who
observed that "nearly all the straight lines we see around us are human
artifacts put there by human labor" (in Ascher & Ascher, 1986, p. 133),
and that the elements of nature, the sky, the sun, the seasons, even the
whirls of the wind, are circular. The associations of masculinity with
construction and domination of nature (Easlea, 1986) and femininity
with reproduction and the cycles of nature (Sanday, 1981) are consistent
with the associations of masculinity with angularity and femininity
with roundness.

Phonetic Symbolism

Although elements of gender duality can be used to characterize
qualities of words, as a rule, research in phonetic symbolism has focused on size, angularity, movement, pleasantness, and warmth, without any attempt to explore their gender associations. Early studies of
phonetic symbolism found that certain vowels and consonants sound
"bigger" than others and when used in a nonsense word are interpreted
by the majority of respondents as referring to large objects (Dogana,
1967; Sapir, 1929). For example, respondents were asked to match
nonsense words such as *kas* and *kis* or *mal* and *mil* with various items of
different sizes. The words with the *a* sound were consistently associated
with large objects, and the words with *i* sounds were associated with
small objects (Sapir, 1929; Tarte & Barritt, 1971). Further studies attempted to eliminate sources of bias such as pronunciation bias by
asking respondents to select the one of two opposing geometric figures
(e.g., large versus small or rounded versus angular) that fit best with
pure tones of varying frequencies. Generally, high tones were associated with angular shapes and low tones were associated with rounded
shapes in English speakers (O'Boyle & Tarte, 1980). In another study,
speakers of Swahili and English associated the more percussive, sharper-
sounding word, *takete,* with an angular geometric figure and the more
flowing word, *uloomu,* with a rounded geometric figure (Davis, 1961).

In a study of speakers of English, Japanese, Korean, and Tamil, Taylor
(1963) demonstrated that informants within a particular language consistently associated certain sounds with certain meanings, but that the

same sounds may have different meanings from language to language. For example, English speakers generally ranked G (as in *gate*) and K as big sounds and T and N as small sounds, whereas Korean speakers classified T and P as big sounds and J and M as small sounds. Taylor hypothesized that individuals learn to associate certain sounds with certain concepts when a language such as English uses a sound such as G more frequently for words that mean very big (grand, gross, grow) than for words that mean very small (grain).

Phonetic Symbolism and Brand Names

Investigators have asked if the sound of a brand name influences consumer perception of the product with that name. Vanden Bergh (1982) and Vanden Bergh, Collins, Schultz, and Alder (1984) found that nonsense names beginning with a plosive consonant such as C, D, G (hard), K, P, or T stimulate higher recall and higher recognition than names that do not begin with a plosive. Schloss (1981) calculated that among the first letters of the top 200 brand names in 1979, the letters C, M, P, S, A, T, B, and K appeared with greater frequency than one would expect from a random selection from the dictionary. And Heath, Chatterjee, and France (1990) found that as the consonant hardness and vowel pitch increased in hypothetical brand names for toilet paper and household cleaners, so did consumer perception of the harshness of the product. Together these studies suggest that harsher or more percussive brand names may have an intrinsic advantage for recall and recognition. However, if consumers transfer qualities of harshness from the brand name to the product, a harsh brand name will be an asset only if strength and harshness are positive qualities in the product, such as an industrial cleanser. A transfer of harshness could be a liability for a product such as baby powder. This suggests that certain words may be appropriate or inappropriate brand names for specific products.

To investigate this question, researchers have asked if there is something in a word that makes the name just seem "right" to consumers as the brand name for a product. Peterson and Ross (1972) asked consumers to rate the appropriateness of various nonsense words for the brand name of a breakfast cereal and the brand name of a detergent. Although they did not investigate which aspects of a word seemed "right" for a given product class, they did find that consumers consistently identified certain words, such as Whumies, with breakfast cereals and other words, such as Dehax, with detergents. Other researchers have demonstrated similar results in the product categories of aluminum foil (Chisnall, 1974), ice cream, and cameras (Zinkhan & Martin, 1987). Respondents have also indicated that certain brand names have personality traits; for example, Hofmeister lager was reported to be "cheeky" and Carlsberg lager was "hardworking" (Alt & Griggs, 1988), suggesting that the dimensions of excess meaning may be extensive and complex.

In our own work, we have studied the inferences that consumers draw from brand names that contain numbers, such as Formula 409 and Product 19 (Pavia & Costa, 1993). Our informants also indicated that certain names were appropriate for certain products and not for others. However, they indicated as well that the strong gender dimensions that numbers, math, and science have in American society extend to the use of numbers in brand names. Brand names with numbers in them were generally considered technical, complex, formulated, and masculine, but these qualities could be reduced if the brand name included a familiar sibilant word (such as Chanel) or if the name was written in flowing script.

With the exception of our study, none of the studies relating phonetic symbolism to brand names has specifically investigated dimensions of gender. However, it is clear that consumers infer certain product qualities based on the brand name (see also Holbrook, 1981), particularly when it is difficult for the consumer to evaluate intrinsic attributes of the product (Mazursky & Jacoby, 1985). Further, consumers use qualities that have strong gender associations, such as harshness, angularity, roundness, and softness, as cues for brand attributes. Consumers also indicate that certain words seem more appropriate as brand names for particular products and for particular geometric shapes. Geometric shapes, in turn, have been associated with gender.

This raises some interesting questions that we shall attempt to explore here. Do the letters of the alphabet have excess meaning, personalities, or dimensions of gender? Can the excess meaning, if it exists, be related to attributes that have been identified in other studies, such as angularity and aural harshness? And does the excess meaning, if it exists, influence consumers' beliefs about products that use nonword sequences of letters in their brand names?

Methods

The research reported here was part of a larger project investigating the excess meaning that consumers associate with brand names containing sequences of letters and numbers. The research questions were characterized by their openness, the direction the informants' answers would lead was unknown, and the methodologies or instruments previously applied to related issues were inappropriate. Consequently, it was not possible or appropriate to define the hypotheses and specific methodologies that would address those hypotheses prior to data collection. Other researchers facing similar problems have used emergent design successfully (Belk, Wallendorf, & Sherry, 1989; Costa & Belk, 1990; McCracken, 1989; Sherry, 1990; Sherry & McGrath, 1989). The approach used in their studies guided the work reported here.

In brief, the course and methods of research were as follows:

1. Nonreactive research involved a literature search for relevant studies, with particular emphasis on the dimension of gender.
2. Initial qualitative in-depth interviews were conducted with adults and children of both genders to elaborate and clarify further dimensions of the research questions.
3. A further literature search was conducted to identify and analyze relevant studies on brand name perception.
4. Eight focus groups were conducted to probe notions about brand names and the perceived appropriateness or inappropriateness of brand names for various products. The focus group informants were students in an evening course in introductory marketing at a state university. The focus groups contained 6 to 10 individuals each.
5. Open-ended questionnaires were administered to 44 MBA students. Participants were presented with nonword sequences of letters identified as brand names of fragrances and were asked to identify the target market and appropriate position for the fragrance with the given brand name.

Although it has been suggested that informant selection for focus groups should emphasize homogeneity as much as possible (Bellenger, Bernhardt, & Goldstrucker, 1989; Levy, 1979), we deliberately constructed the focus groups to include both genders in order to stimulate discussion and represent divergent perspectives, as advocated by Bessell (1971), Kelman and Lerner (1952), Peterson (1975), Smith (1954), and

Tynan and Drayton (1989). Most participants were between 20 and 35 years old and had similar socioeconomic backgrounds.

An open-ended interviewing technique was employed in which further information from informants was elicited primarily through exact repetition of the informant's previous few words in an inquisitive tone. That is, if the informant stated, "The dog ran after the bone," the researcher inquired, "After the bone?" Although the moderators were guided by the agenda of issues to be discussed, appropriate moderating techniques were used to avoid leading questions. Alternative ways of asking questions and probing were also used (Douglas, 1985), and discussion between the two moderators following each focus group reduced bias through investigator triangulation.

This research proceeded from the assertion that "man is an animal suspended in webs of significance he himself has spun" (Geertz, 1973, p. 5). The webs of significance form the structure of an individual's culture and are the shared understandings, attitudes, beliefs, and meanings that the individual experiences. However, a large portion of the culturally shared meanings and symbols lie outside the "objective awareness of members of a given society" (Barrett, 1984, p. 135). Focus groups allow such unexpressed, underlying, culture-based perceptions to be explored. The discussions in the focus groups probed for feelings and attitudes rather than attempting to identify the informants' underlying cognitive processes leading to particular responses. Consequently, the focus groups' texts reflect the informants' shared cultural beliefs about the various research issues.

Drawing from the results that emerged in the focus group data, we selected a list of four hypothetical and three actual fragrance brand names. Told only that fragrances may be targeted to either men or women and to either adults or children, participants were presented with the hypothetical and actual brand names as brand names of fragrances. For each brand name, participants were asked if they were familiar with the brand of fragrance. Those participants who professed no prior awareness of a brand name were asked to identify the target market for the fragrance and to provide a brief description of how the product should be positioned. The informants in this part of the research had not been exposed to the themes from the focus groups, nor had they participated in the focus groups. Each informant completed the task independent of the other participants. The findings from this exercise expanded the focus group data.

As part of emergent design, both relevant and irrelevant dimensions of a phenomenon are identified. In our study, the sequence of research activities outlined above consistently produced the same themes in phonetic symbolism and brand name perception. Recognizing the salience of these factors, we focused the remainder of our research program on investigating these themes in greater depth. However, we maintained openness in both our research formats and ongoing analyses, and alternative explanations emerged and were explored. Thus, as suggested by Kidder (1981), we used both persistent observation and negative case analysis. We also used peer debriefing and member checks at various points in the research process. In addition, to provide a database available to other researchers for analysis, we audiotaped the initial in-depth interviews and the focus groups.

The data obtained through the focus groups and questionnaires were extremely consistent. Closure is achieved in naturalistic inquiry when, through purposive sampling, redundancy occurs (Lincoln & Guba, 1985). The repetitiveness of the data suggested that "closure" had been achieved and that the data could be effectively analyzed.

The Five Salient Attributes of Alphabetic Characters

The focus group informants affirmed the importance of the aural and visual qualities of the alphabetic characters. Consistent with earlier studies, harsh sound and angular appearance were attributes associated with masculinity. Letters that sounded softer or appeared more rounded were deemed to be more feminine. However, the informants identified three other attributes of alphabetic characters that were not explicitly recognized in earlier works. The first of these is associated with aural harshness and is the degree to which a speaker can draw out the pronunciation of a letter. The second newly identified attribute is the letter's placement in the 26-character alphabetic string. The third is the frequency with which the letter is used in the English language. No one attribute is sufficient to identify a letter's excess meaning or gender dimension. Instead, the five attributes appeared to mix together in informants' minds to provide composite assessments. All five of these attributes of letters will be discussed below, with most emphasis placed on the three newly identified features.

With regard to aural distinctions, informants contrasted descriptors such as *smooth, soft,* and *subtle* with *hard* and *harsh.* Aurally harsh, blunt, or hard letters, such as X, T, and K, were believed to be emphatic, powerful, and masculine. In contrast, softer-sounding letters or phonemes such as H, CH, Q, and S were perceived as weak and more feminine. Vowels, in general, were also found to be softer, more open, weaker, and feminine.

According to the informants, the aural softness or harshness of letters is often, but not always, reinforced by visual appearance. In many cases the visual appearance of a letter appeared to be secondary to its auditory impact in determining the letter's gender associations. For example, H is completely angular, yet it is perceived as much weaker and more feminine than the angular letter X. The visual appearance of a letter cannot be discounted, however, because even harsh-sounding letters can be perceived as more feminine if they are written in flowing script. For example, in discussing an advertisement for the product Special K, focus group participants had this exchange:[1]

FG5

M: Well, what's the new Kellogg's product where they have the large K, and they show the woman in the bathing suit? [This is an ad for the product.]

F: Special K.

M: And she ends up in the shape of the K [in the commercial], and they change [her] into the word [for the product] itself. Is K feminine?

F: It doesn't sound feminine.

M: But I think, too, it comes back again to the way they've written it.

M: It's not a block K, it's a big scrolly K.

M: And I think that maybe it [Special K] started out having more masculine appeal, and they wanted to change its image.

The aural harshness and visual angularity dimensions are influenced by the speed with which a speaker can say a letter. For example, in saying the letter S, one may draw out the sound in a hissing manner, whereas the letter X is usually said quickly. Informants associated speed with masculinity, forming complex connections among harshness, bluntness, and quickness. Softer, rounder, more drawn-out sounds were feminine, romantic, and, according to one male informant, wimpy. The quality of speed was often extended to products whose brand names are spoken quickly. For example, because X is said quickly and sounds "fast" it would be appropriate in the brand name for a product that goes fast. On the other hand, W takes a comparatively long time to say and was deemed bulky and industrial, a poor choice for inclusion in the brand name of a sports car. The letter W has the additional liability of being perceived aurally as a vowel because it sounds like "double U":

FG1

M: Now we have a 280 Z. So now we want to show something that's flashy, we're going to put something like that in there or an XT that sounds really fast or something.

F: And an AW wouldn't really . . . it's softer vowels.

FG7

M: Yeah, X marks the spot, like a Z, it's hard, instead of an S, where it flows.

M: Yeah, they're hard sounds too [X and Z], both of them, you know? Like X is a hard sound and Z is a hard sound.

F: Yeah, they're masculine, firm letters.

F: . . . I've been thinking about the difference between the letters that I thought were feminine and the letters that I thought were masculine, and it seems like the similarities and differences are in the sounds. P, T, X, Z, B [the masculine letters], they're consonants, and they're sharp consonants. Where [the feminine ones] A, H, G, M, N, mmmmmmm, hhhhhuh, aaaaah are much softer sounding than kuh, tuh, puh.

FG6

M: Yeah, if we are going to compare letters, N is masculine, M is feminine.

M: I think M, the way you say M, it ends, I don't know, I think it ends on more of a lower, a lower sound, so maybe . . .

F: I think M flows longer, and N just stops.

FG8

M: When you say XY or XZ, they kind of go fast, especially for a sports car, it kind of makes it seem like it's a fast car. That's not like Q.

The speed with which one says a letter was frequently related to the letter's placement in the alphabetic string. Letters at the beginning of the alphabet have a different meaning from those at the end, with the alphabet progressing in complexity from beginning to end. In some cases, attitudes toward various letters were traced to the experience of learning the alphabet. The beginning part of the alphabet is easy for children to learn, and these letters (A, B, and C) are said more slowly, are more basic and simple. The informants believed that saying the alphabet gets tedious somewhere around the middle (M and N) and is difficult to learn at the end (from R onward). Consequently, letters that appear earlier in the alphabet are more basic and simple, are said more slowly, and are potentially more feminine. Letters in the middle are boring or vague, and letters at the end are powerful, dangerous, hard, and potentially more masculine.

FG3

M: More sophistication for R, S, and T, nearer the end.
M: Simplicity seems to be at the beginning, maybe because as the child goes along and you can get the first part and by the time you get clear to the end, you've gone through everything. It's deep.

FG8

M: It seems to me like, at the end of the alphabet, it seems like everybody wants to hurry and get to the end of the alphabet, and then like Z and X, you really whiz through those.

FG1

F: I think you also connote [sic] that [a brand name like ABC1] with something feminine because women and children are a lot of times grouped together. But usually we think of people, when they're thinking of marketing strategies and they're trying to gear toward children, like you said, they use ABC or 123 or stuff like that. And maybe gear toward women too.

Generally, letters that are less frequently used in the English language were believed to have a "unique" quality, especially the masculine letters X and Z. The letter Q was often grouped together with X and Z as a unique letter, although it evokes different feelings. Q is unusual, feminine, somewhat scientific and technical; it does not have the same feeling of speed, power, or masculinity that X and Z have. Although Y is at the end of the alphabet, it is used more frequently in our language and it has a homonym that is an extremely common word—*why*. Letters that were believed to be common were A, B, N, T, L, and the other vowels:

FG3

M: Actually with letters, also if you use a letter that's not commonly used, it also tends to stick a little longer, like if you use a Q, or an X or a Z versus something like an A that's everywhere.

FG6

F: . . . Maybe 'cause they're unusual [X and Z] and that's what their product is, unusual, they have something, you know, out of the ordinary. You don't use Z and X in every single word you write, like you do A's and B's.

FG2

F: Which is why I think the X and Z are kind of unique letters so they're put on cars or something to show that they stand out.
M: . . . Q seems scientific to me.
F: . . . You have to think harder at Q.
M: Like what about M and N. Those are boring.

Finally, when attempting to describe why a certain letter had particular qualities, the informants repeatedly used words beginning with the letter to describe the letter. This lends support to the hypothesis that speakers associate specific sounds with the concepts that the sound is used to articulate. For example, in discussing the letters S and X, informants had these comments (italics added):

FG7

M: I don't think of R as a *soft* thing, like s, *say* s.
F: . . . I think it may even be the form of the letters, the *shape* of the letters.

M: It's more *shapes* than angles.

M: Because of the *shape* and the way it *sounds*, the words say *sensual*, *sexy* [all of this said in a smooth, low voice].

FG8

F: I see that [X] a lot on cars, and it sounds like *sex*.

F: . . . And it could have something to do with when they refer to all the *extras* on a car, or when they talk about *deluxe* models, that they all have kind of an X.

Combinations of Letters

The focus group informants also suggested that when letters with opposing attributes are combined, the combination cancels the individual features. Thus if the feminine letter R, which "signifies softness and comfort" (FG7, M), is combined with the masculine letter X, "The X and the R seem to cancel each other outright" (FG7, M). These opposing characteristics, with their underlying meanings, can signal to the consumer that he or she is purchasing a "well-rounded" product:

FG7

M: . . . That product [Mazda RX7] has two functions; rather than just jet speed, it's got, you know, it's comfortable and pleasurable to be in.

In the following exchange, the informants became engrossed in the idea that letters can express distinct, perhaps human, qualities. Again, synergy is created through the combination of two opposing letters:

FG7

M: . . . If I were going to give G a personality, it would be very shy in the corner, not being noticed.

M: But as soon as you put it with a T, it completely changes. [general agreement]

M: Does GT all of a sudden become more strong than just plain T?

M: Well, T is pretty strong; G isn't. But [GT is] a lot stronger than G.

M: . . . But does the G even add anything to the T?

M: Maybe it tempers it, maybe it softens it a little bit. T is pretty harsh by itself.

Additional Gender Associations of A and X

Although not specifically delineated by the informants, the gender dichotomy also underlies the occasional use of A to denote superiority and X to denote quality and power. A is a relatively less sophisticated, simple letter, and one that is learned early in childhood. In school, a dominant part of childhood and young adulthood, A is a mark of success and X is a mark of failure. The informants felt brand names using an A were often items associated with food preparation, a traditional female task. The number most commonly associated with A is 1, the lowest nonnegative number. In general, the letter A, which was deemed feminine, is a symbol for quality in the sense of excellence and superior grading:

FG4

M: A is more subtle and has to do with the level of quality. You can associate, like A coming first, you are stressing quality as a major feature of this item.

In contrast, brand names with an X are usually constructed by combining X, perhaps some other letters, and a large number. In these instances, X is sharp, harsh, technical, and fast. By the time a child learns X and Z, learning the alphabet is no longer "fun." It is now serious business, and the child realizes that the alphabet is used to make words, to *do* things. The informants associated X with fabricated, complex, powerful products. The masculine letter X is also a symbol for quality in the sense of "more is better." That is, when high quality means high performance, superior speed, or more technology, then X is an appropriate indicator of quality:

FG3

M: I wouldn't want produce marked with an X.
F: I wouldn't want my milk to be unique, I'd want it to be the same.

M: . . . That kind of thing you'd want something that's graded A. 'Cause that means, when you're grading something, that means that's quality, whereas X, that's something that's at the bottom of the line. Unless you come to cars, when X means . . .

M: We're brought up in a school system where the grading system is A to F. A being the best, F being the worst.

FG3

Moderator: If you didn't know anything particularly about the computer systems, how would you rank the IBM PC, the AT model and the XT model. Assuming that you didn't know anything about them, which one would you assume would be the more sophisticated?

M: The XT.

M: XT.

M: That isn't the case, though, is it?

Brand Names for Fragrances

The brand names of fragrances were selected for the following exercise in part because of the approximately 800 fragrances marketed in the United States in 1990, there were 13 fragrances with nonword alphabetic brand names. Many of the 13 potential candidates had additional consumer cues, such as Mr. J, Mr. K, and O de Lancôme. The three real nonword alphabetic brand names that were selected for this part of the study were KL, MCM, and Y. Because the focus groups indicated that combinations of letters may have aggregate meaning, the names K, L, M, and C were also of interest. Consequently, two questionnaires were developed. The first presented the respondent with the brand names K, L, Y, and MCM. Two of these were actual brand names (Y and MCM) and two were components of actual brand names (K and L). The second questionnaire used the brand names M, C, Y, and KL. Again, two names were real (KL and Y) and two were components (M and C). Each time a fragrance brand name was presented, the respondent was asked if he or she was familiar with the particular brand. All brands were unknown to all of the respondents. A total of 21 participants received the first questionnaire and 23 received the second.

A general classification of the target market and positioning that each of the brand names evoked in the respondents is shown in Table 10.1.

TABLE 10.1 Perceived Target Markets/Positions for Fragrances With Various Brand Names

| | Target Market/Production Position | | | | |
| | Male | | Female | | |
Brand Name	Mid to High End	Low End	Mid to High End	Low End	Other
K	7	6	1	7	1 children's low end
L	0	1	16	1	1 unisex low end
					1 unisex high end
					1 children's low end
KL	5	4	9	2	1 children's shampoo
					1 girl's starter perfume
M	18	2	3	0	
C	0	0	9	7	3 children's low end
					2 young girl's low end
					1 girl's and doll's low end
					1 women and children
MCM	12	5	3	0	1 children's middle end
Y	5	3	28	4	2 unisex middle end
					2 children

The phrase "high end" is used for fragrances that were described as very expensive and for the wealthy; the phrase "mid to high end" is used for fragrances that are moderately expensive and available in department stores; the phrase "low end" is used for fragrances that are generally sold in grocery stores, discount stores, and the like. Although the brand name K was deemed an appropriate fragrance for both males and females, as a masculine fragrance it was sometimes associated with wealth (K as an abbreviation for thousand or carat). However, the letter K used alone in a brand name often evoked the image of Kmart for respondents, lending a low-end aura to the product. The letter L was perceived as overwhelmingly feminine and was often associated with love, elegance, and romance. The complex interplay of alphabetic characters is evident in the evaluation of the brand name KL. The harshness of the letter K was tempered by the letter L. Similarly, the femininity of the letter L was reduced by the letter K. The respondents indicated that as a man's fragrance, KL was for active, macho, powerful, tough men; some associated the name KL with "kill." As a fragrance for females, respondents usually targeted KL for professional, on-the-go, independent, successful women.

The brand name M was deemed appropriate for males and was judged to be a masculine, macho scent. The brand M could also be used for upper-class, ambitious, or older women. The brand name C was associated exclusively with women and children, and only one respondent indicated that a fragrance with the name C should be targeted at successful women. The less aggressive images associated with the name C were tempered when the letters M and C were combined into the name MCM. The name MCM may be perceived as masculine for a number of other reasons, among these that the three letters look like a monogram and the movie company with a similar name, MGM, uses a male animal (a lion) for its symbol.

The brand name Y was associated with mystery, supporting the association that the focus groups made between the letter Y and the word *why*. Y was also associated with youth and with saying yes, something the respondents felt was a feminine characteristic. In actuality, all three of the real fragrances, KL, MCM, and Y, are fragrances for women. Y was introduced in 1964 by Yves Saint Laurent and is a mid- to high-end fragrance described by the firm as "delicate and subtle" (Fragrance Foundation, 1990). In 1983, Parfums Lagerfeld introduced KL, which is described as a "seductive gathering of sumptuous flowers, pungent spices and smoldering woods"; in 1989, Michael Cromer Ltd. introduced MCM, which is "oriental with a topnote of modern fruity wood" (Fragrance Foundation, 1990).

Two features clearly distinguish this part of the study from the focus group information. First, the questionnaire restricted respondents to one product category, fragrances. Fragrances rely heavily on marketing and are subject to considerable cultural influence (e.g., someone may feel that fragrances are inappropriate for children regardless of the brand name). However, these results were meant only to provide some additional data to those generated in the focus groups and to act as a starting point for future research. Second, the brand names were presented only in written form, hence effects such as aural harshness or speed of articulation might have been less important to the respondents than shape or other words that may be evoked by the sight of particular letters. In fact, the word association process appeared to be very strong, with description of the fragrance user frequently using the letter of the brand name (e.g., "macho" and "masculine" for M, and "elegant" and "love" for L).

Summary

In this study we asked our informants what commonly held beliefs they shared about the letters of the alphabet rather than why they held specific beliefs. As in previous research, we may point to circumstantial evidence to explain why an attribute such as angularity is masculine or softness is feminine, but no such evidence may stand as absolute proof. Rather than argue this theoretical issue, we have focused on what our informants believe and what this may mean for the naming of products. This study is subject to limitations because the respondents were all students, primarily in the age group 20-35 years old. Most were American; all were living in the United States.

The complex interplay of the five attributes identified by the focus groups may be seen in their evaluation of various letters. The letters that were frequently identified as masculine were X, Z, W, and K. The most masculine letter, X, exhibits the "masculine" aspect of each attribute, being angular, harsh sounding, said quickly, at the end of the alphabet, and used infrequently in the alphabet. The letter W, which receives "masculine" ratings only for angularity and appearance at the end of the alphabet, is masculine but is not as powerful, dangerous, or racy as X. The letter Z, which is angular, the last letter of the alphabet, and used infrequently, is masculine but without the excess meaning of functionality that W has. The letter K appears in the middle of the alphabet but has the masculine attributes of harshness and of being totally angular and said quickly. The fragrance brand name exercise supported the notion that K, by itself, is not perceived as an elegant, feminine brand name. The letters X and Z were uniformly deemed appropriate components of brand names for technical, fast, complex, slightly threatening, male-domain products.

Many of the focus group informants indicated that G (soft), S, O, Q, and A were feminine. The letters G (soft), S, and O are all rounded, can be said softly or drawn out, and are frequently used. The letter S was deemed somehow "better" than G and O, perhaps because of its placement at the end of the alphabet and its familiarity through extremely common usage. The letter Q was the least feminine of this group, perhaps because of its novelty in the language, its use as shorthand for *question*, and its somewhat technical excess meaning. The letter A had a unique place in the informants' minds because of its place of honor in the alphabet, its early association with superior performance in school, its nonthreatening common usage, and its association with quality in traditional tasks. The letter A was deemed appropriate for food products or products in which excellence is not measured strictly by "more is better." Informants believed that letters with soft sounds were feminine and should be used, for example, in the brand names of personal products. This notion was supported in the fragrance brand name exercise, where products named C, L, and Y were strongly associated with women.

The data from the fragrance brand names questionnaire suggest that brand names formed exclusively from an alphabetic character may have excess meaning beyond the attributes identified by the focus groups. This meaning can often be traced to other words beginning with a particular letter, such as an association of K with karat or K mart, M with macho, Y with *why*, and C with children. The excess meaning that comes from using a letter as a stimulus for words beginning with the letter may be at odds with impressions drawn from the attributes identified in the focus group, particularly if the letter is used to identify gender (e.g., M for male, B for boy, W for woman, G for girl).

Taken as a whole, the focus group responses and the fragrance brand name study indicate that consumers perceive excess meaning in the letters of the alphabet. Their beliefs about the letters often have gender dimensions. Further, their beliefs about the letters used in a nonword brand name may extend to the product with that name. This suggests that the consumer evaluation of a product with a nonword alphabetic brand name may be an extremely complex process relying on deep, culture-based notions with potential gender dimensions. Of course, additional research is needed to clarify further the excess meaning of alphabetic characters.

Note

1.   The exact sources of quotes from focus group participants are given using the following notation: FG1 means that the discussion took place during the first of the eight focus groups. M means that the speaker is a male, F that she is female. In a series of quotes from one focus group, ellipses at the beginning or end of a sentence are used to indicate that comments did not follow one another directly, but were nevertheless part of a continuous discussion.

References

Alt, M., & Griggs, S. (1988). Can a brand be cheeky? *Marketing Intelligence and Planning,* 6(4), 9-16.
Ascher, M., & Ascher, R. (1986). Ethnomathematics. *History of Science, 24,* 125-144.

Barrett, R. A. (1984). *Culture and conduct: An excursion in anthropology.* Belmont, CA: Wadsworth.

Belk, R. W., Wallendorf, M., & Sherry, J. F. (1989). The sacred and the profane in consumer behavior: Theodicy on the odyssey. *Journal of Consumer Research, 16,* 1-38.

Bellenger, D. N., Bernhardt, K. L., & Goldstrucker, J. L. (1989). Qualitative research techniques: Focus group interviews. In T. Hayes & C. Tathum (Eds.), *Focus group interviews: A reader* (pp. 10-25). Chicago: American Marketing Association.

Bem, S. L. (1974). The measurement of psychological androgyny. *Journal of Consulting and Clinical Psychology, 42,* 155-162.

Bessell, R. (1971). *Interviewing and counseling.* London: Batsford.

Chisnall, P. M. (1974). Aluminum household foil in the common market: Research for an effective brand name. *Journal of Management Studies, 11,* 246-255.

Costa, J. A., & Belk, R. W. (1990). Nouveaux riches as quintessential Americans: Case studies of consumption in an extended family. In R. W. Belk (Ed.), *Advances in nonprofit marketing* (Vol. 4, pp. 83-138). Greenwich, CT: JAI.

Davis, R. (1961). The fitness of names to drawings: A cross-cultural study in Tanganyika. *British Journal of Psychology, 52,* 259-268.

Dogana, F. (1967). Psycholinguistic contributions to the problem of brand names. *European Marketing Research Review, 2,* 50-58.

Douglas, J. D. (1985). *Creative interviewing.* Beverly Hills, CA: Sage.

Easlea, B. (1986). The masculine image of science with special reference to physics: How much does gender really matter? In J. Harding (Ed.), *Perspectives on gender and science* (pp. 132-158). Philadelphia: Falmer.

Fragrance Foundation. (1990). *The Fragrance Foundation reference guide 1990/1991.* New York: Author.

Geertz, C. (1973). *The interpretation of cultures: Selected essays.* New York: Basic Books.

Heath, T. B., Chatterjee, S., & France, K. R. (1990). Using the phonemes of brand names to symbolize brand attributes. In A. Parasuraman & W. Bearden (Eds.), *AMA Educator's proceedings: Enhancing knowledge development in marketing* (pp. 38-42). Washington, DC: American Marketing Association.

Holbrook, M. B. (1981). Some further dimensions of psycholinguistics, imagery, and consumer response. In A. Mitchell (Ed.), *Advances in consumer research* (Vol. 9, pp. 112-117). Ann Arbor, MI: Association for Consumer Research.

Keller, E. F. (1983). Feminism and science. In E. Abel & E. Abel (Eds.), *The Signs reader: Women, gender and scholarship* (pp. 109-122). Chicago: University of Chicago Press.

Kelman, H. C., & Lerner, H. H. (1952). Group therapy, group work and adult education: The need for clarification. *Journal of Social Issues, 8*(2), 3-10.

Kidder, L. H. (1981). Qualitative research and quasi-experimental frameworks. In M. B. Brewer & B. E. Collins (Eds.), *Scientific inquiry and the social sciences.* San Francisco: Jossey-Bass.

Levy, S. J. (1979). Focus group interviewing. In J. B. Higginbotham & K. K. Cox (Eds.), *Focus group interviews: A reader* (pp. 34-42). Chicago: American Marketing Association.

Lincoln, Y. S., & Guba, E. G. (1985). *Naturalistic inquiry.* Beverly Hills, CA: Sage.

Mazursky, D., & Jacoby, J. (1985). Forming impressions of merchandise and service quality. In J. Jacoby & J. Olsen (Eds.), *Perceived quality* (pp. 139-154). Lexington, MA: Lexington.

McCracken, G. C. (1989). Homeyness: A cultural account of one constellation of consumer goods and meanings. In E. C. Hirschman (Ed.), *Interpretive consumer research* (pp. 168-183). Provo, UT: Association for Consumer Research.

Meyers-Levy, J. (1988). The influence of sex roles on judgment. *Journal of Consumer Research, 14,* 522-530.

O'Boyle, M. W., & Tarte, R. D. (1980). Implications for phonetic symbolism: The relationship between pure tones and geometric figures. *Journal of Psycholinguistic Research, 9*, 535-544.

Pavia, T. M., & Costa, J. A. (1993). The winning number: Consumer perceptions of alpha-numeric brand names. *Journal of Marketing, 57*(3), 85-98.

Peterson, K. I. (1975). The influence of the researcher and his procedure on the validity of group sessions. In E. M. Mazze (Ed.), *Combined proceedings: Spring and fall conferences* (pp. 146-148). Chicago: American Marketing Association.

Peterson, R. A., & Ross, I. (1972). How to name new brand names. *Journal of Advertising Research, 12*, 29-34.

Sanday, P. (1981). *Female power and male dominance: On the origins of sexual inequality.* Cambridge: Cambridge University Press.

Sapir, E. (1929). A study in phonetic symbolism. *Journal of Experimental Psychology, 12*, 225-239.

Schloss, I. (1981). Chickens and pickles. *Journal of Advertising Research, 21*, 47-49.

Schmitt, B. H., Leclerc, F., & Dube-Rioux, L. (1988). Sex typing and consumer behavior: A test of gender schema theory. *Journal of Consumer Research, 15*, 122-128.

Schneider, D. (1968). *American kinship: A cultural account.* Englewood Cliffs, NJ: Prentice Hall.

Sherry, J. F., Jr. (1990). A sociocultural analysis of a midwestern flea market. *Journal of Consumer Research, 17*, 13-30.

Sherry, J. F., Jr., & McGrath, M. A. (1989). Unpacking the holiday presence: A comparative ethnography of two gift stores. In E. C. Hirschman (Ed.), *Interpretive consumer research* (pp. 148-167). Provo, UT: Association for Consumer Research.

Smith, G. H. (1954). *Motivation research in advertising and marketing.* Westport, CT: Greenwood.

Tarte, R. D., & Barritt, L. S. (1971). Phonetic symbolism in adult native speakers of English: Three studies. *Language and Speech, 14*, 158-168.

Taylor, I. K. (1963). Phonetic symbolism re-examined. *Psychological Bulletin, 60*, 200-209.

Tynan, A. C., & Drayton, J. L. (1989). Conducting focus groups: A guide for first-time users. In T. Hayes & C. Tathum (Eds.), *Focus group interviews: A reader* (pp. 30-34). Chicago: American Marketing Association.

Vanden Bergh, B. G. (1982). Feedback: More chickens and pickles. *Journal of Advertising Research, 22*, 44.

Vanden Bergh, B. G., Collins, J., Schultz, M., & Alder, K. (1984). Sound advice on brand names. *Journalism Quarterly, 61*, 835-840.

Weinreich-Haste, H. (1986). Brother Sun, Sister Moon: Does rationality overcome a dualistic world view? In J. Harding (Ed.), *Perspectives on gender and science* (pp. 113-131). Philadelphia: Falmer.

Zinkhan, G. M., & Martin, C. R., Jr. (1987). New brand names and inferential beliefs: Some insights on naming new products. *Journal of Business Research, 15*, 157-172.

11

Gender and Consumption: Transcending the Feminine?

A. FUAT FIRAT

THAT there are close relationships between consumption and gender in contemporary society goes without saying. Who consumes what is still largely dependent on the performance of feminine and masculine roles in many cultures (Gould & Stern, 1989; Schmitt, Leclerc, & Dube-Rioux, 1988; Taylor-Gooby, 1985). However, the historical foundations of the relation ships between consumption and gender have not been systematically studied. The study of the history of relationships between gender and consumption requires an analysis of not only the collapse between the categories of sex and gender—that is, male with masculine and female with feminine—but also the origins of the separations between production and consumption as they relate to gender and sex. In this chapter I will attempt such an analytic recount. A brief discussion of postmodern transformations that seem to be taking place currently in the relationships between gender and consumption follows. I will then attempt to examine the consequences of the break between gender and sex categories—when female and feminine, male and masculine, are no longer exclusive representations—for consumption and the study of consumer experiences.

Consumption and Production

The distinction between consumption and production, as we define these terms today, is one that has been made by modern thought (Mill, 1929; Say, 1964). This distinction depends purely on the meaning of value in classical modern economics, a discipline with close ties to the development of the capitalist system. When the community of definers saw the outcomes from a process of consumption as valuable, they named the process *production*. Otherwise, it was a rather profane (common and ordinary) act of consumption (proper); pure use, devouring, destruction. However, the definition of *value* itself is highly ideological, and not so easy to decide on. Nor is it possible to have an absolute definition. Rather, it is quite relative, to be defined by the culture of the time and society—whether culture constructs this definition through the market, politics, social relations, or a complex combination of such.

Marxist critique of classical political economy pointed out some of the inconsistencies in the definitions (Marx, 1973). Such critique implied that the exact same processes (for example, of nourishment) could be considered production or consumption depending on varying definitions of value, and based on for whom value was created. When consumption activities went on in the homes of the workers in order to replenish their energy for work the next day, this was considered consumption proper. The efforts of the homemaker at home to feed and keep the laborer were not productive. The homemaker was a *consumer proper*, as was the worker when he or she was at home. The worker became a *producer* when in the factory, working for the capitalist, producing commodities. Thus were a capitalist to have, hypothetically, a farm or factory where he or she bred human beings to sell their labor power in the market, thus receiving surplus value within the exchange value for this labor power, to realize and further accumulate capital, the food, clothing, and the like that these workers consumed would have been considered productive, and the eating, sleeping, and so on that went on at this farm or factory would be considered production.

The above narrative, the story of reality in capitalist society, is specific to just that, the capitalist society. This narrative became very much that of modern society, built on capitalism, scientific technology, and the ideology of the market economy. But the development of the market has itself a history. This history is intertwined with the separation of the public and private domains, the articulation of gender categories, the growth of commodity production, and the legitimation of private property. It is also the history of the emergence of the concepts of consumption and production, and the system of values that produces these concepts.

A Common History of Consumption and Gender

Historically, in many cultures, work and play, toil and recreation were largely merged (Cameron, 1973; Udy, 1970; Weber, 1976). Consequently, concepts of leisure and recreation are relatively new (Touraine, 1974). Rather, for many human beings, before the appearance of societies in which substantive and persistent specialization took place, where some decided and others labored, life was a continual and perpetual series of tasks, some more enjoyable than others, but all required for subsistence as subsistence was known to be. With growing commodity production, where tasks began to be performed not just when and where needed, but accumulations occurred for future needs or for trade and barter, especially with the development of markets, the separation of work from consumption time, or when commodities were produced versus used, became a recognized phenomenon (Applebaum, 1984; Udy, 1970).

With greater specialization and mass production came the separation of the home(stead) from the workplace, a separation of the place in which family or household matters were practiced from the location for the running of social or public affairs (Reiter, 1975; Sacks, 1975; Saffioti, 1978). Production increasingly became delegated to the public domain, the factory, office, agency, and so on. Specific cultural myths, forming an ideology, accompanied this transfer of "productive activity" to the public domain. *Useful, creative, value-producing,* important activities were performed in the public domain, and had no place in the private domain, the home. Home was for recreation, leisure, and consumption. The people in the private domain did not *work,* they rested, played, and consumed, performing profane activities that required no expertise or *knowledge of importance.* Such meanings regarding the public and private domains were signified mostly through the valuation practices in society, that is, acts that promoted or demoted, rewarded or condemned, dignified or degraded, glorified or oppressed, remunerated or exploited the tasks done, and those who did these tasks, in the private and public domains. In the public domain, people were making decisions that influenced nations, humanity; they were producing, contributing to the economy and the society, to the welfare of nations. In the private domain, people played and did other insignificant things, such as eat, clean, cook, sleep, and rear children. Production was creation, it added something of value to human lives. It was treated, therefore, as a sacred activity (Polanyi, 1977; Saffioti, 1978).

In societies that later formed the Western civilizations, women came to occupy primarily the private domain and men the public domain. This, in fact, may have been largely the result of many chance occurrences and historical accidents as evidenced in other cultures that did not specialize in the same way (Draper, 1975; Sacks, 1982). With time, these accidental occupations were reinforced by the resulting structures. Essentialist arguments regarding women's biology, childbearing, and child rearing do not seem to hold, given that in many other societies the separation of the public and the private did not occur, or women and men occupied the domains in different proportions, or women dominated the public domain (Rohrlich-Leavitt, Sykes, & Weatherford, 1975; Webster, 1975). In many such cultures, as we specifically know in Africa (Hafki & Bay, 1976), the colonizers would not recognize the women and would refuse to deal with them, forcing the men to take the public roles mirroring those of the colonizers. Thus traditions that were different were forced to change (Boserup, 1970; Sacks, 1982). Even in Western societies, the occupation of the private domain by women and the public domain by men was largely mythical—that is, believed and promoted to be so more than indeed being the case—especially in the experiences of certain subcultures (Lerner, 1973, pp. 240-284). The myth did, however, reinforce a greater separation of men and women into the domains as reflected in the examples of women being forced into the home following the Industrial Revolution in England and following the two world wars in the United States.

Thus categories of gender were constructed on the meanings that generated from the roles attributed to public and private domains. Given the sex specializations into the two domains, the feminine and the masculine collapsed with female and male. Sex and gender became inseparable. Sex defined the biological qualities, but gender afforded them their meanings, roles, and status—in short, their culture. Feminine (female) was the consumer, in the home, the private domain. Masculine (male) was the producer, in the workplace, the offices, the political arena, the public domain. Consequently, given the values and meanings attributed to production, masculine qualities were positive in the culture that developed. Males did things that counted in the accounting of national wealth and income. Women's activities at home were worthless, consumptive, and economically discounted. Therefore, male labor was valuable and merited remuneration; female labor did not merit payment (Gardiner, 1979). Furthermore, such significations of the feminine and the masculine, attached to the public and private domains, males and females, provided a social *order* and determined the *proper* places and positions for men and women to support the ideals of a modern family system, which, in turn, supported a certain economic system and social formation.

Modernity was, indeed, big on seeking and generating order through separating spheres and assigning proper roles and significations to them—as, for example, in the separation of the spheres of science, morality, and art, each working within its own proper logic (Beardsworth, 1992; Franco, 1986; Habermas, 1983). In a majority of cases, modernism tended to separate spheres into oppositional, bipolar categories, as in the case of consumption/production, masculine/feminine, public/private. Such bipolar splitting helped to establish norms for an order through privileging one pole of the opposing categories as good and sacred (e.g., production, subject, active, reason) and the other pole as profane and inferior (consumption, object, passive, emotion). Attaching such superior versus inferior qualifications and meanings to bipolar categories provided the *rational* grounds for identifying the essentials and principles of what was *proper* within the order of things.

In overlapping the categories of feminine, female, and consumer, as well as the categories of masculine, male, and producer, modern Western culture imbued those categories related to the feminine with meanings that represented inferior qualities, whereas those categories related to the masculine represented superior meanings, as illustrated in Table 11.1. The dichotomies shown in the table were used by modernism to establish an order that made sense given certain experiences in modern capitalist society. These categories also aided in establishing norms, a major undertaking in modernity (Habermas, 1983; Keane, 1992; Steuerman, 1992). There existed a void of norms because modernism rejected the norms promulgated by premodern (meta)narratives based on beliefs that a higher spiritual order existed. Also rejected was the idea that norms could be merely given by a higher order, without human inquiry

TABLE 11.1 Significations of Gender

Feminine	Masculine
private	public
home	workplace
consumption	production
Woman (female)	Man (male)
consumer	producer
passive	active
Body	Mind
emotional	rational
sensation	reason
submissive	assertive
Moon	Sun
nature	culture
Profane	Sacred
worthless	valuable
Property	Owner
product (object)	person (subject)
Consumed	Consumer

into the material conditions of life. Because modernity still believed in the existence and necessity of an order, however, the search for and constitution of norms, be they different from those of the earlier order, were considered essential. As Habermas (1983) articulates in his appeal that the project of modernity not be abandoned, this quintessential quest for establishment of norms based on scientific inquiry into the material conditions of human existence had the central purpose of emancipation—the emancipation of the subject (the human being) from both the limitations of nature and exploitation by other subjects.

The female—specifically, in visual culture, the female body—became the representation of the feminine, which was the *ideal* consumer in Western culture. She "went shopping" while he worked. She spent his money or earnings. Her frivolity in buying and consuming became a major topic of jokes in the culture. She was such a consumer that he had always to restrain her appetite for consumables. In the cultural ecstasy of constructing these meanings, the fact that the privacy of the private domain was sheer myth, an illusion, went unnoticed. Indeed, the structure and forms of what went on in the private domain were determined by the politics and culture of the public domain. This determination became more and more forceful as the products bought in the market increased their role at home.

The Market and the Public and Private Domains

In the development of modern culture, the importance of the separations briefly discussed above cannot be overemphasized. Without the separations of home and workplace, public and private, work and recreation, the market is only a site, a location, where trade or barter takes place between tribes or communities. The market, conceptualized as the population of actual and potential customers, consumer units (individuals, households, organizations, and so on), can make sense only given the above separations.

The market was not instantaneously the focus for activities in the public domain, however, when the separations first occurred. Neither was it the dominating force in legitimating culture, meanings, values, and socioeconomic practice that it is in contemporary society. The primacy of politics and social (kinship) relations continued and did not become subordinated to the market for some time. This subordination has increased with the growing transfer of creative activity at home (private domain) to the socially organized workplace (public domain). Creative activity at home has been increasingly substituted by products bought in the market (Fırat, 1987; Fırat & Dholakia, 1977, 1982). Thus activity in the private domain has increasingly become one of following instructions and standards in using these products.

Originally, many of the products produced in the public domain were those that helped creative activities at home. These were products such as sewing machines, raw wool, spinning and knitting tools, agricultural tools, and home building tools. Such products have been replaced by their end products, so that the consumer in the private domain no longer has to create them but finds them in the market ready for consumption (Braverman, 1974; Campbell, 1987; McCracken, 1988; Weinbaum & Bridges, 1979). Now the activity at home is not largely one of creating consumables, but one of *consuming* them. Activities such as gardening, weaving, cooking, baking, and knitting, historically performed at home, have diminished and are consistently substituted with canned foods, ready-made clothing, frozen dinners, packaged bread, and so on. Also, for durable consumables, the market is enlarged not only for supplying the durable itself, but for providing the products to maintain it. Specialized household cleaners to keep the refrigerator, the bathtub, the furniture, and so on odorless and clean are good examples.

The increasing substitution of creative labor at home by *productive* labor in the public domain is good, from a capitalist perspective, because the labor power in the public domain is productive; it creates surplus value and contributes to realization and accumulation of capital and, thereby, to the welfare of nations. The transfer of labor power from home to the public domain, however, did not mean that people (women, who occupied the private domain) were always transferred from the private to the public domain. The transfer was in terms of what Marx calls "abstract" labor, not concrete labor. The actual history of this transfer, of course, is much more complex than can be conveyed here, with women and children being pulled into the factories as cheap labor initially during the Industrial Revolution and then returned home as *pure* consumers, their labor in the workforce being substituted by machines and male workers. The co-optation of family wages and other labor demands for benefits and the like into the political agendas of the industrialists seems to have had much to do with the necessity of mass consumers for a market to grow with growing mass production (Gardiner, 1979; Zaretsky, 1978). Indeed, households had to be populated during the day in order to have continual consumption to absorb the increasing production capabilities in the public domain. So, while they used more and more products produced for the market in the public domain, substituting for the labor they did earlier at home, women were simultaneously returned to the private domain in order to *consume* the products (Braverman, 1974; Campbell, 1987).

Women, forced back to the private domain through social policies in industrialized Western economies, lived extremely paradoxical lives and confronted paradoxical rhetoric and behaviors. Postmodernist claims of paradox in modern life would be well supported by the condition of women in the private domain. First of all, as already mentioned, the so-called private domain was not private at all. Rather, the practices in the public domain and their products, in terms of political-legal outcomes and in terms of products for consumer markets, largely determined life and relationships in the private domain. Women's lives were not private by any means. They were, in many respects, the private properties of men. The feminine that was signified as the consumer became the consumed, commodified, and objectified to be used by men. Husbands owned their wives and all other assets in the household (Saffioti, 1978). A woman could do little without a man's permission (Chodorow, 1979). This happened at the same time much praise and complimenting of women went on in the public rhetoric. As mothers, especially, women were put on pedestals, for raising stout sons and looking after their needy men—even sending them off to "glorious wars."

Other paradoxical circumstances in the private domain were, perhaps, more telling in terms of consumption culture. Although women were praised for undertaking their important social tasks of child rearing and taking care of men, they were belittled for being such consumers. Consuming, after all, was valueless, a profane and banal act. But if they did not consume, their prudence negatively influenced the expansion of the market and, therefore, the wealth (read as capital accumulation) of the nation. They were criticized, made fun of, devalued for being consumers, yet if they were not good consumers, they hurt national economic growth. This contradiction in rhetoric and economy has produced much paradoxical indoctrination of women. They have been given contradicting signs regarding what they ought to be, how they should look, and, more recently, the images they should represent (Butler & Paisley, 1980; Suleiman, 1986). To a large extent, this seems to be an inevitable part of being a consumer.

Contradictions in Modern Significations of Gender

At the same time that the consumer was so paradoxically positioned in modern society, the subject to be emancipated in the central project of modernity was very much defined as the consumer. The subject was the individual who had needs. Satisfaction of these needs through action on objects enabled improvement of life and existence for the subject. As a matter of fact, *improvement of human life by controlling nature through scientific technology* was the central project of modernity (Angus, 1989; Huyssen, 1984). Consequently, as evidenced in such declarations of the project of modernity by all major philosophers (e.g., Descartes, Kant), the role of producer was only a means to support the existence of the subject, the consumer. The producer self of the subject was the self in the moment of providing the *means* for the consumer self, the *end* for which all human action was justified. When, however, the consumer and producer roles were separated and identified with the feminine and the masculine, respectively, much paradox and contradiction was introduced into the system of modern significations and representations

(Doane, 1989). Because the consumer was identified with the feminine, and the feminine was culturally attached with meanings of being an object—object of masculine desire, to be owned and kept at home; to be adorned, embellished, and surrounded by other consumables (Doane, 1989; Flax, 1987; Saffioti, 1978; Suleiman, 1986)—she was also the objectified and the consumed.

Modernity rarely, if ever, noticed the paradoxes; if noticed, they were suppressed and repressed by the modernist rhetoric. At the same time that the consumer was the subject, the act of consumption, a feminine act, was profane; it did not produce any value but only devoured or destroyed it. As a feminine act, consumption was primarily a passive moment, and one that required little reason or the use of mind. Again, primarily a bodily act, consumption was sensual and emotional rather than rational. Even the man, representing the masculine and, thereby, the mind that created and produced, became the performer of bodily functions and fulfiller of bodily needs and desires when at home, in the private domain, during consumption. If he subscribed too much to the roles at home, he was belittled with one of the most degrading terms in modern society: *effeminate.* However, even when a consumer at home, the man had, at least, the redeeming values attached to being the producer in the public domain, as the active and rational, *knowing* being. The producer, therefore, could be proud of productive activity, whereas for the consumer what was consumed was not to be talked about or flaunted.

With the growth of the role of the products of the public domain (products found and acquired in the market) in consumption, lives in the private domain, representing the feminine, increasingly required that women consume market products, fashion items, such as clothing and accessories, or cosmetics. Furthermore, with the growth of *time-saving* or *labor-saving* products in the market, expectations of work from the women at home—in terms of, for example, frequency of washing, cleaning, and cooking—increased, causing them to consume more of these items and to bear greater physical and psychological pressures. In the end, time-saving devices did not decrease the time required by women in consumption activities (Acker, 1978; Ehrenreich & English, 1979; Moore & Sawhill, 1978; Vanek, 1978). Consumers (women), therefore, were being pressured to increase their consumption but were belittled for being consumers, never being rewarded for their expertise in consuming and having to endure a pejorative public rhetoric that kept them silent and in relative shame for their existence. The imprinting of these significations and representations in the conscious and subconscious mentalities of people in modern society has contributed greatly to orientations in marketing, possibly the ultimate institution of postmodernity in contemporary Western civilization.

Consumption and Gender in Postmodernity

There is much speculation that, especially in the advanced capitalist economies of the West, we may be (fast becoming) entrenched in a *postmodern* culture (Angus & Jhally, 1989; Fekete, 1987; Kellner, 1989). Furthermore, there are suggestions that in this postmodern era, the character of consumption and gender may be changing, or that certain characteristics present but suppressed in modernity may be beginning to dominate (Foster, 1983; Kaplan, 1988; Ross, 1988). Specifically, there may be an increasing disintegration of the close connections among sex, gender, and consumption (Firat, 1990).

The conditions of postmodernity and their effects on marketing and consumers have been investigated elsewhere (Firat, 1990, 1991; Sherry, 1990; Venkatesh, 1989). One of the most addressed conditions is *hyperreality*, that is, the becoming real of what was originally hype or a simulation, as well as the inclination of the postmodern consumer to experience or live the simulation rather than the real (Baudrillard, 1983b; Eco, 1986; Wilson, 1989). The realization of the hype or the simulation is facilitated through powerful signification and representation processes that imbue signifiers (verbal, visual, or material signs or symbols that represent things, making them intelligible) with meanings (the signified) different from the original or past meanings. This is possible because, as semioticians at least since Saussure and Pierce have recognized, all signifiers are only arbitrarily linked to the referents that they originally signified (Santambrogio & Violi, 1988). The predominance of continual signification and resignification of signifiers in postmodernity (Foster, 1983), specifically through marketing practices, results in an omnipresence of disjointedness and discontinuity, what many postmodernists discuss as *fragmentation* (Lyotard, 1984; Wilson, 1989). It becomes no longer possible to find centered and unified connections to historical origins or jointedness among the different images represented using the (now remotely) familiar signifiers. Rather, it is the excitement or ecstasy of the fragmented moments of exposure to signs or communication that is sought (Baudrillard, 1983a). In postmodernity, commitment to seeking a central meaning for life experiences, which was a requirement in the modernist sensibility, is transcended (Gitlin, 1989). The spectacle (sensational, exciting [re]presentation of images) takes center stage (Debord, 1983).

The connections between sex and gender are not immune to this omnipresent fragmentation. Enlargement of the market, a locus of fragmentation of all life experiences through the ever-increasing numbers of specialized products, each promoting and necessary as a spectacle for fragmented moments of consumption (Jameson, 1983), both fosters and requires all individuals to take part in the consumption ethic. Males need to take as much part in the *consuming ethic* as the females who have historically been associated with it. Consequently, there is a separation taking place between sex and gender categories that historically had collapsed, as explained above. The historically completed commodification and objectification of the female body, as the representation of the feminine, is being extended to images of the male body as well. The meanings originally attached to the feminine and the masculine are becoming diffused across the sexes, especially in advertising and art (Kaplan, 1987; Kroker & Cook, 1986; Levin, 1988; Tomlinson, 1990).

Postmodern Developments

The changes in the significations of sex and gender were aided by different social and cultural movements and discourses, such as feminism, postmodernism, and countercultural youth movements, which rejected and successfully negated modernist significations. Marketing, increasingly glorifying the act of and ability for consumption, helped these changes, as well as played a role in the transformations in the positions and meanings attributed to consumption. Largely, consumption has become an acceptable activity, even for males, who have been relatively freed from having to represent only the masculine because of the cultural break that has begun to take place between the categories of gender and sex. Furthermore, these contemporary discourses that seem to have gained greater force in popular conscience and, especially, in popular arts of all kinds, such as music and film, tend to invest greater confidence in sensibility and intuition, as well as emotion, because they can provide ample evidence that centuries of emphasis on reason and scientific technology have brought not much other than misery for a large majority of the world's population and depletion and destruction of ecological resources, along with international strife. A limitless zest for production, for control of nature and its resources, has increasingly lost its privileged image. Production and being a producer of *goods* are no longer such lofty efforts. People, especially with the social impact of marketing and advertising as the art forms that command the greatest resources, increasingly tend to (re)present themselves through what they consume. Who one is, is more and more communicated to others, as well as to oneself, by what one has, wears, drives, does during periods of leisure, and so on. The other side of the coin is that in contemporary (Western) culture people largely make their judgments about others on the basis of what others consume and how they (re)present themselves through what they use, wear, and so on. One's *occupation,* or role in production, is merely a conversation topic.

With such a fissure in the consumption/production duality, along with the relative dissolution of other oppositional categories that linked and reinforced the significations of the consumer and consumption, consumption no longer is profane, worthless, and exclusively feminine. Consumption is now an active endeavor. It is the *production* and signification of one's self-image. It is how one constructs and (re)presents (one)self to obtain position(s) in society and maintain livelihood. Furthermore, consumption is increasingly becoming an activity that requires education and planning (Baudrillard, 1975).

It is not yet possible, however, to state that gender categories are lost, or that significations of feminine and masculine are completely changed. Modern significations of gender categories are still very strong. It is just that males and females are now encountering a culture that is much more tolerant of both sexes participating in roles and meanings attached to both gender categories. That is, increasingly, we find both males and females representing the feminine and the masculine during different moments in their lives (males participating in housework, taking on more nurturing roles with children, and increasingly consuming fashion products, cosmetics, and so on, while women are becoming part of the workforce, managers, politicians, and representing masculine qualities in their participation in production in the public domain), finding it possible to move from one (re)presentation of self to another in fragmented moments of everyday life.

Consequently, although postmodernist philosophers, such as Baudrillard (1975, 1981), recognize the meanings of consumption that are different from ones in the modernist (meta)narratives—as in the case of value being created in consumption, sign value, rather than in production, exchange value—such contemporary awareness is not completely transmitted to popular culture, especially in the case of gender significations. A major culprit in this delay is the modern market system, which is able to *marketize* the expressions of feminist, postmodernist, and other countercultural movements. The market system has, indeed, proven to be very resilient in its ability to co-opt many a countercultural movement's expressions by emptying them of their original meanings and translating them into images/products that are marketable (Fırat & Venkatesh, 1993). Currently, the displacement of metanarratives from public consciousness and the disillusionment with universal norms have rendered the market the only locus of legitimation in society. That is, any idea, movement, or even culture can maintain itself only by translating its images, expressions, or messages into marketable commodities. There is no other basis for justifying or validating a claim, in contemporary postmodern culture, than finding a market for it. Even when an idea system, a countercultural movement, resists the marketization/commodification of its expressions, it seems bound to lose to the marketized versions of its expressions when and if this translation is done by other parties—most often, marketing organizations.

This has largely happened to movements such as feminism. Expressions of equality have been appropriated and resignified by companies that make cosmetics and personal care products, for example, in ways that expand the membership in being objectified/commodified to males. Equality between the sexes has, thereby, been resignified to mean that men can equally be objects of oppression, sexual harassment, and the like, and thus equally objectified. Such new significations are used to market products to females by implying access to power through having control over men, or through images of independence from men. On the other hand, products are marketed to men through implications that consumption of such products will make them more presentable and attractive to women. Thus the ploys used to induce females to consume are extended to males. Admittedly, the motivators and appeals used for women and men still adhere much to the ingrained modern meanings attached to gender. These meanings and images still reflect ideas such as that a woman's worth is in her beauty and ability to attract men (Bristor & Fischer, 1993). However, the idea of the necessity to represent oneself as an image, to present oneself as an attractive consumable, seems to be increasing among men also. One reflection of this orientation in women was the objectification of self in order to acquire the power of seduction extended to purchase of body parts through plastic surgery and implants. This trend (e.g., getting implants for biceps and calves) for purposes of *beautification* or *customizing* of body parts is increasing among men as well (Moyers, 1989).

Sex and Gender in Late Modernity

Currently, what we have is more a decoupling of sex from gender and less a deconstruction of gender. There are, however, several reasons to think that a deconstruction of modern gender categories will have to follow. One reason is the emerging transformation of gender categories from simply two, opposing, bipolar ones to multiple ones (Weston, 1991). Even if some may not agree that gender categories other than masculine and feminine have already emerged, the boundaries of masculine and feminine have surely diffused owing to gender crossings (Peñaloza, in press). Gay and lesbian lifestyles, recognition of individuals who cannot be categorized as male or female, and the meanings and expectations attached to both have gone through sufficient changes that their opposition is no longer as clear. Another reason lies in something discussed earlier: the increasing occurrence that both men and women represent the masculine and the feminine in different situations and at different moments in their lives. Because in modernity male and masculine, female and feminine were so tightly identified, fragmented moments of *cross*-representations will definitely *have to* create ambiguity and deconstruction of cultural significations of gender. Already, there are many indications of confusion and, thereby, confluence in gender categorizations.

Production/Consumption

The confluence and confusion in gender promotes a confluence in the conceptualizations of production/producer and consumption/consumer as well, as, historically, these were also tightly identified with gender

(Fırat & Venkatesh, 1993). As mentioned earlier, consumption can no longer be conceptualized as qualitatively different from production. What were defined oppositionally as two separate moments, consumption and production, are just different moments in an ongoing, never-ending process of production/consumption. The likelihood is, therefore, that as this recognition entrenches within the popular culture, the two signifiers, production and consumption, will go through a transformation of signification. They are likely to lose their oppositional meanings, begin to lose their prominence among other signifiers that will come to represent different moments of the same process, and become only two of many categories that define differences (not superiority/inferiority or oppositions) perceived in the process of (re)creation. Again, as indicated earlier, the consumer will be recognized as a producer of self(-image), and these two words (signifiers), *consumer* and *producer*, may also become only two among an array of words that define different acts/roles in the process.

Certainly, the privileging of two oppositional categories among other categories is beginning to fade, and so is the privileging of any category among others. The rejection of privilege by many popular movements is being felt in the loss of privilege for any signifier or category. It seems to be becoming less and less acceptable *naturally* to consider any ethnic group superior to others, any culture *better* or *more advanced* than others—and the list goes on. The preference for recognizing difference rather than superiority/inferiority is clearly becoming culturally popular. One consequence of such development is that production and the roles people play as producers in their jobs, occupations, and workplaces are not as important in defining who they are. Rather, as mentioned before, definition, or *production*, of self(-image) is increasingly dependent on what one consumes. Furthermore, what one consumes is increasingly the basis on which others assess one's position in society and make judgments regarding personality and the like.

With the growing importance of consumption in the (re)presentation of who one is, there is growing awareness on the part of consumers about the necessity to *customize* themselves (Moyers, 1989) for the different situations and roles in which they find themselves. Development of modern society has largely fragmented life spheres, and this fragmentation is not only recognized but emphasized in postmodern culture. Indeed, the separation of the public and private domains in early modernity is extended in contemporary society into more life spheres that present subtle or pronounced differences. Today, an individual participates in home life, work life, shopping life, recreational life, neighborhood life, and a variety of social lives (religious institution social, school social, and more). Each life sphere requires different attention and qualities from the individual and, consequently, in each life sphere a different *persona* is, generally, likely to bring success to the individual. Also, in each sphere the individual will have greater success by "dressing for the occasion." These *transformations*, or customizing, are mostly considered to be natural in contemporary culture, not as violations of character. Simply, it is *normal* and *smart* to do whatever is necessary to get places, as long as one does nothing criminal, and customizing self is by no means considered criminal.

When consumers become conscious of the necessity to cultivate varied self-images, they begin to perceive themselves as marketable items and their consumption becomes a productive means for (re)production of selves (self-images). Such withering of the producer/consumer duality is likely to cause further breakdown of modern gender categories.

Consumer and Gender in the Postmodern

With the breakdown of gender categories, and their further separation from sex, one of the foundations, maybe the most important and effective foundation of motivating consumption, sex or sexual appeal, is likely to go through substantial changes. Foucault (1990) argues that sexuality also underwent a modernization in the sense that a duality was created between the surface and the depth (the hidden, inner), or the appearance and essence of sexuality, during the seventeenth century, later culminating in Victorian morality in Western cultures. Sexuality and the body, which is highly related to sexuality, were relatively open to greater frankness before modernity. With modernity, sexuality moved into the home along with the feminine (represented, especially, by the female body). Along with the body, sexuality began to take on connotations of profanity and baseness, as opposed to the sanctity of the mind and mental activity (Featherstone, Hepworth, & Turner, 1991). On the other hand, sexuality was the most sensual of all sensations in both the rhetoric and the *hidden* discourse. Consequently, it united two most important elements of a spectacle: the *sensual* and the *unknown*, therefore, the *sensational* and *intrigue*. The more sexuality combined these two elements, the more it was likely to create another essential separation for commodification: separation of the objectifiable from everyday activity—the ideas, the visual images, and the accessories from the common act itself. This separation, as in the case of separating the sand painting from the medicinal ceremony, enabled the *sale* of the objects of sex as marketable commodities. And, being already objectified in the image of the feminine, the female was an object of sex as well, depicted in modern art and literature. As Baudrillard (1990) suggests, the female, representing the feminine, had the power of seduction as the object of desire. However, as an object the female was determined not by its own will but by the social will, itself signified by the culture of the modern that privileged the masculine and objectified the feminine in the image that suited the masculine desires.

These images of the feminine largely represented the imaginary of sexuality in modernity and, consequently, signified many of the products that enhanced both masculinity and, much more so, the femininity of the true consumer, the female. Such was the source of many products for consumption, products that were necessary to assure femininity and enable the female to represent the feminine successfully. Correspondingly, although not as many in number, there appeared products to enhance and signify the masculinity of the male. Having relations to many of the most important categorizations in modernity, and given its immediate relationship to sexuality, gender-oriented marketing of almost all consumption took center stage in modernity. That is why the deconstruction of gender in postmodern culture is likely to create radical transformations in both consumer behaviors and marketing theory and practice.

A major issue is the fate of consumer identity when the modern gender order breaks down. The fact that the market system has been successful in co-opting many countercultural movements' expressions by emptying them of their original meanings and translating them into marketable images/products may be an indication that sexuality, however signified, need not be the only or even the most important basis for marketization/commodification and consumption. It could be said that, already, fragmentations in (re)presenting images of self that differ across situations and life spheres have begun to dissolve the need on the part of postmodern consumers to find or constitute a centered, unique, uniform self. Consequently, gender roles that provided the most important *proper* guides for a consistent self may no longer be needed by consumers. As crossing gender boundaries and playfully integrating elements from gendered categories to (re)create or (re)produce exciting, marketable self-images become increasingly acceptable in a postmodern culture of fragmentation, consumers will increasingly employ different guides in (re)producing images. On the one hand, such fragmentation and the breakdown of gendered roles present great potential for liberation from culturally signified and imposed limitations on constructing selves, as well as from requirements of having to be loyal to a single self. On the other hand, the issue of control over images represented by consumers is likely to become a central political and social, as well as philosophical, topic. As in the case of the feminine in modernity, if the objectification of self in representing images that will make self attractive, alluring, seductive, and, therefore, marketable is determined by forces outside of the consumer's control, the emancipatory project of modernity will, indeed, not have been completed. The question may be: Will anyone care about such emancipation in a postmodern culture? If anyone does, will emancipation be possible to achieve given the fragmentation and the necessities of being marketable, of meeting the requirements of catering to the market?

The Possibilities

It could be argued that although the modern (traditional) significations of gender are still forceful, the fragmentation of self(-images) and the fissure between gender and sex categories create complex and paradoxical experiences for consumers, female and male. Marketing organizations, the principal players in representation and communication of images in the market culture, currently seem to be playing on both sides of the fence. Sensing the impact of movements such as feminism and the impending fissure between sex and gender, they are more willing to (re)present nurturing, sensual images of men and assertive, powerful images of women. The roles represented, however, still seem to be gendered in the modern sense. This is reflected in the ways power, attractiveness, and seductiveness images are played for women and men.

When the images played do not propose clear and precise messages as to what is expected of and proper for a woman or for a man, and when the gender categories still represent a dualistic, oppositional quality, both individual consumers and marketing organizations are left with a degree of confusion (Williamson, 1986). As stated before, this affords a degree of independence for the individual. There is a greater possibility for consumers to produce individual meanings for their consumption in a period of confusion, when the speed of acculturation of new sex and gender experiences lags behind the decoupling and decomposition of the old and the emergence of the new. Consumers are allowed to play with, deconstruct, reconstruct, and signify the signifiers (items and practices of consumption) and become active participants in cultural construction (Foster, 1985; Hutcheon, 1988). This is partially observed in the experiences of consumer groups that are generally left out of the targeted markets and, therefore, left to their own devices for representation of (self-)images. When the socially signified and controlled meanings and role expectations are in the process of disintegration/decomposition, this allows relatively greater freedom for individual consumers to control the meanings they attach to and evoke from their experience and existence. When and if the consumers develop a fondness for this newfound freedom, if the acculturation institutions indeed lag behind for a long period, the culture of consumption may, indeed, acquire a different meaning itself. Consumption will, then, no longer be a passive, received, or need-oriented process, but an active self(-image)-construction process. The consumer may then become a product that he or she, as a producer, truly participates in the production of. The role and meaning of the marketing organization will, then, also have to go through a thorough transformation.

This does not, however, signal that the equality and freedom sought by movements such as feminism will necessarily emerge. Rather, as all people are drawn into consumer images historically imbued with feminine significations, they also acquire the remnant commodification and objectification of the feminine. The market may well appropriate and resignify the expressions of equality nurtured in feminist movements, turning all consumers into the *consumed* feminine. The experience of freedom from modern gender categories for both sexes could be very liberating, but it also carries the potential of reinforcing these roles, no longer on the basis of sexual discrimination, but on the basis of both sexes reproducing the ideal images of the *consumer* and the *producer*. The danger here may be that by evolving into these ideal images people will get caught up in the whirlpool of the market and be consumed themselves as the products.

Whatever the consequences, contemporary consumer experiences and behaviors cannot be understood without an understanding of gender and its demise. And it may not be possible to understand the consumers of the future at all without understanding how the decomposing gender categories of the day get to be resignified and represented in a culture of fragmented selves.

References

Acker, J. (1978). Issues in the sociological study of women's work. In A. H. Stromberg & S. Harkess (Eds.), *Women working* (pp. 134-161). Palo Alto, CA: Mayfield.

Angus, I. (1989). Circumscribing postmodern culture. In I. Angus & S. Jhally (Eds.), *Cultural politics in contemporary America* (pp. 96-107). New York: Routledge.

Angus, I., & Jhally, S. (Eds.). (1989). *Cultural politics in contemporary America*. New York: Routledge.

Applebaum, H. (Ed.). (1984). *Work in non-market and transitional societies*. Albany: State University of New York Press.

Baudrillard, J. (1975). *Mirror of production*. St. Louis, MO: Telos.

Baudrillard, J. (1981). *For a critique of the political economy of the sign*. St. Louis, MO: Telos.

Baudrillard, J. (1983a). The ecstasy of communication. In H. Foster (Ed.), *The anti-aesthetic: Essays on postmodern culture* (pp. 126-134). Port Townsend, WA: Bay.

Baudrillard, J. (1983b). *Simulations*. New York: Semiotext(e).

Baudrillard, J. (1990). *Seduction*. New York: St. Martin's.

Beardsworth, R. (1992). On the critical "post": Lyotard's agitated judgement. In A. Benjamin (Ed.), *Judging Lyotard* (pp. 43-80). London: Routledge.

Boserup, E. (1970). *Woman's role in economic development*. New York: St. Martin's.

Braverman, H. (1974). *Labor and monopoly capital*. New York: Monthly Review Press.

Bristor, J. M., & Fischer, E. (1993). Feminist thought: Implications for consumer research. *Journal of Consumer Research, 19*, 518-536.

Butler, M., & Paisley, W. (1980). *Women and the mass media*. New York: Human Sciences Press.

Cameron, K. N. (1973). *Humanity and society: A world history*. New York: Monthly Review Press.

Campbell, C. (1987). *The romantic ethic and the spirit of modern consumerism*. Oxford: Basil Blackwell.

Chodorow, N. (1979). Mothering, male dominance, and capitalism. In Z. R. Eisenstein (Ed.), *Capitalist patriarchy and the case for socialist feminism* (pp. 83-106). New York: Monthly Review Press.

Debord, G. (1983). *Society of the spectacle*. Detroit: Black & Red.

Doane, M. A. (1989). The economy of desire: The commodity form in/of the cinema. *Quarterly Review of Film & Video, 11*, 23-33.

Draper, P. (1975). !Kung women: Contrasts in sexual egalitarianism in foraging and sedentary contexts. In R. R. Reiter (Ed.), *Toward an anthropology of women*. New York: Monthly Review Press.

Eco, U. (1986). *Travels in hyperreality* (W. Weaver, Trans.). San Diego, CA: Harcourt Brace Jovanovich.

Ehrenreich, B., & English, D. (1979). *For her own good: 150 years of the experts' advice to women.* Garden City, NY: Anchor.

Featherstone, M., Hepworth, M., & Turner, B. S. (Eds.). (1991). *The body: Social process and cultural theory.* London: Sage.

Fekete, J. (Ed.). (1987). *Life after postmodernism: Essays on value and culture.* New York: St. Martin's.

Firat, A. F. (1987). The social construction of consumption patterns: Understanding macro consumption phenomena. In A. F. Firat, N. Dholakia, & R. P. Bagozzi (Eds.), *Philosophical and radical thought in marketing* (pp. 251-267). Lexington, MA: Lexington.

Firat, A. F. (1990). The consumer in postmodernity. In R. H. Holman & M. R. Solomon (Eds.), *Advances in consumer research* (Vol. 18, pp. 70-76). Provo, UT: Association for Consumer Research

Firat, A. F. (1991). Postmodern culture, marketing, and the consumer. In S. MacKenzie & T. Childers (Eds.), *Marketing theory and applications* (pp. 237-242). Chicago: American Marketing Association.

Firat, A. F., & Dholakia, N. (1977). Consumption patterns and macromarketing: A radical perspective. *European Journal of Marketing, 11,* 291-298.

Firat, A. F., & Dholakia, N. (1982). Consumption choices at the macro level. *Journal of Macromarketing, 2,* 6-15.

Firat, A. F., & Venkatesh, A. (1993). Postmodernity: The age of marketing. *International Journal of Research in Marketing, 10,* 227-249.

Flax, J. (1987). Postmodernism and gender relations in feminist theory. *Signs, 12,* 621-643.

Foster, H. (Ed.). (1983). *The anti-aesthetic: Essays on postmodern culture.* Port Townsend, WA: Bay.

Foster, H. (Ed.). (1985). *Recodings: Art, spectacle, cultural politics.* Port Townsend, WA: Bay.

Foucault, M. (1990). *The history of sexuality: An introduction* (Vol. 1). New York: Vintage.

Franco, J. (1986). Gender, death and resistance; Facing the ethical vacuum. *Chicago Review, 35*(4), 59-79.

Gardiner, J. (1979). Women's domestic labor. In Z. R. Eisenstein (Ed.), *Capitalist patriarchy and the case for socialist feminism* (pp. 173-189). New York: Monthly Review Press.

Gitlin, T. (1989). Postmodernism: Roots and politics. In I. Angus & S. Jhally (Eds.), *Cultural politics in contemporary America* (pp. 347-360). New York: Routledge.

Gould, S. J., & Stern, B. B. (1989). Gender schema and fashion consciousness. *Psychology and Marketing, 6,* 129-145.

Habermas, J. (1983). Modernity: An incomplete project. In H. Foster (Ed.), *The anti-aesthetic: Essays on postmodern culture* (pp. 3-15). Port Townsend, WA: Bay.

Hafki, N. J., & Bay, E. G. (Eds.). (1976). *Women in Africa.* Stanford, CA: Stanford University Press.

Hutcheon, L. (1988). *A poetics of postmodernism: History, theory, fiction.* New York: Routledge.

Huyssen, A. (1984). Mapping the postmodern. *New German Critique, 33,* 5-52.

Jameson, F. (1983). Postmodernism and consumer society. In H. Foster (Ed.), *The anti-aesthetic: Essays on postmodern culture* (pp. 111-125). Port Townsend, WA: Bay.

Kaplan, E. A. (1987). *Rocking around the clock.* New York: Methuen.

Kaplan, E. A. (Ed.). (1988). *Postmodernism and its discontents.* London: Verso.

Keane, J. (1992). The modern democratic revolution: Reflections on Lyotard's "The postmodern condition." In A. Benjamin (Ed.), *Judging Lyotard* (pp. 81-98). London: Routledge.

Kellner, D. (1989). *Jean Baudrillard: From Marxism to post-modernism and beyond.* Stanford, CA: Stanford University Press.

Kroker, A., & Cook, D. (1986). *The postmodern scene: Excremental culture and hyper-aesthetics.* New York: St. Martin's.

Lerner, G. (Ed.). (1973). *Black women in white America: A documentary history.* New York: Vintage.

Levin, K. (1988). *Beyond modernism.* New York: Harper & Row.

Lyotard, J.-F. (1984). *The postmodern condition: A report on knowledge* (G. Bennington & B. Massumi, Trans.). Minneapolis: University of Minnesota Press.

Marx, K. (1973). *Grundrisse.* New York: Vintage.

McCracken, G. (1988). *Culture and consumption: New approaches to the symbolic character of consumer goods and activities.* Bloomington: Indiana University Press.

Mill, J. S. (1929). *Principles of political economy.* London: Longman, Green.

Moore, K. A., & Sawhill, I. V. (1978). Implications of women's employment for home and daily life. In A. H. Stromberg & S. Harkess (Eds.), *Women working* (pp. 201-225). Palo Alto, CA: Mayfield.

Moyers, B. (Host). (1989, November 8). Image and reality in America: Consuming images (Episode of *The public mind*). Public Broadcasting System.

Peñaloza, L. (in press). When boys will be boys and girls won't: A look at the nature of gender boundaries and their impact on marketing research. *International Journal of Research in Marketing.*

Polanyi, K. (1977). *The livelihood of man.* New York: Academic Press.

Reiter, R. R. (1975). Men and women in the south of France: Public and private domains. In R. R. Reiter (Ed.), *Toward an anthropology of women* (pp. 252-282). New York: Monthly Review Press.

Rohrlich-Leavitt, R., Sykes, B., & Weatherford, E. (1975). Aboriginal woman: Male and female anthropological perspectives. In R. R. Reiter (Ed.), *Toward an anthropology of women* (pp. 110-126). New York: Monthly Review Press.

Ross, A. (Ed.). (1988). *Universal abandon? The politics of postmodernism.* Minneapolis: University of Minnesota Press.

Sacks, K. (1975). Engels revisited: Women, the organization of production, and private property. In R. R. Reiter (Ed.), *Toward an anthropology of women* (pp. 211-234). New York: Monthly Review Press.

Sacks, K. (1982). *Sisters and wives.* Urbana: University of Illinois Press.

Saffioti, H. I. B. (1978). *Women in class society.* New York: Monthly Review Press.

Santambrogio, M., & Violi, P. (1988). Introduction. In U. Eco, M. Santambrogio, & P. Violi (Eds.), *Meaning and mental representations* (pp. 3-22). Bloomington: Indiana University Press.

Say, J.-B. (1964). *A treatise on political economy.* New York: A. M. Kelly.

Schmitt, B. H., Leclerc, F., & Dube-Rioux, L. (1988). Sex typing and consumer behavior: A test of gender schema theory. *Journal of Consumer Research, 15,* 122-128.

Sherry, J. F., Jr. (1990). Postmodern alternatives: The interpretive turn in consumer research. In H. Kassarjian & T. Robertson (Eds.), *Handbook of consumer theory and research* (pp. 548-591). Englewood Cliffs, NJ: Prentice Hall.

Steuerman, E. (1992). Habermas vs Lyotard: Modernity vs postmodernity? In A. Benjamin (Ed.), *Judging Lyotard* (pp. 99-118). London: Routledge.

Suleiman, S. R. (Ed.). (1986). *The female body in Western culture.* Cambridge, MA: Harvard University Press.

Taylor-Gooby, P. (1985). Personal consumption and gender. *Sociology, 19,* 272-284.

Tomlinson, A. (Ed.). (1990). *Consumption, identity and style.* New York: Routledge.

Touraine, A. (1974). Leisure activities and social participation. In M. R. Marrus (Ed.), *The emergence of leisure.* New York: Harper & Row.

Udy, S. H., Jr. (1970). *Work in traditional and modern society.* Englewood Cliffs, NJ: Prentice Hall.

Vanek, J. (1978). Housewives as workers. In A. H. Stromberg & S. Harkess (Eds.), *Women working* (pp. 392-414). Palo Alto, CA: Mayfield.

Venkatesh, A. (1989). Modernity and postmodernity: A synthesis or antithesis? In T. Childers (Ed.), *Proceedings of the winter Educators' Conference.* Chicago: American Marketing Association.

Weber, M. (1976). *The agrarian sociology of ancient civilizations.* London: New Left.

Webster, P. (1975). Matriarchy: A vision of power. In R. R. Reiter (Ed.), *Toward an anthropology of women* (pp. 141-156). New York: Monthly Review Press.

Weinbaum, B., & Bridges, A. (1979). The other side of the paycheck: Monopoly capital and the structure of consumption. In Z. R. Eisenstein (Ed.), *Capitalist patriarchy and the case for socialist feminism* (pp. 190-205). New York: Monthly Review Press.

Weston, K. (1991). *Families we choose: Lesbians, gays, kinship.* New York: Columbia University Press.

Williamson, J. (1986). *Consuming passions: The dynamics of popular culture.* London: Marion Boyars.

Wilson, E. (1989). *Hallucinations: Life in a post-modern city.* London: Hutchinson Radius.

Zaretsky, E. (1978). Capitalism and the evolution of the family. In R. C. Edwards, M. Reich, & T. E. Weisskopf (Eds.), *The capitalist system* (pp. 69-73). Englewood Cliffs, NJ: Prentice Hall.

About the Authors

Amardeep Assar is Assistant Professor of Marketing at the School of Management, Binghamton University, in Binghamton, New York. His research in consumer behavior has primarily been concerned with decision making in families His work has appeared in *Advances in Consumer Research* and in a report of the Marketing Science Institute. He is currently studying aspects of gender in the context of spousal allocation of household tasks, as well as voluntary simplification of consumption patterns.

Gary J. Bamossy is Professor of Marketing at the Vrije Universiteit, Amsterdam. His research activities are in the area of cross-cultural consumer behavior, and have focused on effects of country of origin information on product evaluation and choice; materialism among expatriates and children; ethnicity, cultural identity, and consumption; and methodological issues in cross-cultural consumer behavior research. He is coeditor of *European Advances in Consumer Research, Advances in*

Public and Nonprofit Marketing and *Marketing in a Multicultural World: Ethnicity, Nationalism, and Cultural Identity* (Sage).

George S. Bobinski, Jr., is Assistant Professor of Marketing at the School of Management at Binghamton University in Binghamton, New York. His research interests include family decision making, particularly for baby boomer couples. His work in this area has been published in *Advances in Consumer Research*, the proceedings of the annual meeting of the Association for Consumer Research. Currently, he is examining gender issues related to allocation of household tasks, financial tasks, and patterns of voluntary simplicity.

Janeen Arnold Costa is Assistant Professor of Marketing, David Eccles School of Business, and Adjunct Assistant Professor of Anthropology, University of Utah. She received her Ph.D. in cultural anthropology from Stanford University in 1983 and undertook a postdoctoral position in marketing at the University of Utah in 1987. Having taught for several years in social anthropology, she joined the marketing faculty at the University of Utah in 1989. Her research focuses on social and cultural dimensions of consumer behavior and marketing, including assessment of the role and influence of culture, gender, class, ethnicity, and cross-cultural marketing, particularly in the context of tourism. She organized and chaired two conferences on gender and consumer behavior in Salt Lake City in 1991 and 1993. Her research has been published in the *Journal of Marketing, Advances in Consumer Research, Research in Consumer Behavior, Advances in Nonprofit Marketing, Anthropological Quarterly,* and numerous other books and conference proceedings. She edited the published proceedings of both the Salt Lake City gender conferences, and is coeditor of *Research in Consumer Behavior* (Volume 6) and *Marketing in a Multicultural World: Ethnicity, Nationalism, and Cultural Identity* (Sage).

A. Fuat Fırat is Professor of Marketing at Arizona State University West. He received his degree in economics (Licencié en Economie) from the Faculty of Economics, University of Istanbul, in 1970, and his Ph.D. in marketing from Northwestern University in 1978. He has held academic positions at Istanbul University, University of Texas at Dallas, University of Maryland, McGill University, and Appalachian State University. His research interests cover areas such as macro consumer behavior and macromarketing; postmodern culture, marketing, and the consumer; feminist studies in consumer research; marketing and development; and interorganizational relations. His work has been published in a number of journals, including the *International Journal of Research in Marketing, Journal of Macromarketing, Journal of Marketing, Journal of Organizational Change Management*, and *Journal of Economic Psychology*, as well as in several edited books. His article, "Consumption Choices at the Macro Level," with coauthor Nikhilesh Dholakia, won the *Journal of Macromarketing* Charles Slater Award. He has coedited two books, *Philosophical and Radical Thought in Marketing* and *Marketing and Development: Toward Broader Dimensions*. He has also been coeditor of two special issues of the *International Journal of Research in Marketing* on postmodernism, marketing, and the consumer.

Eileen Fischer is an Associate Professor of Marketing in the Faculty of Administrative Studies at York University, North York, Ontario, Canada. She joined York in 1988 after receiving her Ph.D. in marketing from Queen's University in Kingston, Ontario. Her empirical research in the field of consumer behavior has focused on the nature and implications of the gender socialization of consumers. With coauthors, she has explored the ways in which women's socialization encourages them to take responsibility for consumer activities (such as gift shopping and gift giving) associated with developing and maintaining interpersonal relationships, and the ways in which such activities may help women to define and reinforce their social identities. Her more conceptual work deals with feminist issues in the discipline, and with less familiar approaches to research—such as hermeneutics—that may prove useful to those seeking to conduct feminist inquiry in the field. Her empirical and conceptual work has been published in such outlets as *Journal of Consumer Research, Psychology and Marketing, International Journal of Research in Marketing*, and *Advances in Consumer Research*.

Brenda Gainer is an Assistant Professor of Marketing in the Faculty of Administrative Studies at York University in Toronto, Canada. She joined the faculty at York after completing her Ph.D. there in 1992. Her main research interests are in the field of consumer behavior, particularly sociocultural influences on consumer behavior. A major portion of her research to date has been devoted to gender issues. In a recent study she investigated the relationships among gender, biological sex, and product involvement; her work has also focused on the relevance of the study of gender to such topics as ritual and home shopping, rites of passage, fat and body image, community formation, philanthropy, and arts attendance. A second main focus of her research is interpersonal influences on consumption, particularly social networks; in a recent study she examined the impact of social relationships on the consumption of shared services. Her work has appeared in the *Journal of Business Research, Psychology and Marketing, Services Industries Journal, Advances in Consumer Behavior,* and *Journal of Arts Management, Law and Society.* Before embarking on an academic career, she worked as a marketing manager in the arts. She continues to work as a consultant to arts organizations in strategic planning and marketing research, and pursues academic research also in the area of consumer behavior toward the arts.

Suzanne C. Grunert is currently Associate Professor in the Department of Marketing at Odense University, Denmark. Previously, she was a Research Fellow in the Department of Information Science, Århus School of Business, Denmark, and a Research Associate at the Department of Consumer and Home Economics, University of Hohenheim, Germany. She has degrees in nutritional science and sociology from the University of Bonn, Germany, and a Ph.D. in social sciences from the University of Hohenheim. Before starting her position at Hohenheim, she was affiliated with the Food Aid Department of the Commission of the European Communities in Brussels, Belgium. Her main research interests are in consumer behavior from an economic psychology perspective, especially eating behavior and environmentally relevant aspects of consumption, personality theories, cross-cultural insights into consumers' values, and methodological issues in social science research. Her writings include a recently published book on emotions and eating as well as numerous articles. She is the Economics and Behavioral Science Book Review Editor for the *Journal of Consumer Policy.*

Morris B. Holbrook is the William T. Dillard Professor of Marketing, Graduate School of Business, Columbia University, New York, where he currently teaches courses in communication and in consumer behavior. He earned his bachelor's degree in English at Harvard in 1965. Both his MBA (1967) and Ph.D. (1975) are in marketing from the Columbia Business School. His research applies a broad range of methods from the social sciences and humanities to issues related to communication, consumer esthetics, semiotics, hermeneutics, and other aspects of symbolic behavior. Besides his articles in various marketing journals, his work has appeared in publications devoted to research on consumer behavior, semiotics, cultural economics, the arts, aesthetics, psychology, organizational behavior, communication, leisure, and related topics. He has recently coauthored two books with Elizabeth C. Hirschman: *Postmodern Consumer Research: The Study of Consumption as Text* (Sage, 1992) and *The Semiotics of Consumption: Interpreting Symbolic Consumer Behavior in Popular Culture and Works of Art* (1993). Under his own steam, he has just published *Daytime Television Game Shows and the Celebration of Merchandise: The Price Is Right* (1993). He is especially proud of contributing what he believes to have been the first sustained treatment of feminist perspectives in the consumer-research literature (in his presidential address to the ACR Conference in New Orleans).

Paul G. W. Jansen is Professor of Industrial Psychology at the Department of Business Administration of the Vrije Universiteit, Amsterdam. In addition, he is consultant for the Corporate Staff for Management Development of the Royal PTT Nederland NV. He graduated, cum laude, in 1979, with specializations in mathematical psychology and work and organizational psychology. His research activities are in the areas of management assessment and development, testing and scaling theory, and research methodology. He has published a book on assessment centers titled *Assessment of Managers. Effectiveness of Assessment Center Methods for the Selection and Development of Managers* (in Dutch; 1991). He is coeditor of *Selection Research in Practice* (in Dutch; 1991) and *The Assessment Center: An Open Book* (in Dutch; 1993). He has published more than 60 articles in Dutch, English, and German books and journals.

Patricia F. Kennedy is an Assistant Professor at the University of Nebraska, Lincoln. She has worked as an Account Executive at Montgomery Advertising Agency in Portland, Oregon, and as Assistant Convention Sales Manager at Walt Disney World. She has published articles in *Current Issues and Research in Advertising, Research in Marketing, Journal of Services Marketing, Journal of Consumer Marketing, Psychology and Marketing,* and *Advances in Consumer Research.* Her research interests lie in the promotion area, specifically, advertising's effects on children and what information children get from advertising, advertising's effects on individuals' self-esteem, gender- and age-related differences in responses to advertising, and values information in marketing communications and the interaction between individuals' value systems and this information.

Tina M. Lowrey is Assistant Professor in the Department of Marketing, Rider University. In addition to her research interests in ritualistic consumption and gift-giving behaviors, she is currently undertaking a major project focusing on psycholinguistic aspects of advertising. Her work has been published in the *Journal of Consumer Research, Journal of Consumer Psychology*, and *Psychology and Marketing*.

Mary C. Martin is a doctoral candidate in the Marketing Department at the University of Nebraska, Lincoln. Her research interests include determining the effects of advertising on consumers, public policy implications, and the role of gender in consumer behavior. Recently, she published a paper in *Psychology and Marketing* concerning the effects of advertising on female preadolescents and adolescents. She has presented papers at conferences of the American Marketing Association and the Association for Consumer Research, and at the Second Conference on Gender and Consumer Behavior in Salt Lake City, Utah, 1993. She was a fellow at the 1993 AMA Doctoral Consortium held at the University of Illinois at Urbana-Champaign.

Cele Otnes is Assistant Professor in the Department of Advertising, University of Illinois at Urbana-Champaign. Her research interests center on consumer rituals in American culture. Her work has been published in the *Journal of Consumer Research, Journal of Business Research*, and *Journal of Popular Culture*.

Teresa M. Pavia is Associate Professor of Marketing at the University of Utah. She received her Ph.D. in mathematical statistics from the University of Maryland. She made the transition from statistics to marketing while doing market forecasts and new product development at Bell Labs and Bell Communications Research. The focus of her research is on various aspects of product policy and product management. Products are developed within learned cultural environments, and consequently even things such as product design, product position, and product brand name may provide insight into learned cultural norms. It is this perspective that led to the work explored in her chapter in this volume.

Barbara B. Stern is Professor of Marketing, Faculty of Management, Rutgers, The State University of New Jersey, where she has been a faculty member since 1986. She received her B.A. from Cornell University, a Ph.D. in English from the City University of New York, and an MBA in marketing from Fordham University. She is on the editorial boards of the *Journal of Consumer Research, Journal of Advertising, Journal of Consumer Marketing, Journal of Promotion Management,* and *Consumption, Culture, and Markets: A Journal of Critical Perspectives.* Her research has introduced principles of literary criticism into the study of marketing, consumer behavior, and advertising. Additionally, she has focused on gender issues from the perspective of feminist literary criticism, using feminist deconstruction to analyze values encoded in advertising text. She has published articles in the *Journal of Marketing, Journal of Consumer Research, Journal of Advertising, Journal of Current Research in Advertising,* and other publications. She has been active in feminist research since the 1970s, when she developed a women's studies course at Saint Peter's College in Englewood Cliffs, New Jersey. In 1984, she applied her interest in feminism to her second career in marketing by developing a course called "Women in Managerial Roles," which won the Leavey Award for Excellence in Private Enterprise Education from the Freedom Foundation. In 1992 she won a grant from the Teaching Excellence Center in Newark to develop a course titled "Feminist Issues and Marketing."

Alladi Venkatesh (Ph.D., Syracuse) teaches in the area of marketing at the University of California, Irvine. His research interests include gender issues in marketing, the diffusion of information technologies to households, work at home with computers, and cross-cultural and postmodern developments in marketing. His doctoral dissertation was selected as part of the Landmark Dissertation Series in Women's Studies, and was published in 1985. His publications on gender issues and work at home have appeared in the *Journal of Consumer Research, Advances in Consumer Research, Journal of Advertising Research, Gender and Consumer Behavior,* and *Management Science.* He recently spent six months each in India and Denmark studying cross-cultural aspects of consumption and the impact of new technologies on households and consumers. He is an editor of a new journal, *Consumption, Culture and Markets.*